'This book covers the landscape of qualitative research in a way that inspires the reader new to the subject and stimulates the experienced researcher to think more deeply. Even after 20 plus years' involvement with research, I found my knowledge both challenged and increased.'

Sally Ford-Hutchinson, Global Planning Director, DMB&B

'Stimulating, entertaining and provocative. This has to be the definitive book on qualitative research. It is a must for anyone involved in research and will be central reading for anyone entering the communications industry, whether researcher, planner or buyer. Wendy has left the research industry with a qualitative bible which even highly experienced researchers will wish to keep by their side for reference.'

**Richard Pike, Head of Qualitative Research (UK),
The Research Business International**

'This book will remind everyone what qualitative research is meant to be about and how it ought to be done – things we too easily forget.'

Paul Feldwick, Executive Director of Planning, BMP DDB

'Goodthinking is the perfect name for this great new book. The book helps researchers to think in new and exciting ways using an approach which is both theoretical and practical. Wendy makes it clear that the skill of the researcher, whilst dependent on good technique, is ultimately judged by the quality, originality and clarity of the thinking. Another essential for the qualitative researcher.'

Laura Marks, Research and Planning Consultant

Goodthinking

Goodthinking

A Guide to Qualitative Research

Wendy Gordon

Admap

First published 1999

Admap Publications
Farm Road
Henley-on-Thames
Oxfordshire RG9 1EJ
United Kingdom
Telephone: +44 (0) 1491 411000
Facsimile: +44 (0) 1491 571188
E-mail: admap@ntc.co.uk

A CIP catalogue record for this book is available from the British Library.

ISBN 1 84116 030 X

Typeset in 11/14pt Sabon by Admap
Printed and bound in Great Britain by Redwood Books Ltd, Trowbridge.

Contents

Introduction

The reason for this book

Over a decade ago, in 1988 to be accurate, I wrote a book with Roy Langmaid called *Qualitative Market Research: A Practitioner's and Buyer's Guide*. We decided to write it because there wasn't a book of its kind – one that drew together the practical and theoretical understandings of two experienced qualitative practitioners about the contemporary applications and processes of qualitative market research. The book was republished in 1989 and has not been edited since that time.

During the 1990s, the book's reputation grew through word of mouth to such an extent that it had precious currency with qualitative practitioners and requests for copies began to come from ever-widening geographic circles – Europe, the US, South Africa, Australia, New Zealand and, more recently, Eastern Europe and Asia. The level of interest in the book reflects the belief among international qualitative practitioners and buyers that the UK model of qualitative thinking and processes constitutes best current practice – a sound benchmark from which to adapt the principles to suit any particular country.

Over the years I have trained many qualitative researchers in the UK and abroad, and also conducted seminars with advertising agency planners and research buyers within companies about how to enhance the practice and value of qualitative research. Not surprisingly, my thinking and practice has evolved in response to the changing demands of research in order to meet the needs of users in the complex marketing environment of today. The book published over ten years ago no longer reflects the reality of my approach. So I decided to write another, very different one.

This book is a very personal effort to explain how I *think* about human beings and their relationship to brands, communications and the delivery of service, and hence what I *do* as a qualitative researcher. My credentials for attempting to do this are 30 years of experience that span the birth of qualitative research as we know it, its unprecedented growth and subsequent maturity as a recognised and valid component of the marketing toolbox.

I did not wish to write an academic text book that exhaustively acknowledges and references the large number of authors who have published books and articles on fmcg or service brands, communication and research. Instead I wished to write an easy-to-read guide that points out the fundamental nature and highlights of the qualitative territory as I see it. Like guidebooks to foreign places, there are those weighty volumes that rigorously describe every church and building of interest, provide information on the weather, travel conditions, culture, religion, shopping, doctors, dentists and food. Then there are those that select certain highlights of the country or city, aiming to help the visitor obtain the most memorable experience.

My intention is the latter – a personal guidebook that I hope will become well-thumbed, providing practical knowledge and guidance. It will include references to those authors who have shaped my thinking, Web sites that have caught my interest and other arenas in which qualitative thinking has a significant role to play.

I have a reputation as being an innovative research practitioner and a sound thinker about the business of brands. Researchers call me an inspirational teacher. This has not come about through a greater amount of intelligence than anyone else but, if true, has developed through a passion for qualitative research and the commitment to share as much of it as possible with as many people as I can – both within and outside the research world. I have always been predisposed to question conventional wisdom and to find better ways of problem solving and it is these motivations that have now led me to want to share my years of experience with you.

I hope that you succeed in merging my map of the world with yours, in challenging my assumptions, in moving the discipline onwards and upwards while, at the same time, enjoying yourself in the search for insight – for in the final analysis that is what qualitative research is all about.

Wendy Gordon
1999

Acknowledgements

I would like to thank a small number of people for the time they gave me so generously while I was writing this book.

Lesley Thompson is an excellent qualitative researcher whom I admire. She read each chapter twice, challenged my point of view and willingly contributed additional thoughts and examples.

Amanda Mullard had been in qualitative research for only a few months when she agreed to read the draft chapters. Her comments were invaluable in ensuring that the book would be useful to young and enthusiastic qualitative researchers as well as older and more experienced ones.

Hazel Macmillan designed the cover and layout of the book. She understood and responded intelligently to my request that the experience of reading this book be simple and friendly as well as attractive and interesting. Thank you.

A big thank you to Rachel Harvey who helped produce the book and put up with my complaints about the pains of writing and the annoying habits of my computer. Ro Pocock took over where Rachel ended – another angel to edit the text and ensure that the references were cross-checked.

Finally, a thank you to Yehudi who never failed to encourage me when my creativity seemed to hit a low spot or to listen to me when I was flying high on ideas. And, as always, my thanks go to my children – Gabi and Paul, Nick and Tanya – for their unfailing support in my endeavours.

I would like to dedicate this book to my Mum whose curiosity about the world outside her own encouraged me to spend my life trying to walk in other people's shoes.

Qualitative Research – New or Old Discipline?

Chapter one

Introduction

Writing a history of qualitative research theory, methods and practice for those interested in qualitative marketing research turned out to be far more difficult than I imagined it would be for three reasons.

First, after reading Social Anthropology at the University of the Witwatersrand in Johannesburg, South Africa, which I completed in 1963, I became completely divorced from the academic world. Thus my present-day understanding of the academic antecedents of commercial qualitative research is very minimal. I am aware that I have been influenced by ideas and theories from other disciplines, but this has been indirect, mainly through working with a wide range of people with different backgrounds from myself and through attending conferences and reading books.

'I have an ethnocentric view of qualitative market research, which is based on a life-long career in this field in the UK.'

Second, I have an ethnocentric view of qualitative market research that is based on a life-long career in this field in the UK. That is not to say that I have not travelled widely to other countries or co-ordinated qualitative research projects across continents, but my exposure to other ideas and thinkers from different parts of the world has been limited, particularly where language is a barrier.

Third, it is not easy to uncover the history of qualitative research as applied to the study of the relationship people have with products, brands, services and environments, in those countries of the world where there has been experience of this kind of research. There are papers presented at conferences that discuss methodological issues or provide case study material, but there is little available that tells us when commercial qualitative research first came into being, why it did so at that time, who the main pioneers were, what theoretical stances shaped the development of the discipline, how many practitioners there were four decades ago compared to today and so on.

This chapter is essentially a personal history based on my experience and choice of reading material. It is 'context-bound' by a specific research culture, a time period (1963–1998) and geography (UK).

I hope that readers in other parts of the world will be able to use this history as a mirror in which to see which parts of the image match and which do not. For, in the final analysis, all history and all research, qualitative or quantitative, is subjective and interpretative. We select what we notice and what we do not, and what meanings we place on these observations, according to our unique map of the world – this historical perspective is no different.

'In the final analysis, all history and all research, qualitative or quantitative, is subjective and interpretative.'

New or old discipline?

The tradition of ethnography (the science describing the ways of life of humankind), which is based on qualitative methods of enquiry, extends from the ancient Greeks to 15th and 16th-century Westerners who attempted to understand the origins of culture and civilisation by regarding 'primitive' people as living examples of 'the great chain of being' that linked contemporary culture with its pre-historic beginnings. The racial, cultural and moral diversity of peoples throughout the world posed a problem for post-Renaissance Europeans, since the wide range of ways of life, belief systems and values challenged the fundamental tenets of Christianity.

'The racial, cultural and moral diversity of peoples throughout the world posed a problem for post-Renaissance Europeans.'

The ethnographic accounts of Western missionaries, explorers and colonial administrators were heavily biased by the mind-set of the conquering civilisation, and their descriptions of the practices of 'the primitives' reveal as much or even more about the prevailing practices and belief systems of the West then they do about the primitive culture being described. This form of value-laden ethnography continued until well into the 20th century and provided anthropologists with the foundations for many of the major theoretical debates of the second half of this century. The subsequent series of revolutions in ethnographic thinking, resulting in the contemporary post-modern stance, is beyond the scope of this chapter but makes relevant reading particularly for those qualitative researchers and users involved in cross-cultural studies. See *The Handbook of Qualitative Research*, Chapter 2 (1).

In addition to the ethnographic tradition there have been many other historical influences on qualitative methods and thinking. Most people who are involved with qualitative research today, either as buyers or practitioners, are unlikely to have had an extensive formal academic background in any of the human disciplines such as sociology, anthropology, social sciences (education, communications, social work), or to have studied the methods and research practices of ethnography, participant observation, cultural studies, psychoanalysis, semiotics and the narrative analysis methods in cinema and literary studies. Nor are they likely to have been exposed to the approaches of archival, material culture, historical and document analysis in history, biography and archaeology, or the discourse and conversational analysis of communications and education.

> Yet this is the pedigree of qualitative research theory, methods and practice – the combining of many genetic strands – of which we are unaware. The history of research traditions is not linear and straightforward: 'It is more like a Diaspora, a story of the dispersion and migration of ideas from one spot to another, one thinker to another' (1, p.20).

'Formal training is almost non-existent and occurs by serendipity.'

My experience of training and exchanging views with many researchers both in the United Kingdom and in other parts of the world over the years suggests that, as a professional group, we are oblivious to the fact that qualitative research is a very old discipline with a huge body of literature from which we can learn. Most of us have arrived at the doors of qualitative research by travelling down a road beginning with a broad-based arts, science or business degree (with perhaps a few modules covering any of the subjects described above) and then gaining experience by learning 'on the job' either as a buyer and user or a trained practitioner of qualitative research. Formal training is almost non-existent and occurs by serendipity in terms of the academic or philosophical orientation of a young person's successive mentors and role models.

For this reason, qualitative marketing research, as applied to contemporary commercial and social problems, exists like a goldfish in an empty glass bowl, separated from its impressive academic heritage, credentials and authority, and therefore vulnerable to challenge.

The following sections attempt to summarise the many influences on qualitative research from both academic and commercial historical perspectives.

An academic historical perspective

The Handbook of Qualitative Research, edited by Norman K. Denzin and Yvonna S. Lincoln (1) was published in 1994 and consists of 586 pages. There are sections on qualitative methods and traditions, major paradigms and perspectives, strategies of enquiry, methods of collecting and analysing empirical materials, and interpretation, evaluation and presentation issues. It ends with a section on the future of qualitative research. The authors represent disciplines as diverse as sociology and education, medicine and communication, anthropology and policy studies, and come from three continents. The aim of the two editors was to compile a handbook which:

> *... represents the distillation of knowledge of a field ... a benchmark volume that synthesises an existing literature, helping to define and shape the present and future of that discipline. In metaphoric terms, if you were to take one book on qualitative research with you to a desert island (or to study for a comprehensive graduate examination), you would choose a handbook.*

The existence of this huge tome surprised me. As a practitioner of qualitative research – my career for the last 30 years – I had no idea that such a handbook was available. The next surprise was that there is nothing in the index that refers to qualitative market research or any commercial context that I recognise! Even the so-called 'father' of qualitative research, the motivational researcher Ernest Dichter, is not mentioned.

This simply confirms that the worlds of academia and business are separate – as far apart as two planets in different galaxies. It is my

'This simply confirms that the worlds of academia and business are separate.'

'The decade of the twenties saw the work of sociologists from "the Chicago School" establish the importance for the role of qualitative research in understanding the group life of human beings.'

belief that the two planets have influenced each other indirectly, and will do so more directly in the future, due to the efforts being made today by many academic institutions and commercial organisations to exchange learning and practice.

Qualitative research has had a history in the human disciplines, particularly in anthropology where the work of Boas, Mead, Malinowski, Bateson, Evans-Pritchard and Radcliffe-Brown formed the foundation of the fieldwork method whereby an observer went into another culture to study the customs, habits, beliefs and behaviours of another society. The decade of the 1920s saw the work of sociologists from 'the Chicago School' establish the importance for the role of qualitative research in understanding the group life of human beings. From then onwards, to this very day, qualitative research has been applied to disciplines as diverse as medicine and policy development in Labour Britain.

Qualitative research is defined as:

> ... a field of inquiry in its own right. It cross-cuts disciplines, fields, and subject matter. A complex, interconnected family of terms, concepts, and assumptions surrounds the term 'qualitative research' (1).

Some of these disciplines have already been mentioned above. Others include the traditions of positivism (the assertion that objective accounts of the world can be given), post-structuralism (the assertion that language is an unstable system of referents and thus it is impossible ever to capture the meaning of an action, text or described experience), and cultural and interpretative studies (a complex field that merges critical theory, feminism and post-structuralism).

Denzin and Lincoln thus describe qualitative research as:

> ... *multi-method in focus, involving an interpretative, naturalistic approach to its subject matter. This means that qualitative researchers study things in their natural settings, attempting to make sense of, or interpret, phenomena in terms of the meanings people bring to them. Qualitative research involves the studied use and collection of a variety of empirical materials – case study, personal experience, introspective, life story, interview, observational, historical, interactional and visual texts – that describe routine and problematic moments and meanings in individuals' lives. Accordingly, qualitative researchers deploy a wide range of interconnected methods, hoping always to get a better fix on the subject matter at hand.*

The editors make a number of relevant points in the introduction to the book.

- Qualitative researchers often invent new tools depending on the problem: 'choice of research practices depends upon the questions that are asked, and questions depend on their context'.

- Objective reality does not exist – the truth cannot be captured. There is no value-free science: 'research is an interactive process shaped by [a researcher's] personal history, biography, gender, social class, race and ethnicity, and those of the people in the setting'.

- Qualitative research as a set of interpretative practices does not value one single methodology over any other – it has no theory that is distinctly its own.

'Objective reality does not exist – the truth cannot be captured. There is no value-free science.'

Phases of development

The development of qualitative research in the 20th century is divided into a number of phases.

Objectivism and positivism at the end of the 1800s

Objectivism and positivism have their roots in the Renaissance and developed through Galileo, Descartes, Newton and others. By the late 19th century there was an endemic belief that the world could be entirely understood and explained by fundamental laws, expressed as mathematical equations representing rational relationships. This is the school of reality seeing man as a machine which responds to stimuli in an entirely rational, predictable manner, or more bleakly being 'balls of rock and fire rolling through space' (anon). This is in stark contrast to early Greek understanding of all aspects of life as holistically related, and the mysticism that lived through to the Middle Ages. To quote Descartes:

> *We reject all knowledge which is purely probable and judge that only those things should be believed which are perfectly known, and about which there can be no doubts.*

The traditional period (early 1900s to World War 2)

This was the time when qualitative researchers wrote 'objective' colonialising accounts of field experiences that were reflective of the positivist scientist paradigm. Early pioneers of this method of enquiry, such as Malinowski and Margaret Mead, wrote accounts of the alien world of the Trobriand Islanders and the people of Samoa, which were published as objective accounts of the cultures studied. The 'Lone Ethnographer' (2) of these times organised his observations and interpretations according to four beliefs: a commitment to objectivism and collusion with imperialism; a belief that the ethnography would stand alone like a museum exhibit; evidence of the culture studied; and finally a belief that what was studied was unchangeable. This

'Objectivism and positivism have their roots in the Renaissance and developed through Galileo, Descartes, Newton and others.'

model of thinking also assumed that the researcher could translate his fieldwork into general theories of the human condition.

The Chicago School emphasised the 'slice of life' approach to qualitative enquiry and developed an approach which placed a narrated life history as the central text. This gave permission to the qualitative researcher to re-present the story, using the language of ordinary people, as an example of objective truth. The way in which many qualitative research reports are presented using verbatim quotes to illustrate points made by respondents (those people being studied) derives directly from this school of research.

It is worthwhile pointing out that, although the assumptions of the traditional period of qualitative research have been seriously challenged by academics, they remain free of criticism by most buyers, users and practitioners of commercial qualitative market research today. The positivist interpretation of human behaviour lingers on. We are all guilty of reducing the complexity of human motivation, behaviour and attitudes to simplistic 'decision trees' or 'stimulus response' models of interpretation.

'We are all guilty of reducing the complexity of human motivation, behaviour and attitudes to simplistic "decision trees" or "stimulus response" models of interpretation.'

The modernist phase (World War 2 to the 1970s)

This phase was characterised by an effort to formalise qualitative methods and to make its methods as rigorous as those of quantitative research. Researchers sought rigour by searching for probabilities (as in statistics) which could support arguments concerning the likelihood, frequency or nature of the conclusions of the study. Methods included combining open-ended and semi-structured interviewing, participant observation and the careful analysis of materials in a standardised quasi-statistical form.

This phase of qualitative discourse in the academic world strongly influenced the commercial world of research as well, resulting in the fierce debates and, even worse, slanging matches, that occurred between advocates of qualitative and quantitative methods.

Merging boundaries (1970 to 1986)

'Qualitative research is a series of creative and interpretative acts. Qualitative interpretations are constructed.'

The lines between the humanities and the social sciences merged and it became difficult to separate truth from fiction. Norman Mailer wrote documentaries that read like fiction, Carlos Casteneda wrote parables that seemed like ethnographic accounts and the essay appeared as an art form to replace the scientific article. The main academic issue of this time was the question of the author's presence in the interpretative text – how could any text be authoritative if there are no hard-and-fast rules concerning the 'truth', 'objectivity' or 'best practice'?

Crisis of representation (the mid-1980s)

During this period, issues of gender, class and race became important. Questions about whether or not a qualitative researcher can ever capture the lived experience were raised, since an experience, it was argued, is created in the social text written by the researcher. This is called the crisis of representation – meaning that the field worker is so enmeshed in the arena of enquiry that he or she is a central character alongside the people and the experience being studied. Shakespeare's famous quote seems to sum up the academic debate of this time: 'All the world's a stage, And all the men and women merely players; They have their exits and their entrances; And one man in his time plays many parts ...'.

The legitimacy of qualitative research, in terms of reliability, validity and ability to generalise, again became problematic despite the fact that these terms have been constantly redefined in each phase of development.

The art of interpretation (the late 1980s)

Qualitative research is a series of creative and interpretative acts. Qualitative interpretations are constructed. The researcher first creates a 'field text' consisting of notes, observations, records and documents, and moves from this to the creation of a 'research text' which is the interpretations and notes based on the fieldwork. This is then recreated into a 'working text' which contains the researcher's attempts to make sense of what he or she has experienced and learned. Finally, the researcher produces the 'final text' that comes to the reader and that may assume several forms: realistic, impressionistic, formal, critical, literary or analytic.

The process of creating and recreating interpretations of the findings of research is 'both artful and political ... There is no single interpretative truth ... there are multiple communities each having its own criteria for evaluating an interpretation' (1).

Where next? (The 1990s and beyond)
In the academic corridors of qualitative research the current model of thinking goes like this:

> The concept of the aloof researcher has been abandoned' and 'The individual enters the research process from inside an interpretative community that incorporates its own historical research traditions into a distinct point of view. This perspective leads the researcher to adopt particular views of the "other" who is studied. At the same time, the politics and ethics of research must also be considered, for these concerns permeate every phase of the research process (1).

The Handbook of Qualitative Research ends with five basic themes, which define the future of qualitative research. These are: positivism and post-positivism; the crises of representation and legitimisation; the treatment of the Other and the Other's voice; conflicts between science and religion; and the implications of new technologies for qualitative research.

Some of these will be examined in the final section of this chapter.

'The individual enters the research process from inside an interpretative community that incorporates its own historical research traditions into a distinct point of view.'

A commercial historical perspective

We owe our knowledge of the beginning of commercial qualitative market research in the United Kingdom and its relationship to that practised in the United States, to Bill Schlackman who originally worked with the founder of motivational research, Ernest Dichter, in the US. Bill Schlackman is a clinical psychologist and trained psychotherapist and was instrumental in developing qualitative methods based on clinical procedures in the United Kingdom. He was also my first mentor and guide and I owe him a debt of gratitude for his unique form of training and for passing on to me his passion for qualitative research. This section draws heavily on a chapter he wrote for a book entitled *Qualitative Research in Action* published in 1989 (3) as well as the book commissioned for the celebration of the 50th anniversary of the Market Research Society in the UK (4).

How did qualitative research develop as a tool for commercial clients – in other words by what route did it separate itself from its academic applications and become an applied science?

The early years (the first four decades of the 20th century)

'Charles Booth is generally credited with being the first person to develop a social survey which relied on qualitative inter-viewing methods.'

Charles Booth is generally credited with being the first person to develop a social survey that relied on qualitative interviewing methods. He conducted a comprehensive study on the social and economic conditions of Londoners, which was later published, called *Life and Labour of the People in London (1902–1903)*. It was based on survey research interviews supplemented by ethnographic observation and unstructured interviews.

This study was copied by other cities within and outside the United Kingdom over the next few decades, the most famous of which was R. S. Lynd and H. M. Lynd's *Middletown* (1929) and *Middletown in Transition* (1937).

The use of observation, personal documents and informal interviews in social studies was evident in the work of Thrasher (5) who based his study of gang members on about 130 qualitative interviews and also Nels Anderson (6) whose study of hoboes relied on informal in-depth conversations.

During the same period of time and leading up to World War 2, interviewing in survey research and opinion polling was used increasingly as a tool to quantify data. During the war, there was a big increase in survey research. Sociologists were hired by the US armed forces and more than half a million American soldiers were interviewed on their mental and emotional lives, with the results reported in a four-volume study – *Studies in Social Psychology in World War 2* (7). This work had a great impact and led to the widespread use of systematic survey research. This coincides with the Modernist phase in academic qualitative research discussed earlier in this chapter.

'Dichter vehemently challenged conventional methods of survey research with what he called the "motivational research system".'

The European influence

In another part of the world and coming from a very different background, a number of social scientists escaped from Vienna between 1933 and 1939 and all ended up working in New York as research specialists in the fields of social science or marketing research. Their names were Hans Ziesel, Herta Hertzog, Paul Lazarsfeld and Ernest Dichter. Ziesel and Hertzog worked for McCann-Erickson in New York. Lazarsfeld became Professor of Social Studies at Columbia University and simultaneously was managing director of the Bureau of Applied Research at Columbia, which had commercial clients for whom it conducted research. Ernest Dichter also worked for an advertising agency before joining the Columbia Broadcasting Service.

Dichter in particular vehemently challenged conventional methods of survey research with what he called the 'motivational research system' – a methodology designed to answer the more fundamental 'why' questions of human behaviour using quantitative and qualitative indirect questioning techniques. This was because he was strongly influenced by Freudian psychology with its emphasis on the interpretation and analysis of human motives stemming from the insight, training and experience of the analyst rather than from what the individual actually said and believed.

While the others were more cautious in their rejection of the survey methods of the time, they did support his 'non-directive' (used synonymously with the word 'indirect') and 'qualitative' interviewing approach as a legitimate method of gaining insight and understanding. Dichter regarded himself as a 'cultural anthropologist' and used qualitative interviewing (both group and individual interviews in particular), as the basis from which to make interpretations of the underlying motives that drive people's behaviour.

It is worth emphasising that the phrase *motivational research* thus carries with it an emphasis on psychoanalytical interpretation, while *qualitative research* is more technique and methodology bound.

'Motivational research carries with it an emphasis on psychoanalytical interpretation, while qualitative research is more technique and methodology bound.'

We know from 'The history of UK qualitative research, according to Bill Schlackman' (8) that Dr Ernest Dichter was practising as a psychological consultant in 1953. He wrote a report called 'Why men read *Time* magazine' which Schlackman (a student earning money as a delivery messenger) read in a coffee bar instead of delivering it to its destination! By 1955, Dichter had built a big motivational research business, called the Institute for Motivational Research. After a year of working in the States, Dichter sent Schlackman to the UK to work with his partner David Collins, and with Tony Lee, in the Motivational and Social Research Centre. A few years later, Dichter decided to set up his own company in the UK, called Ernest Dichter Associates, which Schlackman ran before setting up on his own as William Schlackman Limited in 1961. The use of group discussions became the primary methodology around this time although individual interviews were widely used.

Resistance to motivational methods

Returning to the 1950s, social scientists like Paul Lazarsfeld never fully accepted motivational research and tended to view the role of qualitative interviewing as a necessary preliminary stage to more formal, rigorous, quantitative surveys based on large samples, not as a stand-alone methodology.

He was not alone in his suspicion of motivational research. In the mid-1950s, the Dichter model of thinking clashed with that of Politz – a German psychologist who was a strong proponent of statistics and experimental design in surveys. The quantitative–qualitative 'war' began at this time and carried on through the 1960s and 1970s both in the United States and in the United Kingdom.

Sampling the Universe (4), a book describing the growth, development and influence of market research in Britain since 1945, suggested three reasons for the fact that qualitative methods aroused such hostility in the early years. The first was that many of the 'founding fathers' of survey research in the UK had worked for the government during and after the war and were trained in disciplines with a strong quantitative tradition and a high regard for statistics. The small quota samples of qualitative research were anathema to these research professionals for whom membership of the Association of Incorporated Statisticians was more highly rated than membership of the Market Research Society.

The second influence was the need for the new discipline of 'marketing research' to establish its professional credentials and to be seen to 'keep its nose scrupulously clean' (4, p. 165). The strong influence of the modernist phase in the social sciences reverberated in the world of commercial research, illustrated by the clash between two individuals: Henry Durant believed that scientific measurement is all, 'that empirical methods in the social sciences should be predominantly quantitative', but was opposed by Tom Harrison of Mass Observation

'Many of the "founding fathers" of survey research in the UK had worked for the government during and after the war and were trained in disciplines with a strong quantitative tradition.'

who believed that scientific measurement (statistical consistency) can be misleading. It therefore should be seen as 'a check, corrective and extension of the qualitative approach' (4, p. 165).

The final hostile influence was the poor reputation and image of motivational research in the United Kingdom. The discipline was linked with stories of expensive marketing disasters as a result of using psychologists to provide deeper insight into the motivations and behaviour of consumers. There are apocryphal stories about Dichter's interpretation that the female shape of the Coca-Cola bottle was the underlying reason for the success of the brand. Another was the recommendation to General Mills that in order to sell its cake-mix packages successfully it must ensure that the housewife had something to do – a fresh egg to add – in order that she, as the cake-maker, felt fulfilled rather than guilty.

Dichter's insights were often brilliant but were not based on empirical thoroughness and attention to the data.

Harry Henry, in the 1988 introduction to his book *Motivation Research* (first published in 1958), looked back and said:

> *The reason why motivation research tends to be regarded as being no longer relevant is that most people associate it with the somewhat idiosyncratic practices of Ernest Dichter and his followers (of which it was once said 'Very interesting, but why do they call it research?').*

And again:

> *When motivation research is used to establish, firmly and unequivocally, that a housewife is more likely to buy a product if it is packed in a blue wrapper than a red one, it is doing a useful and worthwhile job; when it goes further,*

to discover that she prefers blue to red because she was frightened by a bull in early childhood, it is simply wasting time and resources. (9, p. 31)

Bill Schlackman believed that Dichter over-sold motivational research by claiming that large-scale surveys and statistical analysis were unnecessary. And Dichter's followers, according to Schlackman, made personal interpretations of the issues (which were projected onto the data) resulting in very erroneous findings. To make matters even worse, these were derived from poorly constructed and inadequately controlled samples in terms of size and representation.

The reputation of motivational research lingered in the United States for many years and it is only in the last ten years that 're-launched' qualitative research is now becoming valued as a discipline in its own right.

In 1964, when I first joined William Schlackman Limited, the UK business was thriving. Schlackman always conducted extended groups, believing that it was impossible to employ a psychological and psychodynamic approach to elicitation and interpretation of consumer responses within a one-and-a-half-hour timeframe. He taught me the fundamentals of human psychology applied to marketing research: people will not share feelings and thoughts with a researcher if these are in any way embarrassing to self-esteem; that people always try to 'look good' (rational, intelligent, helpful); that some attitudes and emotions are difficult to put into words; that 'rationalisations', 'ambivalence', 'justifications', 'projections' are part of everyday human life and that integrity in one's relationship with respondents is paramount.

He truly believed that qualitative studies could stand alone and guide strategic decision making. He also acknowledged the essential role of survey research and quantitative verification of qualitative findings,

'The reputation of motivational research lingered in the United States for many years.'

but only in particular cases such as when the client requires 'frequencies' of attitudes and behaviours of market segments. As a trainee in the company, I was expected and trained to work with both methodologies – a training programme that disappeared in the mid-1970s as specialisation developed.

In other parts of the world the use of qualitative research methods and the reputation of the discipline has depended on the local history of commercial marketing research combined with influences from abroad. For example, in South Africa qualitative methods were used commercially in the early 1960s both by advertising agencies and market research companies to understand the complexities of marketing products in a multi-racial and multi-lingual society. A quantitative backlash occurred later (as in the US and UK) and only now, in line with other parts of the world, is a more balanced view beginning to prevail.

The birth and exponential growth of qualitative research (1976 to 1989)

The term 'motivational research' thus became a liability to those practitioners using qualitative methods very successfully for major clients who were marketing products and services to customers. The term 'qualitative research' took its place and, without the baggage of the past, qualitative research was embraced by marketing and advertising professionals as the most sensitive tool with which to develop marketing strategies and executions.

'Qualitative research was embraced by marketing and advertising professionals as the most sensitive tool with which to develop marketing strategies and executions.'

It is worth clarifying the terms 'motivational research' and 'qualitative research' as they are not synonymous. The term 'motivational', used by Dichter and Schlackman, is psychoanalytical in origin and refers to the interpretation of 'material' (the text or conversations) of the study based on an understanding of the unconscious and subconscious dynamics of human behaviour. The phrase 'qualitative research', which replaced the previous terminology in the mid-1970s, refers to a methodology (primarily focus groups and depth interviews) and a cognitive model of analysis based firmly on the 'data' derived from the interview processes. This model of thinking held that:

- consumers are able to tell you what they do, feel and think, particularly with the aid of indirect questioning techniques which allow the interviewer to probe more 'heartfelt' responses

- the role of the researcher is to encourage consumers to respond to various stimuli relevant to the client, such as early advertising concepts, pack mock-ups, competitive advertising, brands in the category, and to summarise this information so that the client can make a decision

- qualitative researchers can be drawn from any background – clinical psychology or psychoanalytical training is no more valid for good qualitative practice than a business degree or a diploma in theatre studies

- the data can be rigorously analysed by revisiting the conversations between interviewer and respondent(s), through listening to the audio-tapes and/or reading transcripts of the interview and carrying out a formal content analysis

- recruitment quality is very important – respondents in a group discussion or series of interviews must be representative of the target market – in terms of category or brand usership, demography, geography and psychographic or attitudinal profile (optional)

- the protocol (the sample design and criteria, the stimuli, the discussion guide, the audio-taping of the conversations)

'The role of the researcher is to encourage consumers to respond to various stimuli relevant to the client.'

can be standardised and therefore the approach can be applied consistently across international boundaries and cultural differences

- the research report – the written findings at the end of the project – containing evidence (quotes, verbatims, transcripts, diaries, consumer 'drawings' and responses to projective tasks) is objective. It is empirical evidence of the target group studied.

'The popularity of qualitative research is best illustrated by the "professionalisation" of the discipline.'

The popularity of qualitative research during this period is best illustrated by the 'professionalisation' of the discipline. In 1982, the Association of Qualitative Research Practitioners (AQRP) was formed with the aim of providing qualitative researchers with their own forum for the exchange of ideas and for 'promoting confidence in qualitative research within the rest of the survey research industry'. It produced a Code of Conduct covering technical and ethical standards and soon began to run its own training courses and seminars focusing on qualitative methods and issues. AQRP began with ten founder members in 1982 and by 1985 had 250 members. It now has 950 members.

An equivalent professional organisation, the Qualitative Research Consultants Association (QRCA) was founded a year later in 1983 in New York City by a small number of professionals. It is a non-profit organisation which embraces the objectives of enhancing the professionalism of qualitative marketing research and social research, promoting and maintaining the highest standards of ethics and integrity in its work; broadening awareness and appreciation of qualitative research within the marketing research community and providing a channel for communications. The growth in members and chapters grew as rapidly as in the United Kingdom and it now has international connections with more than 550 members in 36 states and on five continents.

In other parts of the world, qualitative research interests were served by the professional society that represented both qualitative and quantitative disciplines. It is only very recently that specialist professional bodies have been founded in Australia and New Zealand, for example, to perform the same role as AQRP and QRCA.

It is interesting to examine the definitions of qualitative research that were written in the 1980s by practitioners of the discipline:

> *Qualitative research is usually exploratory or diagnostic. It involves small numbers of people who are not sampled on a probabilistic basis. They may, however, be selected to represent different categories of people from a given target market or section of the community. In qualitative research no attempt is made to draw hard and fast conclusions. It is impressionistic rather than definitive* (10).

And:

> *At a simplistic level 'Qualitative research' answers such questions as 'What', 'Why' or 'How' but it cannot answer the question 'How many' and it is centrally concerned with understanding things rather than with measuring them ... In general terms, qualitative research:*
>
> *– involves small samples of consumers which are not necessarily representative of larger populations*
> *– employs a wide variety of techniques to collect data, not simply a structured question-and-answer format*
> *– relies on interpretation of the findings which is an integral part of the data collection and indeed begins well before the fieldwork commences at the briefing*
> *– allows access to the ways in which consumers express themselves* (11).

'Qualitative research is defined by methodology, which is synonymous with the depth interview and group discussion.'

What is common in these definitions is that qualitative research is defined by methodology, which is synonymous with the depth interview and group discussion. The definitions implicitly or explicitly differentiate between quantitative sampling and statistical validity, and qualitative small-scale target sampling methods, making it absolutely clear that one is not a substitute for the other.

During the late 1970s and early 1980s, many practitioners began to disseminate information about the role and practice of qualitative research by writing articles, speaking at conferences and seminars, and conducting training sessions aimed both at users and buyers, as well as training researchers. The emphasis was on distinguishing the role and applications of qualitative research, thereby ensuring that those involved with its output understood the 'horses for courses' evaluation that needs to be made in deciding whether to employ a qualitative or quantitative methodology to a research problem.

'Many practitioners began to disseminate information about the role and practice of qualitative research.'

Peter Sampson, in a section in the *Consumer Market Research Handbook* entitled 'The uses and abuses of qualitative research' written in 1986, describes ten common examples of the use of qualitative research techniques. This list, with the exception of the last point, clearly illustrates the predominantly cognitive model of thinking, which evolved in the step change between motivational and qualitative research practice:

- to obtain some background information where absolutely nothing is known about the problem area or product field in question

- in concept identification and exploration

- to identify relevant or 'salient' behaviour patterns, beliefs, opinions, attitudes, motivations, etc.

- to establish priorities among categories of behaviour and psychological variables like beliefs, opinions and attitudes

- generally defining problem areas more fully and formulating hypotheses for further investigation and/or quantification

- during a preliminary screening process in order to reduce a large number of possible contenders to a smaller number of probable ones

- to obtain a large amount of data about beliefs, attitudes, etc. as data input for multivariate analysis studies

- conducting post-research investigations of 'post mortems' to amplify or explain certain points emerging from some major study, without having to repeat on a large scale

- in piloting questionnaires to test comprehension, word forms, the 'memory factor', etc.

- where we cannot discover in a simple, straightforward way like direct questioning, why people behave as they do because the field of enquiry is personal or embarrassing in some way. In these circumstances some 'oblique' approach is called for, where projective questioning techniques may be used in a qualitative research setting (10).

'My memory of the time between 1976 and the recession at the end of the 1980s was that there was relatively little criticism of this new form of qualitative research.'

My memory of the time between 1976 and the recession at the end of the 1980s was that there was relatively little criticism of this new form of qualitative research. However, there were a few strong attacks that deserve a mention primarily because they focused practitioner attention on their own practices and underlying belief systems.

'The underlying emotional aspects that drive consumer behaviour are not easy to articulate in response to a direct question.'

A major debate took place after Gerald de Groot delivered a paper called 'Deep, Dangerous or just plain Dotty', which he presented at an ESOMAR seminar on qualitative research methods in Amsterdam in 1986 (12). The paper raised issues about the subjectivity of qualitative research, its lack of 'validity' (compared to quantitative surveys) and attacked the use of projective techniques such as 'thought bubble' completion tasks and other less commonly used construction techniques such as clay modelling or psychodrama. The paper suggested that qualitative questioning should be 'direct' and that interpretation should be based on a strict and literal analysis of responses.

This paper resonated with many buyers and users of qualitative research, for whom doubts about moderator/interviewer subjectivity, 'mysterious projective techniques' (which were used with no explanations of the background theory or evidence of usefulness), anxieties about the replicability, 'generalisability' or validity of qualitative research at different points of time or in different parts of the world, had generally not found an avenue for public expression.

The mid-1980s, like the Californian gold rush, was a time when new qualitative researchers either operating independently or in small companies, staked their claim to expertise overnight. Instead of one researcher being involved in the project from start to finish, the newer researchers began to share responsibility for fieldwork and interpretation for two reasons: speed and sharing of insight. This led to accusations by experienced researchers (who had been trained in the 1970s) of the 'industrialisation' of qualitative research – the danger of it becoming a mechanical process manned by different people. Poor training and lack of professionalism became a major issue that was taken up by the newly formed AQRP resulting in courses designed to improve moderating, data analysis and interpretation skills.

The opposite point of view to that of de Groot has been expressed by Peter Sampson, Monica Bhaduri, Bill Schlackman, Paul Heylen and others who agree with the saying that 'people do not mean what they say, nor say what they mean' (10, 14). This is not because people wish to lie (although sometimes they are economical with the truth), but because the underlying emotional aspects that drive consumer behaviour, attitudes and choice are not easy to articulate or express verbally in response to a direct question. Therefore, projective approaches, enabling techniques and other forms of facilitation such as the extended creativity group (a term coined by Peter Cooper) are essential tools rather than gimmicks.

This view had been eloquently expressed by Judie Lannon and Peter Cooper a few years earlier in a paper called 'Humanistic Advertising: a holistic cultural perspective' (13) – a seminal paper that had a long-term influence and influenced me and many other researchers at the time. The paper drew on many different disciplines (modern social anthropology, communication studies, transactional analysis, neuro-anatomy and psychology) to make the point that it is not what brands and advertising do to people but rather what people do with brands and advertising.

> *Brands have practical, rational values, but what makes them distinctive and unique are their symbolic values. Advertising operates more effectively at the symbolic, intuitive level of consciousness. To design such advertising and to check on its effectiveness in the market place requires methods for opening up the inner world of what consumers do to advertising, their play and imagination, the language it speaks, its social values, and so on* (13).

'Brands have practical, rational values, but what makes them distinctive are their symbolic values.'

Lannon and Cooper called this approach the 'holistic-cultural' model and suggested that qualitative methods are most useful because:

> *... they allow us to see the world as consumers experience it: from their frame of reference, with their own words, gestures and behaviour. Qualitative methods allow us to explore cultural concepts such as beauty, pain, fun, hope, play – as they are defined and experienced by real people in their everyday lives* (13).

This had the effect of giving permission to researchers to draw inspiration from whatever discipline or theory seemed helpful for the problem at hand. Over the next few years Lannon and Cooper's reputations as excellent researchers and thinkers helped the 'coming out' and legitimising of those qualitative techniques (particularly projective techniques) that were in use at the time.

'It is not what brands and advertising do to people but rather what people do with brands and advertising'

The age of bricolage – the nineties

'Bricolage' is a term quoted by Denzin and Lincoln, which emerged in academic writing of the 1990s and is defined as follows.

A pieced-together, close-knit set of practices that provide solutions to a problem in a concrete situation ... It is a contraction that changes and takes new forms as different tools, methods, and techniques are added to the puzzle (1, p. 2).

And further:

... the qualitative researcher ... uses the tools of his or her methodological trade, deploying whatever strategies, methods, or empirical materials as are at hand. If new tools have to be invented, or pieced together, then the researcher will do this. The 'choice' of which tools to use, which research practices to employ, is not set in advance. The choice of research practices depends upon the questions that are asked, and the questions depend on their context.

'The choice of research practices depends upon the questions that are asked.'

The same process seems to be taking place in commercial qualitative research. The fundamental difference in orientation between the humanistic-cultural model on the one hand and the cognitive descriptive model on the other, led gradually to a segmentation of qualitative research by research objectives, methodology and interviewing techniques and, importantly, by researchers. Buyers of research could choose particular individuals whom they knew were most able to conduct one or other type of research or whose work would fit most comfortably into the organisational culture of the company. There are two distinct approaches, as described below.

Descriptive and diagnostic – cognitive research

- Essentially positivist in orientation (empirical, based on facts and experience).

- Detailed descriptive information on category/brand behaviour and attitudes as well as straightforward diagnostic feedback of consumer response to new product concepts, pack designs, new service propositions, new advertising executions or campaigns, staff attitudes, customer satisfaction criteria, response to brochures, promotions and point-of-sale material, attitude generation prior to questionnaire design and so on.

- Single methodology, most commonly the group discussion (generally less than two hours in length) or depth interviews for low-penetration brands or difficult-to-interview respondents (e.g. business-to-business research, high-income professionals).

- Small samples: four to six groups in total.

- Minimal use of projective questioning and tasks.

- Research stimuli standardised and simple (e.g. verbal concepts, animatics, new product concepts drawn as rough scamps with little or no emotional imagery).

- Formalised and standardised group discussion guide/interview guide prepared in collaboration with the research buyer/user to which the moderator(s) are expected to adhere.

'Descriptive research provides an account of the subject under study – a commentary.'

Descriptive research provides an account of the subject under study –
a commentary, a record, a representation of 'the data' generated by
the process of interviewing 'respondents'. Such accounts are regarded
by those who produce them and those who commission the research
as 'objective' and 'truthful', 'factual' and 'accurate'. They provide an
essential tool for decision making, since facts brook no argument.

Descriptive and diagnostic qualitative research is institutionalised in
many organisations and those researchers whose main body of work
falls into this category are rigorous in ensuring that their reports are
as objective as possible. This can be partially achieved through accurate recruitment (so that the correct people are being interviewed),
pair moderating so that both researchers can 'check out' the generality
and interpretation of responses, tape-recording or videoing the group
discussions so the 'data' are on record, inviting 'the client' to observe
the groups in progress and, finally, content analysing the transcripts of
the interviews/group discussions in a systematic way. The final report
(including verbatim quotes to illustrate how respondents expressed
themselves), which includes details of the sample, recruitment criteria
and other material used (e.g. concepts shown, respondent diaries and
so on), forms a complete record of the study.

'Descriptive and diagnostic qualitative research is institutionalised in many organisations.'

Explanatory and interpretative: humanistic–cultural

- Essentially ethnographic, psychological and anthropological in orientation – acknowledging the context of
people's day-to-day lives and the social/cultural group to
which they belong; an interpretative naturalistic approach
to the subject matter.

- Explanations and interpretations of the complex relationship people have with brands (fmcg, service, financial,
retail, corporate); services (airlines, banks, insurance
companies); corporations; communications (above and

'Explanatory and interpretative qualitative research acknowledges that all human beings create meaning from objects, events and relationships within a context.'

below-the-line, environments) paying attention to the multi-dimensional nature of the relationship particularly at the level of symbolism and emotional values.

- Interconnected methods such as combinations of group discussions (usually extended), direct and participant observation, individual interviews (in-home), interactive workshop sessions combining consumers and staff, qualitative panels, video recordings of context and behaviour.

- Larger samples because of multi-methods but also because the target market is broken down into tightly defined segments in order, for example, to understand their differing relationships with the brand.

- Maximum use of projective and enabling techniques often requiring participants to complete tasks prior to the interview/group session.

- Complex jigsaw of stimulus material designed to be appropriate for the target group or culture within which the work is taking place – brands and products, advertising both within and outside the category, below-the-line material, video concepts, mood boards, TV scripts and storyboards, music tracks and so on.

- Flexible and facilitative outline of the process for the group discussion, with discretion left to the research moderator to use whatever techniques or stimuli he or she regards as appropriate at that time.

Explanatory and interpretative qualitative research acknowledges that all human beings create meaning from objects, events and relationships within a context and that people have very different priorities from that of marketing, advertising and research professionals. Nothing has an unchangeable meaning – meanings alter depending on the who, when, where, why and how of the particular individual and the context. It accepts that the observer/researcher plays a part in making these meanings explicit within the framework of his or her own theoretical stance.

'Meanings alter depending on the who, when, where, why and how of the particular individual and context.'

This theoretical stance is part of what the researcher offers to the buyer and user of the end product – a particular view (based on background and experience) through which the empirical information is channelled. This is why qualitative research buyers choose particular researchers for particular problems – it is more to do with accepting that his or her view of the consumer–brand relationship might be a useful way to solve a problem than it is to do with appreciation of his or her moderating skill.

The age of bricolage is well established as we come to the end of the 1990s. Modern-day qualitative practitioners and users will adopt concepts and methods from any writer, philosopher, school of theory or discipline they come across, cherry-picking ideas and models of thinking that bear relevance to the increasingly complex problems they face. Some that are fairly common are neuro-linguistic programming, the Landmark Forum (run by Landmark Education Ltd), semiotics, brainstorming, synectics, systems thinking, organisational learning, communications theory and collaborative computer technology. There are probably many other influences to which we are all exposed, particularly now that people working in marketing, advertising and research commonly use the Internet.

The millennium and beyond
It is likely that the age of bricolage will continue, resulting in the segmentation of qualitative research becoming more complex.

Companies will be able to choose exactly which researcher or research company (or indeed someone who does not consider himself a researcher at all) will be best suited to the problem and therefore, increasingly, qualitative researchers will have to make their underlying thinking and assumptions public and accountable.

'Communities of qualitative researchers will soon exist in cyberspace, freed from the boundaries of country and space.'

If your skill is moderating group discussions then this is your selling point. Perhaps, you consider that your expertise lies in understanding corporate brands and that you have both the experience and the academic and contemporary knowledge about brands to claim a unique advantage over someone else? Alternatively, your skills lie in idea generation using brainstorming techniques and collaborative software technology. None of us can possibly know everything, nor be the right researcher for every problem, and the sooner we acknowledge this the better it will be for the buyers of our expertise since they will know what they are getting.

What else is likely to change?

Already technology has radically changed the face and structure of quantitative survey research. Qualitative practice is bound to change dramatically, too, over the coming years. Electronic and video technologies, interactive and collaborative software systems for video and computer, laptop mobility and modems connecting researchers to each other or to their offices will transform every part of the process of qualitative research. New methods for analysing 'material' will emerge – analysis software packages already exist – and researchers are already grappling with how to conduct 'legitimate' research using the Internet.

Communities of qualitative researchers will soon exist in cyberspace, freed from the boundaries of country and culture – a process that will propel the exchange of learning even faster. Interviewing will no longer have to be face to face but will take place in cyberspace with the resultant text 'growing' by itself. When texts are thus constructed, who is the writer and who is the interviewee? How will our Code of Conduct have to be rewritten to cope with issues of confidentiality, quality standards and the rights of respondents?

Returning to the rigours of science and academia, there is a growing body of work by respected academic scientists working in the field of quantum physics who are grappling with explaining the human condition via quantum theory; systems thinking is one branch of this. The dominant themes are as follows.

- The act of observation, in itself, influences the outcome at a quantum level. There can be no such thing as a totally dispassionate and separate observer.

- A nuclear particle is therefore neither a particle nor a wave, or is both simultaneously, depending on your point of view.

- Classical Cartesian/Newtonian physics rapidly breaks down at the sub-atomic level and, indeed, only works approximately at the macro level by discounting innumerable other variables.

- Quantum physics describes the world in terms of *patterns*, *possibilities*, *connections* and, above all, *relationships*. Essentially, it describes the interconnectedness of all things, including environments and the behaviour, thoughts and emotions of others as well as ourselves.

'Quantum physics describes the world in terms of patterns, possibilities, connections and, above all, relationships.'

We seem to have returned to the holistic model of thinking of the early Greek philosophers!

On a completely different paradigm (or perhaps not) is the influence coming from what is disparagingly referred to as the 'spiritual supermarket' of New Age ideas. I Ching, numerology, hypnosis, angel cards, intuition and even the idea of the jacuzzi focus group have been discussed at conferences on qualitative research. The point is that practitioners of qualitative research are more likely than most to have explored the burgeoning area of personal development and so cannot fail to be influenced by seminars, workshops and books on these subjects that have now become mainstream and accessible.

One of the issues high on the agenda of academic qualitative researchers is understanding the voice of 'the Other'. As commercial qualitative researchers, particularly in the shrinking world of global marketing, one of our most important remits is to understand and explain how people of a different social group, culture and country think, feel and behave. I am not aware that we qualitative researchers have ever interrogated the degree to which we filter the interpretations about 'the Other' through the 'superiority' lens of our individual social class, ethnic background, gender and religion. Our academic counterparts have struggled long and hard with this issue and now believe that qualitative researchers are more humble than they were in the past.

'One of the issues high on the agenda of academic qualitative researchers is understanding the voice of "the Other".'

> *We know that our texts have specific locations. We know that they represent – whether in some hidden way or openly – our baggage as individual social scientists. We care less about our 'objectivity' as scientists than we do about providing our readers with some powerful propositional, tacit, intuitive, emotional, historical, poetic, and empathic experience of the other via the text we write* (1).

I would contend that the majority of qualitative researchers and the buyers and end users of the qualitative 'product' hold the traditional view that:

... there is a separate and distinct 'social reality' 'out there' somewhere, separated from those who experience it, and that it is the scientists' job to uncover this separate reality, and report on it, for that is the essence of 'Truth' (1).

This, for me, is the biggest challenge that we face in the future for, unless we do, we will find credibility in the role and applications of qualitative research continuing to erode, simply because expectations of what qualitative research can deliver are neither realistic nor informed.

This theme is developed in the next chapter, which covers the wave of disillusionment threatening to put qualitative research back into the dark ages of the 1950s and 1960s.

'The majority of qualitative researchers hold the traditional view that ... there is a separate and distinct "social reality" "out there".'

REFERENCES

1. N. K. Denzin and Y. S. Lincoln (eds), *The Handbook of Qualitative Research*, Sage Publications, 1994.
2. R. Rosaldo, *Culture and Truth: The Remaking of Social Analysis*, Beacon, 1989.
3. S. Robson, and A. Foster, *Qualitative Research in Action*, Edward Arnold, 1989.
4. C. McDonald and S. King in J. Goodyear (ed.), *Sampling the Universe*, NTC Publications Ltd in association with the Market Research Society, 1996.
5. F. M. Thrasher, *The Gang: A Study of 1,313 Gangs in Chicago*, University of Chicago Press, 1963 (original work published in 1927).
6. N. Anderson, *The Urban Community: A World Perspective*, Hewry Holt, 1959.
7. R. K. Merton (ed.), *Studies in Social Psychology in World War 2*, Ayer Co., 1974.
8. W. Schlackman, 'An historical perspective' in S. Robson and A. Foster (eds), *Qualitative Research in Action*, Edward Arnold, 1989.

9. H. Henry, *Motivation Research*, MCB University Press, 1988.

10. R. Worcester and J. Downham (eds), *Consumer Market Research Handbook*, ESOMAR, 1986.

11. W. Gordon and R. Langmaid, *Qualitative Market Research: A Practitioner's and Buyer's Guide*, Gower, 1988.

12. G. de Groot, *Deep, Dangerous or just plain Dotty*, ESOMAR, 1986.

13. J. Lannon and P. Cooper, 'Humanistic Advertising: a holistic cultural perspective', *International Journal of Advertising*, Vol. 2 No. 3, July/August 1983.

14. P. Sampson (ed.), *Qualitative Research Through a Looking Glass*, ESOMAR, 1998, pp. 18–22, 30–43.

FURTHER READING

The Directory and Handbook of Qualitative Research, AQRP 1997–1998.

ESOMAR, Qualitative research seminar, Geneva, September 1990.

P. Fleury, 'New Qualitative Studies' in P. Sampson (ed.), *Qualitative Research Through a Looking Glass*, ESOMAR, 1998.

H. Marianpolski, 'Ethnography as a Market Research Tool' in P. Sampson, (ed.), *Qualitative Research Through a Looking Glass*, ESOMAR, 1998.

K. Oyhe, 'Cross Cultural Qualitative Research' in P. Sampson (ed.), *Qualitative Research Through a Looking Glass*, ESOMAR, 1998.

W. Sykes, and M. Collins, 'Quality in Qualitative Research' in P. Sampson (ed.), *Qualitative Research Through a Looking Glass*, ESOMAR, 1998.

Summary of Significant Dates in the Development of Qualitative Research

	Academic	Commercial
1900	*Traditional Period*	*The Early Years*
	Ethnographics	Social surveys
		Survey research
	Slice of life – Chicago School	Opinion polling
		European Influence
1940	*Modernist Phase*	Dichter, Ziesel, Hertzog
	Formalising qualitative research	
	– quasi-statistical 'rigour'	
1950		*Resistance to Motivational*
		Research
		Lazarsfeld
		Politz–Dichter clash
		Institute for Motivational
		Research 1955
1960		Quantitative–Qualitative war
		William Schlackman Ltd 1961
1970	*Merging Boundaries*	
	Carlos Casteneda	
	Norman Mailer	Birth of Qualitative Research 1976
1980		AQRP/QRCA (1981/83)
	Crisis of Representation	
	Feminism, literacy criticism –	
	gender, race, class issues	Cognitive descriptive vs.
		Humanistic cultural
	Art of Interpretation	
	'No single truth'	
1990	*Bricolage* ◀------------▶	*Bricolage*

Qualitative Research – Warts & All

Chapter two

The United Kingdom has spearheaded the growth of qualitative research as a legitimate research discipline and has seen an unprecedented increase in the number of qualitative research companies and independent practitioners. Other parts of the world, notably the US, Europe, Australia, South Africa, New Zealand and Asia, have all had different histories of qualitative research development in response to variations in the marketing, advertising and research cultures of each country. Only in the last decade, with the energy provided by large multinationals determined to be more effective in marketing global brands across borders, have common issues come to the surface.

As we come to the close of the millennium, qualitative research is buoyant. The Association of Qualitative Practitioners (AQRP) has nearly 1,100 individual members, compared with 400 six years ago. In the UK, qualitative research accounts for 20–25% of all market research and it is estimated that the qualitative market is worth around £156 million per annum in the UK. Laura Marks, ex-chairperson of the AQRP, claims that the market might become even larger if it were professionally audited.

'Recent growth has been fuelled by the use of qualitative techniques in many areas outside the traditional enclave of marketing and advertising.'

Recent growth has been fuelled by the use of qualitative techniques in many areas outside the traditional enclave of marketing and advertising: politics, broadcasting, the press, the arts, law, academia, government, local government, trade unions and even the monarchy. Its primary applications are in strategy or policy development, monitoring of public and internal employee attitudes and opinions, meeting tastes and preferences, and understanding and developing communications. Qualitative research is shaping the world we live in more fundamentally than ever before.

The previous chapter described the origins of qualitative research and the wide range of disciplines that have influenced its form. It also described the primary applications of qualitative research that are still relevant today and will continue to be so as long as there are human beings on this earth who think, feel and act, and who need to understand how to meet people's needs or influence their behaviour.

This chapter is concerned with a wave of disillusionment (stronger in some parts of the world than others) among supporters of this discipline in relation to its role, practice and effectiveness in the development and implementation of brand, communications or product strategies. There is also disappointment with its usefulness as a predictive tool in understanding the impact of change. In order to understand why these antipathetic views now exist, it is worth following the relationship of qualitative research and advertising in the UK in the hope that researchers in other parts of the world can better anticipate warning shots across their bows and take preventative action.

'In the early 1970s, fast, flexible and responsive qualitative research evolved from the more time-consuming and weightier motivational research.'

In the early 1970s, fast, flexible and responsive qualitative research evolved from the more time-consuming and weightier motivational research. The new adaptation developed in response to the birth and growing influence of the discipline of advertising planning which began to take hold in advertising agencies in a public way around the second half of the 1970s. The crucial role of qualitative research was to provide nuggets of insight about the nature of the relationship people have with a brand which, when translated and distilled through the planning process, provided both a background of understanding and a source of inspiration leading to creative and relevant advertising.

One of the most useful contributions made by planning when still in its infancy was the think planning cycle (see Figure 1) – a model still widely used today. The cycle divides the process of developing advertising into distinct phases and indicates clearly both the research methodology and objectives that best fit each phase. (For further discussion of the think planning cycle see Chapter 9.)

Planning in the UK has grown and evolved, emerging in different ways according to agency philosophy. Some agency planners conduct their own qualitative research believing that, through their greater understanding of the advertising process and their closer relationships with the creative department, their skills and experience make the

Figure 1: Think Planning Cycle

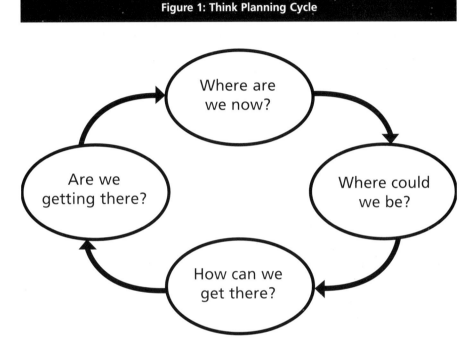

qualitative study more directly actionable. Other agency planners prefer to outsource all qualitative research, remaining closely involved and using researchers known to be empathetic to the needs of advertising agencies and their clients. Some agencies have planners as founding partners and have therefore instilled planning into the core philosophy of the agency, while others do not believe in planning specialisation within agencies, preferring to outsource planning skills through planning independents.

At the present time in the UK there are in the region of 450 planners who are members of the Account Planning Group, which produces a regular newsletter, holds training courses and seminars and has introduced the Creative Effectiveness Awards to acknowledge the contribution of planning to great campaigns.

In other parts of the world, the discipline of planning is at various stages of sophistication. Many American agencies, after a slow and somewhat suspicious start, are now convinced that planners can make a significant contribution to effective advertising. Planning is growing in other parts of the world as well with the spread of multinational agencies and the demands of worldwide branding strategies and global or 'glocal' executions.

Returning to the UK, the decade between 1978 and 1988 saw a boom in qualitative research evidenced by the many new specialist agencies that came into existence, as well as in the growth of independent qualitative research practitioners. It was a time when advertising development involved consecutive stages of qualitative research. 'Rough' creative work was generated to explore several different routes (in the early stages), followed by the use of a number of different campaign executions (presented in the form of animatics, narrative tapes or storyboards), to assess which creative idea best met the strategy.

'Planning is growing in other parts of the world as well with the spread of multi-national agencies and the demands of worldwide branding strategies and global or "glocal" executions.'

During the 1980s there were a number of other streams which fed the fast-flowing river of qualitative research. In brief, these were:

- the adoption of the planning model by other consultancies, such as packaging design, corporate identity, new product development

- the entrance of new advertisers who needed to understand the consumer–brand relationship in a very different context from that of fmcg (packaged goods), e.g. financial services, retailers, IT companies

- the impact of the sale of Rowntree brands in 1986, which brought into vivid relief the potential asset value of strong brands and the power of brand building, a process to which qualitative research is particularly well suited

- the dominating power of the multiples and resulting pressure on all brands from own-label competitors, leading to recognition of the importance of brand differentiation and new product development

- the growth of pan-European and worldwide research for global brands which tended to be co-ordinated from one country – often the UK – which was able to provide the expertise and the resources to conduct substantial studies across the world in a very short time period; co-ordination expertise also existed in European research companies as well as the UK; by 1995 international research accounted for £277 million spent in Europe, 34% up on the previous year, while UK domestic research only saw an 8% rise in the same period

- growing consumer sophistication about the worlds of advertising and marketing, fuelled by coverage in the media of basic terminology and concepts as well as books such as Peter York's *Sloane Rangers*.

'The 1980s was the decade of "conspicuous consumption" and "greed is good".'

The 1980s was the decade of 'conspicuous consumption' and 'greed is good', where people lived as if they were the badge brands that they displayed. These brands were far less about rational or functional qualities than the less tangible facets of imagery, especially brand personality. Since qualitative research is ideally suited to exploring and developing these facets (and the purchasers of qualitative research were arguably among the most obsessive personal consumers of status brands), the boom in qualitative research was a reflection of the times.

'For the first time in two decades, qualitative research as a discipline, and qualitative researchers as deliverers of that discipline, are being criticised and devalued.'

At the end of the decade, the recession in the UK hit hard. If the 1980s were a fertile breeding ground for qualitative research, then the opposite could be said to be true for the first half of the 1990s. In the face of the recession, there was something faintly obscene about trying to build brands on intangible values and the obsession with 'looking good'.

Much of the bread-and-butter work that made qualitative specialist agencies very profitable and viable ceased overnight. The world changed. Businesses, across all sectors, adopted the term 'accountability' with a vengeance. The impact on qualitative research practice was enormous. Reduced research budgets slimmed down marketing and research departments and pressure on the bottom line meant that only essential projects were commissioned.

These necessitated consultation with a number of stakeholders, all of whom formulated questions and issues which the research project was required to answer. The areas of responsibility and expertise of these stakeholders was broad – communications in general, advertising in particular, trade relationships, promotions, sponsorship, merchandising, packaging, corporate identity, customer loyalty initiatives and so on. The load of expectations and demands that each qualitative project was expected to carry became more and more onerous and this is one of the fundamental reasons for the disappointment in performance – a situation that continues to this very day.

Qualitative research has been found wanting. For the first time in two decades, qualitative research as a discipline, and qualitative researchers as deliverers of that discipline, are being criticised and devalued. Stakeholders are looking at other experts to help highlight issues and show the way forward: marketing, NPD, management, change, communications and planning consultancies are stepping on qualitative toes. There is also a growing number of brainstorming and synectics specialists who offer authority, experience and the possibility of innovation – a heady promise for jaded marketers. Lastly, many more clients, both advertisers and advertising (as well as other marketing service) agencies, are undergoing basic training in order to conduct qualitative research themselves. This includes screening new products, dipstick research for diagnosis, research for advertising and product development, employee attitude pilots, trade interviews and so on.

As with any fundamental change, there are many contributing factors, in addition to the evolutionary developments described above. Qualitative researchers as individuals, and the professional bodies that represent them, have been myopic and inward-looking and thus compounded the problems that now face this research speciality.

The next section discusses some of the other factors that have undermined the effectiveness of qualitative research in the 1990s.

'Qualitative researchers as individuals have been myopic and inward-looking.'

Qualitative research has become process driven

Qualitative research has become formulaic, obsessed with quality standards, recruitment, (mal)practice, 'quantitative' sample design and other process factors.

Qualitative recruitment issues and problems have become the centre of focus for many of the trade and professional bodies involved in research, advertising and marketing. Many hours of work from a small number of dedicated people who care deeply about quality standards have been devoted to improving standards in the following areas: training for qualitative recruiters, payment and contracts, centralised record-keeping of respondents, blacklisting of poor-quality recruiters, back-checking procedures, the geographic spread of recruiters across the country, telephone panels, the relationships of recruiters to individual researchers and to companies, confidentiality, video protocols and the interviewing of children.

'Qualitative research has become formulaic, obsessed with quality standards, recruitment, (mal)practice, "quantitative" sample design and other process factors.'

Importantly, the Professional Code of Conduct for Qualitative Research developed by ESOMAR and the Market Research Society together with the Association of Qualitative Researchers, has made qualitative processes and practice both legitimate and explicit. (A summary of the code is included in the reference section and should be mandatory reading for practitioners and buyers of qualitative research all over the world.)

Despite all this excellent work to improve the very foundations and structures of the discipline, the old chestnut of the cheating qualitative recruiter and the panel of professional respondents who collude in making a living by masquerading as different brand users at focus groups each week, still receives periodic and sometimes hysterical coverage in the trade publications or on conference platforms.

Even today, there is media suspicion of qualitative research. Since the 1997 election, the idea of the 'focus group' has become public property, courtesy of the Labour Party communications machine. In some sectors of the press this has been expressed as cynicism that the views of 'eight ordinary people' (about government, politics, the monarchy, our lives) are being manipulated to 'sell' decisions to the general population.

In a business context, people who find themselves at odds with its philosophy and practice often use the spectre of the dishonest respondent to attack qualitative research. At present there is a concern over whether segments of the population that tend to be critical of advertising *per se*, should or should not be excluded from advertising qualitative research – a debate that focuses on sampling criteria.

Sample design – the number of focus groups (or other interviewing units), their make-up and geographical location – is the subject of much agonising by buyers and practitioners of research at the start of a project. Practitioners are professionally responsible for ensuring that the sample design and recruitment criteria are appropriate, but when this becomes nit-picking and obsessional, it is usually a sign that the buyer or practitioner feels anxious about the project and they then displace this nervous energy by exerting control over the process. The more inexperienced or junior the project controller (buyer/client-side researcher), the more likely this is to happen. This leads to over-defined samples and impossible recruitment criteria, which result in focus groups that have an in-built self-destruct mechanism that can derail the project.

While all of these quality controls and continuing improvements are undoubtedly important, they are 'hygiene factors', like the safety procedures British Airways undertakes in flying people across the world. The inspiration for great qualitative work and the search for the nuggets of insight that make clear how to leverage the brand–consumer relationship do not lie in process factors.

'Sample design – the number of focus groups, their make-up and geographical location – is the subject of much agonising by buyers and practitioners of research at the start of a project.'

The mechanisation of qualitative research

'Innovative qualitative methods of finding and interviewing people are not like groceries in a cash-and-carry wholesaler that can simply be piled into a trolley and used by anyone.'

Now that qualitative research and planning have become established jobs or careers within their industries, they are surrounded by a variety of rules, processes, procedures and techniques which enable practitioners to do the job. My concern here is that these processes were invented by a previous generation after much trial, error and soul-searching. This generation of researchers and planners passed down their thinking to the 'second' generation. However, this 'second' generation passed down the process to the current generation without the thinking and reasoning behind it. The danger is that recent entrants to both research and planning approach research as a mechanistic procedure rather than a dynamic process (1).

Projective techniques are an illustration of this. Qualitative researchers both guard their own toolkit of projective techniques and copy those learnt from others as if this was the answer to the meaning of life. In the US and elsewhere I have often been asked: 'What's new in projective techniques?' in the same tone that one might ask 'What's new in information technology?'. Training sessions are held on projective techniques – not a bad idea in itself – but the emphasis is on the 'doing' of projective techniques, not the thinking underpinning them. They have become detached from the theoretical background on which they are based and thus become toys rather than tools.

This is plain silliness. Projective techniques do not guarantee access to the truth. They are simply ways to enable the person or the group being interviewed to get in touch with the jumble of thoughts, feelings and behaviour attached to the subject of the enquiry (see Chapter 6).

Innovative qualitative methods of finding and interviewing people and ways of asking questions directly and indirectly are not like groceries in a cash-and-carry wholesaler that can simply be piled into a trolley and used by anyone who pays the money. They are the intellectual property of the discipline and, like the tools of management consultants, are only effective when the user has both rigorous formal training and considerable practice and experience.

The sanitisation of real human beings

The most sanitised part of contemporary qualitative practice is the viewing room that has become almost synonymous with qualitative research. Viewing rooms were born in the US and have spread throughout the world, changing the face of qualitative market research, particularly in the UK. Previously it was common to conduct groups in the neighbourhood homes of recruiters. The underlying assumption was that a group, held in a suburban home, provided a safer and more homely environment for the members; the event being more like a coffee evening or small local get-together than a business meeting.

The model in the US is completely different. Viewing rooms came into being to allow the client team to see for itself how people talk about their products, brands and new ideas. Focus groups, observed in this way, are positioned as a forum for rational debate and fact finding. (See Chapter 4 for a discussion on the psychodynamic model of groups versus the rational model.) Viewing rooms in America look like board rooms rather than living rooms and have a very business-like feel, communicated through the behaviour of the staff, the decor and the location.

'Viewing rooms came into being to allow the client team to see for itself how people talk about their products, brands and new ideas.'

Rapid growth in the number of viewing studios has led inevitably to variations in quality – there are many excellent ones but also others with below-par audio-visual equipment, untrained hostessing, poor professional standards and inadequate facilities both sides of the one-way mirror. As a result, the Viewing Facilities Association (UK) was formed in 1995, and this organisation exerts pressure on studios to improve standards and to comply with the MRS Code of Conduct.

While viewing facilities allow access to the target market in a way that can challenge the thinking of the brand team, and allow the observation of real people talking about the brand, responding to the advertising or new product ideas, and exchanging points of view, often the creature comforts behind the screen, the voyeuristic nature of the experience and the politics of different party agendas interfere with the process of genuine open-minded listening.

Observers often misbehave behind the mirror, laughing raucously or discussing other business matters, listening only periodically to parts of the discussion. Participants may become suspicious, aggressive or may posture and show off for the benefit of the unseen audience. Group dynamics are complicated by the fact that the environment is business-orientated and unrelaxed. From the point of view of the moderator there are two groups interacting simultaneously – one behind the mirror and one in front of it – which is a difficult process to manage. Finally, there is huge pressure on the moderator to run 'a good group' – an entertaining group with many memorable sound bites for the observers to take to work or to friends the next day.

'People in viewing rooms are observed away from their homes, shopping environments and neighbourhoods leading to a vacuum in which their verbal utterances take on meanings that do not reflect reality.'

An important concern is: who are these people sipping wine and eating peanuts while discussing toilet cleaning products or advertising work-in-progress for a bank? People in viewing rooms are observed away from their homes, shopping environments and neighbourhoods leading to a vacuum in which their verbal utterances take on meanings that do not reflect reality. Reported behaviour is the content of the discussion rather than the real behaviour that takes place at point of purchase or consumption, involving the complex dynamics that determine choice of brand for a particular set of circumstances.

The loss of contact with real life, manifested by the distancing of the consumer to the other side of a one-way mirror, stems from an inherent problem of attitude: who is the consumer? We all use jargon like: 'the average consumer', 'our consumer', 'consumer motivation', 'consumer typologies'. We study consumer behaviour as David Attenborough studies gorilla behaviour – sometimes in hushed awe and sometimes with cruel laughter. By using the word 'consumer', we attempt to objectify human beings and persuade ourselves that we understand people as individuals, when in fact we have often drawn stereotypical and numerically based approximations.

A conspiracy

One of the most frequent expectations of qualitative research is that it should indicate how people will respond to an unborn concept – the foetal advertising campaign, pack design, corporate identity, new product idea, range extension, service initiative or brand to be revitalised with new meanings and values. At the time of the research, the 'real thing' has not yet been born. It is like showing an unborn baby to whole lot of strangers through a scanner machine: the baby is obviously human, alive and moving but it is also featureless, lacking colour and certainly without personality. Taking the analogy further, we are then asking this panel of strangers to tell us whether or not they are interested in this baby, whether or not they might like to baby-sit for a few days, what his/her personality might be like and how the baby compares to other children and small babies they know!

Yet this is exactly what happens with the so called 'stimulus material' that is so widely used in qualitative research. Embryonic concepts are used to predict the nature of consumer response to the advertising campaign or executions, new product ideas, corporate identity schemes or brand propositions. Prediction in this case does not mean sales forecasts (although a positive indication is often transmuted into high sales expectations); rather it means to anticipate or to envisage likely response. Stimulus material conveys a premise or hypothesis that needs to be explored. The material in itself is not reality (see Chapter 8).

'There are relatively few people who are experienced or authoritative enough to bring the inadequacies of stimulus material into full view.'

Many planners, practitioners and clients know that stimulus material can be misleading, yet it is rarely talked about openly. There are relatively few people who are experienced or authoritative enough to bring the inadequacies of stimulus material into full view and to manage expectations effectively. This fuels disappointment in the practice and promises of qualitative research.

Clients, planners and researchers are guilty of collusion in other ways. There is a conspiracy that prevents people from being open about the qualitative process for fear of bringing the discipline into disrepute. We complain but continue to conduct research using the ubiquitous focus group, we cut sample sizes to a minimum (two per country on some international studies), and we hijack the original objectives and include other issues in the research discussion – packaging, brochures, a few more executions! We allow long 'questionnaire' discussion guides to be written, which detract from exploring stimulating thoughts that arise from the interaction of a number of people, and we continue to recruit middle-class compliant individuals from 'nice' areas of London, New York, Johannesburg or Manchester, shutting our eyes to the fact that the target market is not being represented.

'Young people with less than one year's experience in business are thrown in at the deep end and asked to moderate group discussions.'

If this is not enough, we are also guilty of lack of training – among planners, researchers and clients who are now conducting some of their own 'screening' or dipstick projects. Young people with less than one year's experience in business are thrown in at the deep end and asked to moderate group discussions. They are not given practical help in how to expose stimulus material, what projective techniques to use, how to deal with group dynamics and how to work out which responses are important and which are not. They are not given any theoretical background and are unaware of recent developments in qualitative research. Not surprisingly a young client said recently: 'Well ... qualitative research is really easy ... all it is is chatting to a few people for an hour or so.' No wonder the expertise in qualitative research is being undermined!

Finally, there is a big squeeze on time and budgets, which has led to a condensation of the planning cycle. Nowadays, the discipline of separating strategy development from execution is often missing. In terms of the ideal brand planning cycle, we are often asking the question 'where could we be?' at the same time as 'how are we going to get there?', i.e. disentangling strategy from creative ideas and executions, whether these be advertising, new product, promotions or other solutions to the defined strategy. Sometimes we are even doing the whole developmental cycle in one go – answering the fundamental questions about the consumer relationship with the sector and the brand in the same piece of research as pricing, in-store behaviour and alternative pack designs. It is a minefield that only the most experienced researcher can begin to negotiate and, even then, mistakes can be made.

'There is a big squeeze on time and budgets, which has led to a condensation of the planning cycle.'

Where do we go from here?

A change in orientation and practice is necessary if we are to develop a meaningful understanding of how to develop brands, communications, service delivery and products in the advanced brand marketing environment of the late 1990s and beyond. This change means a rethink of what fieldwork actually is, and certainly requires a redefinition of the contract we have with respondents (including a change of terminology).

'A change in orientation and practice is necessary if we are to develop a meaningful understanding of how to develop brands.'

The re-orientation can be tackled from four directions:

- the need to get closer to an individual's relationship with a product, brand or service we are studying, as and when behaviour actually occurs

- the need to develop a holistic approach that allows us to understand the brand relationship in different contexts and over time

- the need to enter into a different kind of contract with people who participate in research – one that is more open and based on partnership

- the need to adapt qualitative techniques and develop new approaches to help companies plan strategies, brands and products for the future – not simply next year but five to ten years ahead.

Getting closer to real behaviour

This involves excursions into the real world – observing, listening, talking and being aware of the broader cultural context in which the brand behaviour is taking place. It involves observation alone or combined with accompanying people (recruited from the target market) while they shop or cook, while the family goes out at the weekend, going clubbing or drinking in different kinds of places from one's normal repertoire, shadowing the extended process of selecting and booking a holiday. It can take the form of involvement in other activities such as eating, ironing, choosing gifts, visiting dealers for a new or used car and so on.

Naturally the interviewer is not invisible and his or her presence needs to be acknowledged in the process. Fieldwork such as this demands trained observation and rapport skills together with expertise in recording the behaviour on video or audio-tape. There are important practical issues to do with recording, coding and analysing the information in addition to technical expertise in filming and editing. The theoretical fieldwork guidelines of anthropology are more relevant than traditional qualitative training, which is derived from the discipline of psychology and group therapy.

In the conventional group discussion or depth interview it is easy for people to play back the image-related aspects of a brand (certainly useful and encouraged by the projective techniques used by most qualitative researchers), but they are less likely to remember the real impact of price, promotions, packaging or the dominant need state determining choice of brand.

'Being there' captures the moment-to-moment relationship people have with brands. It can illustrate how brands get lost in the back of kitchen cupboards, how people use packaging in-store in a tactile way, how women interpret healthy eating by demonstrating to the interviewer the contents of their fridge or freezer. It allows research to place what people say, do and think in the context of family dynamics, neighbourhood and broader cultural influences.

This kind of qualitative enquiry involves leaving behind the sanitised safety and profitability of group discussions and crossing into the messy lives of real human beings. It means being flexible, internalising the research brief, doing away with discussion guides and stimulus

'"Being there" captures the moment-to-moment relationship people have with brands.'

material; it means spending time in the field; it means rethinking the very nature of qualitative research – who does it best, what should it cost and in what form should the output be?

A more detailed discussion of this approach is included in Chapter 3.

Developing a more holistic and longitudinal approach

This allows us to understand how people relate to a brand in many different contexts. Repertoires change over time and, by understanding behaviour at the level of the individual, we can gain valuable insights into the way in which the tools of mass marketing integrate in their influence. This type of work is particularly useful in providing genuine insight into product categories and brands where there are different points of interface with the brand or where there is a decision-making chain of events.

'Adopting a family with whom the researcher builds a relationship can help one understand how people choose a car for instance.'

Adopting a family with whom the researcher builds a relationship can help one understand how people choose a car, for instance, or their relationship with photography and all the purchases that are involved. By entering into a long-term contract with the individual or family which is transparent, the relationship develops to the point that both researcher and participant(s) are involved, as partners, in the search for understanding.

Both of these approaches to fieldwork have a role to play at the strategic planning stages of development. They add reality to the process of market analysis which is so fundamental to the development of effective brand communications.

Citizens' juries have become established in the political arena and are an example of this contextual approach. A sample of people, representing the population at large, is brought together as a large group. They are presented with information and asked to debate and then vote on an issue. Further information and 'evidence' is then presented to the group and, after debate, another vote is taken. This method allows politicians the opportunity to understand how different types of information sway and influence public opinion, leading to decisions regarding the best way to communicate policy or government initiatives to the country as a whole. Citizens' juries can be used to understand how different contexts of understanding shape opinion.

The way we think about people
The word partner, rather than consumer or respondent, is the key to optimising the contribution of the target market to the development and evaluation of advertising. There is the need for a more experiential approach, which engages the client and its agencies with the people who buy and use the brand, or do not as the case may be. All human beings can be resourceful and creative given a sympathetic environment to problem solving.

> Research will begin to reflect this realisation by being increasingly transparent and by sharing the enquiry agenda with respondents. People will often be told what the task is and the groups be run more like 'workshops' (2).

In practical terms, this means that part of the qualitative research process can be more interactive, using brainstorming, synectics and other workshop techniques with expert facilitators. There are all sorts of ways that the barriers between client and agency professionals and 'ordinary people' can be broken down prior to the interactive session taking place. For example, pairs of people (professional and target market), can be asked to visit a number of supermarkets to explore a category fixture in the light of the brand being explored, or given a reel of advertising film for a category outside the purpose of the workshop and asked to analyse the ads according to criteria that are relevant to both of them. Smaller groups can be asked to work on expressing 'brand essence' or positioning statements or could be given

'The word partner, rather than consumer or respondent, is the key to optimising the contribution of the target market to the development and evaluation of advertising.'

the task of finding the best way to represent a new campaign using different forms of stimulus material. Whatever the problem, by working as partners, the outcome is grounded in reality.

Interactive 'research' has practical implications. What constitutes the 'data'? How should the outcomes be recorded? How can the hypotheses and insights be explored with more conventional research approaches? Is it research at all and, if not, what should we call this type of work?

'The greatest challenge of all for the long-term health of the discipline is to focus on the future.'

The greatest challenge of all for the long-term health of the discipline is to focus on the future. Qualitative research, like quantitative research, relies heavily on the past, on behaviour and attitudes that occurred months or a year ago or attitudes formed either early in life or in response to the times. How then can qualitative research help clients envision the future? How can the techniques and methodologies it has developed, and is developing now, be used to show clients the shape of things to come?

Qualitative researchers are uniquely equipped to offer this essential service to clients. We are able to integrate large amounts of information of different kinds, unlike quantitative research which has to bear in mind sampling, questionnaire design, question wording and other factors in fusing different data sources. We have the rigour and discipline to assess which elements of new knowledge are anecdotal and which represent a growing trend. We have access to experts around the world, whether consumer experts, fashion experts, youth experts or techno-experts, to name but a few. We can work with cross-functional teams of marketing, communications, design and R&D specialists to paint likely scenarios of the future and visualise them in a way that human beings can imagine. We can brainstorm and brandstorm these ideas into development thus having a far more senior role in the team than pure ad hoc research project responsibilities.

But we can only do this if we have integrity, courage and expertise combined with the intention to escape from the narrow world of qualitative research into the broader business context.

All qualitative practitioners and the users who value its contribution need to work together to ensure that it does not lose its way. We need to invest in the training of users as well as practitioners in order to increase the understanding and sensitive use of established and new qualitative methodologies; we need to close the distance gap between ourselves as professionals and people like ourselves who buy the brand and services in which we are interested; we need to re-orientate ourselves in how we think about fieldwork and how we behave with 'respondents' and, most importantly, we need to be future-focused. Only then can qualitative research regain the excitement and inspiration that it achieved in the early 1980s.

'All qualitative practitioners and the users who value its contribution need to work together to ensure that it does not lose its way.'

REFERENCES

1. R. Pike, 'Qualitative Advertising Research: The Gap Between Theory and Practice', *Admap*, IPA, MRS Seminar: How to make Advertising Research Work Harder, 1997.
2. Roddy Glen Special Report, 'Qualitative', *Research* magazine, May 1998.

FURTHER READING

A. Hedges, *Testing to Destruction, A Fresh and Critical Look at the Uses of Research in Advertising*, IPA, 1974.

C. A. Restall, and R. Auton, 'From Passivity to Interaction? The Future of Qualitative Research', 49th ESOMAR Congress, Changing Business Dynamics: The Challenge to Marketing Research, September 1996, pp. 281–293.

A Review of Qualitative Methods

Chapter three

Introduction

There has been a growing trend over the last five years among both buyers and practitioners of qualitative research to search for more innovative and creative methodologies to crack complex marketing or business problems. There are two reasons for this. First, the disillusionment with conventional qualitative group discussions and depth interviews (discussed in Chapter 2) has led to a search for new ways to reveal insight. Second, there is a mistaken belief that new methods have more power to 'delve beneath the skin of the consumer', 'reveal the true needs and drivers of consumer behaviour' or 'reach the truth'.

'Innovation in itself brings the practitioner and end user no closer to the truth.'

It is probably true that a new method of interviewing the target group or the relevant application of a new projective technique might provide a different perspective, one that may enrich the picture obtained through the conventional methods. Innovation in itself, however, brings the practitioner and end user no closer to the truth – because it would seem that there is no single truth to be found! Truth, as discussed in Chapter 1, is a relative concept and the best we can achieve as researchers is a multi-faceted view of the problem from which we make the best interpretation.

This chapter reviews the qualitative methodologies that are in use today and offers criteria of evaluation so that the most relevant combination can be chosen for the problem in hand.

The debate

'Participant observation and ethnography, where the researcher enters the consumer's world, reflect our need to understand the cultural context surrounding purchase and consumption.'

There has been a growing debate among qualitative practitioners about the limitations of the 'focus group' (as it has come to be known) and the individual interview compared to ethnographic, observational or interactive methodologies. For some strange reason, these latter approaches have been called 'alternative' – rather like aromatherapy and acupuncture are called 'alternative medicine' – and yet they are based on the sound academic principles of scientific research described in Chapter 1. The term 'alternative' has brought with it an underlying suspicion in some quarters that these methodologies are simply marketing tools and 'gimmicks' for research agency promotion rather than the result of a genuine need to find more robust, relevant and insightful means of understanding the complexities of human behaviour.

> *Participant observation and ethnography, where the researcher enters the consumer's world, reflect our need to understand the cultural context surrounding purchase and consumption, the experiential dimension of brands, and the importance of symbolic meaning to the post-modern consumer.*
>
> *Experiencing context is the critical step ... a participating experience with its myriad of details creates and recreates authenticity and coherence in the world being studied* (1).
>
> *In contrast, focus groups, which import respondents to the researchers world, have their roots in the experimental, laboratory-based, traditions of social psychology and the group dynamics work of the psychotherapists* (2).

These two orientations are neither right nor wrong – they simply produce different perspectives. The psychological or psychotherapeutic model tends to be wary of surface responses and consumer explanations of the reason-why underlying behaviour; hence the extensive use of projective questioning and techniques to aid interpretation. The sociological and anthropological models accept the face validity of people's behaviour and their explanations of it and use the contextual frame of culture to develop an interpretation.

Methodology – what are the choices?

There are four types of qualitative methodology:

- the group interview

- the individual interview

- observational methods

- interactive workshops.

'The depth versus breadth argument is generally cited to justify choice of a group versus an individual approach.'

The depth-versus-breadth argument is generally cited to justify choice of a group versus an individual approach. Individual interviews are believed to provide more detailed information of the attitudes and behaviour of the individual while group discussions are claimed to provide breadth in terms of the range of behaviours and attitudes between individuals attending the group.

The group interview

There are many different variants of the group interview but the group discussion or focus group is the most commonly used method around the world. This consists of seven to nine people in the UK and ten to twelve in the US, who have been recruited according to a pre-determined set of criteria such as age, gender, life stage, social class, and product, service or brand usership. Conventional group discussions last under two hours in length. At the most simplistic level, each group discussion has a moderator (or facilitator) whose role it is to create an environment in which participants feel safe enough to share their attitudes, behaviour, thoughts and feelings with a number of strangers. Moderators are trained to:

- guide the discussion over a number of topic areas that are of interest and relevance to the paying client

- recognise important points of view and encourage the group to explore and expand on these

- deal with group dynamic processes effectively (see Chapter 4)

- internalise the research objectives of the study so that he or she can listen carefully and, at times, play back his or her understanding to the group to check meaning and interpretation

- use forms of questioning, research material, stimuli, tasks and exercises with discrimination to enable the members of the group to articulate thoughts and feelings that they may not be used to accessing or expressing.

The most common reasons for adopting a group approach are:

- a less intimidating environment than the individual interview (3) since most human beings welcome 'safety in numbers' when confronted with an unusual event, together with an atmosphere that generates feelings of anticipation, excitement and energy (2)

- a way of encouraging people to build on each others' views, expressing similar or opposing experiences, attitudes, thoughts and feelings within clearly defined parameters

- a method that highlights the range of behaviours, attitudes and points of view between people within a relatively

'Moderators are trained to guide the discussion over a number of topic areas that are of interest and relevance to the paying client.'

short period; a time-efficient way of obtaining consumer feedback, suited to time-poor executives

- 'live' research which can be observed through a one-way mirror or video relay system, by members of the client organisation so that they can experience customer response, consumer vocabulary, attitudes, accounts of behaviour, perceptions of the market and reactions first-hand

- a window into the cultural and social experiences of the group

- a 'laboratory' in which the responses of the group to a wide range of different stimuli (advertising, packaging, products, brands, brochures, below-the-line material) can be explored.

The argument against using the group interview approach alone may involve any or several of the following reasons.

'"Expert" participants will intimidate those with less experience, making an unbalanced group.'

- People have different levels of knowledge and understanding – 'expert' participants will intimidate those with less experience, making an unbalanced group, e.g. financial confidence and sophistication, home decorating and DIY capabilities, gourmet cooking.

- Social norms and the need to conform to an ideal which is socially or politically correct will predominate, such as teaching children road safety, bottle versus breast feeding, parental discipline, eating healthy food, racial attitudes.

- Detailed behaviour and attitudinal histories are required, e.g. tracing the pattern of car ownership, sequential

'The mini-group may overcome problems of embarrassment, expertise differences and recruitment difficulties.'

processes of finding a mortgage for a new home, deciding which holiday to go on this year compared with previous years, exactly how a product is used etc.

• Intimate subject matter (sexual behaviour, sanitary protection, body odour, constipation), or personal financial situations (wealth management, insurance, pensions), where disclosure is potentially embarrassing in front of strangers or observers.

• Difficult-to-recruit respondents such as highly paid senior management, farmers, pre-selected names from company listings, minority brand users, the homeless, people who travel a great deal.

• Complex political and social issues such as 'the meaning of motherhood today', 'gay parenthood', 'surrogacy', 'the portrayal of men in the media', 'work and the next millennium'.

• Matters of fashion and taste where personal preferences are likely to be extremely varied, e.g. music, decor, fashion.

Variations in the group interview method – such as the mini-group, friendship group, extended group, 'conflict' group, reconvened group and sensitivity panel – have all been developed to overcome the perceived limitations of the basic format.

The *mini-group* consists of four to six people and usually lasts for a shorter length of time. It may overcome problems of embarrassment, expertise differences and recruitment difficulties.

Friendship groups are usually recommended for children and teenagers where problems of shyness can be overcome by recruiting a group of friends or pairs of friends. Often this approach means that a greater number of groups needs to be conducted; the mini-group format is a solution.

The *extended group* (or 'extended creativity group') may last as long as four hours or even longer and allows sufficient time for respondents to participate in tasks and exercises such as words and pictures, psychodrama, brand mapping, exploring advertising both inside and outside the category of interest, brand personality exercises, and so on (see Chapter 6). This method can overcome problems of embarrassment or political correctness since greater attention can be paid to forming the group and creating a safe environment for disclosure. It also allows for a wide range of research objectives and stimuli.

'The conflict group is designed to highlight the differences between people and to use this "clash" to understand the core issue.'

The *conflict group* is designed to highlight the differences between people and to use this 'clash' to understand the core issue or to explore with the group if and how these differences can be resolved or negotiated. The moderator thus makes it explicit in the forming phase of the group that people have been recruited with very different viewpoints and agendas and that the task for the group is to explore the nature of these differences. For example, a group could be constructed with people who buy and passionately support British brands (e.g. cars, appliances and airlines) versus those who actively prefer European, Japanese or other non-British brands in order to understand the nature of the 'Britishness'.

Moderating skills need to be finely honed in order for this kind of group to be productive since the group can become stuck, locked in conflict and hostility, to the detriment of the research process.

The *reconvened group* is one of the most useful and under-used variations of the group interview. A group is recruited for two sessions separated by one week. The first session covers some of the key topics, usually the more straightforward ones. During the interim week the group is asked to conduct a number of exercises. These are designed to sensitise the members of the group to certain aspects of their own or other members of their families' or friends' behaviour and to come back to the group with a mini-analysis of their observations. For example, the members of the group might be asked to visit two different retail environments and make observations about the display of goods, the behaviour of the shop assistants, the behaviour of other people in the store and details of the environment. A group might be asked to stop doing something that they take for granted like drinking tea, cleaning the toilet, driving the car. This kind of behavioural change highlights vividly the key drivers of attitude and behaviour.

'At the reconvened session, it is noticeable how much more involved people are with the subject and the aims of the research.'

At the reconvened session, it is noticeable how much more involved people are with the subject and the aims of the research. They are more willing to disclose and share 'heartfelt' thoughts and feelings and thus many of the topics become easy to discuss.

The *sensitivity panel* is a psychodynamic group interview process first described by Bill Schlackman in 1983 (4). A number of people are invited to attend a series of group discussions exploring various subjects over a period of time. During these sessions, they are 'taught' how to access hidden thoughts and feelings – those that might be repressed for one reason or another or have become highly defended. They learn such techniques as free association, analogy generation, 'gestalt dialogue' and stream of awareness, and require almost no preparation to engage in a new subject. The fact that the group members come to know each other facilitates an atmosphere of rapport and this intimacy enables 'sharing' to take place, since the trust level between them is high. This kind of approach is valuable if the moderator has the appropriate experiential training and theoretical understanding of psychoanalytical theory and group psychology.

Sensitivity panels are not the same things as qualitative panels. The latter is a sample of people, usually customers of an organisation (such as a bank or a credit card company), who have been recruited to a panel and have agreed to attend a group discussion or to conduct an interview, when asked. Bank or credit card behaviour of each individual is well documented and thus groups or interviews can be conducted with people whose behaviour is fact not fiction. Panel members can be interviewed once or several times. Panels do decline over a period of time and thus they constantly need to be 'topped up' with new members.

There may be even more variations than those discussed above. The underlying principle is the same: each variant has evolved in response to a particular limitation of the basic group discussion or 'focus group'. None are the magic answer to greater truthfulness. In combination they provide a more colourful picture of the behaviour and attitudes of a target group.

The individual interview

The individual interview has had a chequered history in contemporary qualitative market research. In the early days of motivational research it was the primary 'deep digging tool' and still is according to Chrissie Burns (5) who, like many experienced qualitative researchers, believes that this methodology has an important complementary role to play alongside group interview methods.

For the purposes of definition, the individual interview is a conversation conducted between a trained qualitative researcher or depth interviewer and a 'respondent' selected according to agreed criteria (age, life stage, gender, social class, marital status, usership profile etc.). It can last anywhere between half an hour and two or more hours, depending on the nature of the enquiry.

Generally, the standard 'depth' interview is an hour in length and is conducted in the home of the recruiter, in the respondent's own home or place of work, in an agreed venue (pub, club, retail environment), or in a research facility. The place influences the nature of the

'Each variant has evolved in response to a particular limitation of the basic group discussion or "focus group". None are the magic answer to greater truthfulness.'

interview in the same way that the venue effects the nature of the group discussion.

Over the past two decades, use of the individual 'depth' interview has declined as the popularity of the 'focus group' has risen. This is due to a number of reasons:

- the nature of the information obtained in a 'one-on-one' interview is believed to be similar to that elicited in a group discussion when, in practice, it is very different

- the lack of entertainment value for the observers of a 'depth interview' compared to a group discussion is often an underlying reason for a preference for the latter

- a mistaken belief that it is easier to interview one person alone rather than a group of eight to ten people and hence depth interviews are considered a suitable training ground for young and inexperienced researchers to test their wings; this can lead to naïve research recommendations based on reportage rather than interpretation

- buyers often balking at the relative costs of depth interviews compared to group discussions, as they do not place enough value on a senior practitioner conducting them, nor appreciate the complexity and the chameleon-like qualities that are needed.

One of the fundamental problems is that individual interviews are usually advocated *instead* of group discussions – in other words the two methodologies are seen to be in opposition rather than being used to enrich and complement one another.

'Over the past two decades, use of the individual "depth" interview has declined as the popularity of the "focus group" has risen.'

In the UK particularly, practitioners prefer to recommend group discussions rather than depth interviews for the simple reason that, in terms of time and energy, they are more profitable.

Generally speaking, the individual interview is considered appropriate for sensitive subject matter such as redundancy, medical problems, relationship difficulties or intimate hygiene products where it is important to understand in some detail how the individual's attitudes and behaviour evolved over time. Today, in the West, it is relatively easy to encourage a group of people to talk about AIDS or sanitary protection but this is not the case in all cultures. The findings of the experiment in methodology discussed later in this chapter suggest that the nature of the information and understanding is different depending on whether it was approached through the vehicle of a group interview or an individual interview.

The individual interview is also useful for product categories, brands and services where overclaiming or underclaiming is likely to occur. This happens in many product categories, even those that appear to be straightforward, like the use of spices in cooking. Women will often overclaim on creativity and experimentalism in preparing food just as people over or underclaim about the amount of wine or whisky they drink.

'In the UK particularly, practitioners prefer to recommend group discussions rather than depth interviews for the simple reason that they are more profitable.'

While the same dynamic occurs in the individual interview, it is easier for a well-trained moderator to detect it and to work out how to enable the individual to show his or her 'private face' (5).

Individual interviews can help reconstruct the process of decision making. For example, the step-by-step process of choosing a telecom supplier including the influence of advertising, direct mail, point of sale, word of mouth and advice of family and friends and so on can best be tackled through a one-to-one approach. A historical reconstruction and review of key events in the process is difficult to achieve in the group interview. There is no time to elicit the necessary level of detail for each member of the group and contamination by the views of other members of the group, who tend to make value judgments as the individual is speaking, interferes with the flow.

Sometimes it is relevant to try to find out whether a particular point of view or behavioural trait is idiosyncratic or common. By conducting 20–30 individual interviews it is relatively easy to come to a conclusion about this. If this sample supports the findings of previous group discussions, the combination of the two approaches is robust enough to eliminate a follow-up quantitative exercise (provided the objective is to understand proportions rather than to obtain percentages).

'Researching communication in a group is a frustrating experience – the brightest individual "gets it quickly" and articulates it for the group.'

Communication issues connected with press advertising or brochures, magazine readership behaviour, participation in product promotions and response to promotion mechanics (e.g. 10% extra versus BOGOF – Buy One Get One Free) or any other instance where the relationship between the stimulus and the individual is uniquely individual, benefit from this kind of interview (5). Researching communication in a group is a frustrating experience – the brightest individual 'gets it quickly' and articulates it for the group. The moderator never knows how many other members of the group would have absorbed the same message or expressed it in the same way.

Behaviour such as cleaning the car, cooking a curry, taking photographs on a day out, drinking behaviour in a club or watching television as a family cannot be tackled through the conventional focus group – members reconstruct a 'memory amalgam' of behaviour rather than the real behaviour. Here, the individual interview needs to take place in the real context, not in a research venue, office or front room.

Difficult-to-interview respondents are best interviewed individually, perhaps because of geographical dispersion (farmers, people who buy from catalogues, lists of customers), status (managing director, CEO, head of finance, IT and telecoms directors, journalists, opinion formers etc.), expertise and knowledge, and low penetration purchasing.

Individual interviews can also be used as a pre-quantification exercise in order to ensure that a questionnaire designed for a survey reflects consumer or customer vocabulary or that the list of attitude statements or behavioural variations that are to be included in 'closed questions' represent the key parameters of the market.

There are variations on the basic interview format: mini-depth interviews, semi-structured interviews, pair interviews and family interviews, as follows.

Mini-depth interviews are short – between 20 minutes and half an hour and are used to explore a very focused issue such as the communication effectiveness of an advertisement or some other stimulus (pack design, brochure, promotion, visual, icon, logo), or the presence or otherwise of a comprehension problem. In a short time, someone can be shown an advertisement (or any stimulus) several times and responses explored in an open and flexible way.

Mini-depths are also used alongside conventional survey research, particularly central location pre-tests, to provide 'flesh to the bones' of quantitative survey data. Sometimes, a respondent who has already completed the main questionnaire can be re-interviewed by a qualitative researcher in order to understand the responses in more depth or a 'fresh sample' can be recruited to complement the main survey.

Semi-structured interviews are usually conducted by trained quantitative field interviewers using an open-ended questionnaire. The

'A respondent who has already completed the main questionnaire can be re-interviewed by a qualitative researcher in order to understand the responses in more depth.'

interviewer is trained on probing techniques and rapport skills but is required to ask the question exactly as it is written and not deviate with follow-up questions of his or her own. This kind of interview is used extensively in business-to-business research as well as medical, agricultural and pharmaceutical research where large numbers of interviews are required.

Semi-structured interviews can provide a useful 'booster' sample for conventional individual or group interviews especially where there are many cells in the sample.

Pair interviews are self-explanatory. A pair of respondents – best friends, spouses, co-habitees, employees, mother and daughter (or some other family combination), or users of the same brand are inter-viewed simultaneously. These interviews are useful for gaining insight into the dynamics of purchase decision making that often occur between family members or friends, or can help to create a less intimi-dating environment for the interview than a one-on-one, and are therefore frequently used as the interviewing format for children and teenagers.

Family interviews are similar to pair interviews except that the whole family is interviewed either separately, in pairs or all together (some-times in all three ways). Understanding the dynamics of a family rela-tionship around food, watching television, leisure activities or parental discipline is not easy. Any one spokesman for the family (mother, father or one of the children) has a particular perspective, which may or may not be shared by the others. The 'push-me, pull-you' dynamics of parent and child can best be explored using this interview format.

The AQRP runs a training course each year called 'An Introduction to the Principles and Practice of Qualitative Research' in which one of the modules is the 'depth interview'. The notes from this course make useful reading for those who have not conducted many depth

'Semi-structured interviews can provide a useful "booster" sample for conventional individual or group interviews especially where there are many cells in the sample.'

interviews. Written by Joanna Chrzanowska, the module covers:

- the importance of planning the interview beforehand and ensuring that it has an introduction, a warm-up, open-ended questions to find the unexpected, a topic outline and stimuli to generate response

- learning the relevant skill set such as personal presentation; clarity of communication; dealing with someone of a different age, sex, social class or background; listening skills; creating trust; drawing someone out; non-verbal awareness; dealing with dominating, arrogant, passive, withdrawn or uninterested interviewees; making assumptions too quickly; generalising – to name but a few.

'Self-awareness is crucial – prejudice is often highlighted in the individual interview dynamics.'

Chrissie Burns (5) adds yet more: knowing when to challenge; the manner of executing challenge; what to challenge and how to become aware of one's own role in reinforcing game playing; performing well within the safety net; and 'withholding'.

- 'Know thyself' – what are you bringing to the interview? What personal baggage? How quickly do you judge people by their appearance? How tolerant are you of those less or more intelligent than yourself? Self-awareness is crucial – prejudice is often highlighted in the individual interview dynamics.

- The importance of the introduction – people do not know what to expect when they agree to be interviewed. They may try to please, believe there is a correct answer, respond as they would to an authoritarian parent, a dismissive schoolteacher, an indulgent friend or a flirtatious stranger. There are no cues from other members of the group and certainly no benchmarks as to the level of sharing they should give. In a depth interview, just as in a

'Non-verbal communication is very powerful in a one-to-one, particularly body language, pacing, mirroring, time and space language.'

group discussion, it is essential to give the respondent the reason for the interview, confidentiality reassurances, some personal information about yourself, indications of the kind of conversation you wish to have and a time limit.

- Non-verbal communication is very powerful in a one-to-one, particularly body language, pacing, mirroring, time and space language (see also Chapter 5).

- Understanding the psychosocial dynamics of human relationships is essential to good interviewing. There are different roles people play in an individual interview – all of which are worth thinking about in terms of how to interact with someone who has taken on a particular way of being. There are those who are 'over-talkative', 'withdrawn or passive', 'emotional', 'cut-off', 'know-it-all', 'a complainer' or 'self-deprecating' for example. All of these are symptoms of past baggage, responses to anxiety at being the focus of attention, finding the subject difficult to talk about, or a manifestation of the games people play (see Chapter 5).

Observational methods

There are two types of observation: 'simple observation' and 'participant observation'. In approaches using simple observation, the observer functions impartially, almost as a machine, recording details of individual behaviour. However, no human being is a machine and therefore at some level, unconsciously, selective perception takes place.

Nowadays, video recorders are used to record the behaviour of individuals in public places like airports, shopping centres and retail store environments. Places where people consume products and services are suited to observation: restaurants, bars, theme parks, holiday venues, tourist attractions, hotel lobbies and garage forecourts.

Much new work is being conducted at 'the moment of truth', that is, the moment when someone selects a product from the shelf. Several advertising agencies in London have set up specialist units to conduct observation studies for clients. BMP DDB Needham is currently engaged in an innovative commercial observation exercise that involves members of its specialist unit – Culture Lab – living with a selected number of British families for two weeks at a time.

In the early 1980s, the BBC conducted a famous experiment on the television-watching habits of the nation. A video camera was installed in the television itself, which filmed the viewer(s) as they watched the programmes. Viewer reactions could be linked to the programme watched (6). Of course, the 'subjects' had given permission but it was clear from the footage that, over a period of weeks, they forgot about the existence of the camera. One of the key findings was that people rarely watch television with absolute concentration: they talk, eat, sew, read, walk in and out and interact with the announcers and advertisements. There was much footage that could not be shown!

The primary emphasis of this type of observation is recording what human beings do, not what they say they do. There is a great deal to be learned from this type of work for this reason alone.

The following extract is from an article by Malcolm Gladwell originally published in *The New Yorker* magazine on 4 November 1996.

> *... when potential shoppers enter a store, it's going to take them 10 or 15 paces to adjust to the light and refocus and*

'People rarely watch television with absolute concentration: they talk, eat, sew, read, walk in and out and interact with the announcers and advertisements.'

gear down from walking to shopping speed. [Paco] Underhill calls that area inside the door the Decompression Zone, and the thing he tells clients over and over again is never, ever put anything of value in that zone – not shopping baskets or tie racks or big promo-tional displays – because no one is going to see them ... Underhill believes that ... customer interaction with any product in the Decompression Zone will increase at least 30% once it's moved to the back edge of the zone and even more if it's moved to the right ... one of the funda-mental rules of how humans shop is that upon entering a store the shopper invariably and reflexively turns to the right...

'The main disadvan-tage of simple observation is that we can find out how people behave in a particular context or situation but not why they do so.'

The recommendations that stem from pure observational research can be enormously helpful provided there is a large enough database. Underhill's observations go back 20 years and therefore are based on a sufficiently robust sample of observations.

The main disadvantage of simple observation is that we can find out how people behave in a particular context or situation but not *why* they do so.

Observation supplemented by interviews, studies of records or conver-sations with other experts is called participant observation. This is defined as a process of research that 'looks at social phenomena from the inside as well as from the outside' (*The Dictionary of Sociology*). Participant observation is based on rigorous methods developed for cultural studies and involves establishing a rapport in a way that helps to watch, record and understand behaviour. Importantly, researchers need to learn to distance themselves from their own cultural or social 'baggage' and at the same time be aware that their very presence is altering the behaviour taking place.

How many observations make a robust sample? There is no absolute answer but a few suggestions are:

- enough to represent the target market that is being observed

- enough to represent the process or segments of the process (e.g. arriving at an airport, stages of the embarkation process)

- enough to represent changes in behaviour over time (e.g. different times of the day or week)

- enough to represent different cultural perspectives (international studies).

'Researchers need to learn to distance themselves from their own cultural "baggage" and at the same time be aware that their very presence is altering the behaviour taking place.'

There are two main ways of setting up this kind of methodology. The first is to re-recruit an individual or group and enrol them in the process. For example, a qualitative researcher is given permission to accompany the individual(s) through the process under investigation – a teenage nightclub, a mother-daughter shopping spree, a friendship group 'hanging about the city on a Saturday', a woman shopping for groceries at the supermarket and so on. The researcher observes and asks questions at different points in time in order to understand what the individual might be thinking or feeling at that moment or why an event is taking place.

The second way is to obtain permission from the retail outlet and observe people over a period of time. The researcher selects a range of behaviours to explore and asks questions for clarification: 'I noticed that you took quite a time to order your meal and then asked the waitress to come back a few times, could you tell me what was going on?' or 'I noticed that you picked up a number of packs and seemed to be reading the backs before choosing which one to put in your trolley. Can you tell me what was running through your mind?'

Observation is far more difficult than it appears. The researcher first needs to be familiar with the environment and types of behaviour, then he or she needs to notice patterns of behaviour, particularly the most frequent ones, and then to validate the importance of these through talking to the people involved.

'Participant observation is becoming an increasingly widely used qualitative methodology.'

The information can be recorded by audio-tape, written notes or video. It is then captured for later analysis and can be edited for illustration to the client or used as stimulus in further research (perhaps using a group interview method).

Participant observation, variously called 'Being There' (a term used by The Research Business *International*) or 'Accompanied Trips' (*AQRP Handbook*, e.g. accompanied shopping, drinking, eating, cooking) is becoming an increasingly widely used qualitative methodology with the following applications.

- *Process stories* – visiting a showroom for a new car demonstration, taking the car on a test drive, being 'sold' the car by the salesman. Travelling to Paris on Eurostar from the time of departure at London Waterloo to arrival at *Gare du Nord* (buying a ticket, arrival at the station, boarding the train, the journey, buying a snack and so on).

- *Extended relationships* – with a brand, product or service over time, such as following the photographic endeavours of a new camera owner over a period of six months including buying film, collecting the prints, showing the photographs to people, storage and many other associated activities.

- *Brand context* – and all the cues in the environment that communicate messages and influence choice of brand or product, e.g. male toiletries, storage of brands in the home, 'alcopop' usage in a pub.

- *'Moment of truth' and the point-of-sale influences* – when someone purchases or experiences a product or service, a number of factors have an important role in the choice: merchandising, point of sale, promotions and advertising (so do spaces and places). The interior design and layout of environments such as shopping centres, record stores, book shops and urban spaces all play a part in choice, although the influence is often subliminal.

There are many issues to be resolved in this relatively new application of qualitative methods for commercial market research:

- training qualitative researchers in film technology

- confidentiality issues such as the ethics of filming people without their initial permission

- the nature of video 'data' and how they should be analysed and presented to clients so that their limitations are well understood.

'All human beings can be a problem-solving resource if given enough time and the right environment.'

In January 1999, AQRP and BMP DDB Needham arranged a forum on ethnographic and observation methods which was attended by a small number of practitioners and academics currently involved or interested in these qualitative methods. The purpose of the forum was to explore the range of approaches currently in use and to make explicit the theoretical and professional issues involved.

Interactive workshops

These take many shapes and forms. The basic premise is that all human beings can be a problem-solving resource if given enough time and the right environment.

Interactive workshops came about as a development of 'extended creativity groups' that encourage respondents to engage with a complex problem and use techniques to enable the group to 'work' through problems because the issues and parameters have been made clear. Most importantly, they came about through a change of attitude (discussed in Chapter 2) whereby researchers came to realise that, by treating people as 'laboratory subjects from which to extract information and responses', the contribution of customers and consumers was undervalued. People can be willing problem solvers, especially those who have relevant experience to contribute.

'Interactive work-shops are helpful for brand problems (such as deciding whether or not a dormant or old-fashioned brand should be revitalised).'

Usually, a workshop consists of both consumers, people from the company sponsoring the project and representatives of its agencies such as R&D, the advertising agency, the design company, market researchers and any other professionals who may have an area of expertise to offer.

The session takes place in a facility large enough to hold 'break-out' sub-groups so that combinations of the large group can work at the same, or on different, tasks or problems. Workshops often last a whole day or may be broken up into two sessions, one with consumers in the evening – observed by the team, followed by a brainstorming workshop with the wider team the next day.

This methodology requires that the facilitator is well trained in brain-storming techniques and that he or she also has the skill to handle large groups, since the numbers can reach 20 people or more. Interactive workshops are helpful for:

- new product development programmes

- brand problems (such as deciding whether or not a dormant or old-fashioned brand can be re-vitalised)

- exploring the consumer–company interface

- understanding the issues involved in internal employee–management relationships.

The output of these workshops is usually a vast number of flipcharts or Post-it notes. One of the roles of the facilitator is to record the progress of the workshop and to provide a summary for the team to revisit as the project develops.

'People can be willing problem-solvers, especially those who have relevant experience to contribute.'

A comparative methodology experiment

'The ethnographic
method (participant
observation) was
based on videoing
the process of toilet
cleaning combined
with respondent
explanations to the
researcher while
engaged in
the process.'

In 1997, The Research Business *International* sponsored an experiment to compare the nature of the similarities and differences in qualitative 'information' derived from three methodologies (2). These were conventional group discussions of two hours duration, accompanied shopping preceded by in-home individual interviews and participant observation using video and 'field notes' conducted in home at two different points in time. In the latter case, the respondent was asked not to clean the toilet for as long as possible in order to heighten awareness of the key issues!

The subject was toilet cleaning attitudes and behaviour, chosen because it is an intimate and personal topic which would stress test the different methodologies. The research objectives were extensive:

> ... to understand consumer behaviour and attitudes to cleaning the toilet, the role of the family, the products used, the purchase cycle and context, the imagery of the main brand players, indications of possible brand partners and idea generation for new products.

Not surprisingly, each methodology has its strengths and weaknesses. The experiment proved the value of mixed methodologies in providing richness of information, depth of understanding and unique insights, the three elements required of qualitative research.

The ethnographic method (participant observation) (7) was based on videoing the process of toilet-cleaning combined with respondent explanations to the researcher while engaged in the process. Video was also used to record the individual interview that took place before and after the toilet cleaning exercise which covered the other topics of relevance.

This methodology brought the consumer alive for the client and convincingly demonstrated real people, in real toilets, using real products and expressing thoughts and feelings closely connected to the task itself. The respondents played an active part in the research, offering insights of their own. In this sense the participant became 'lay researcher' or 'co-researcher' rather than 'respondent'.

The very act of 'behaving' (i.e. cleaning the toilet) releases personal insights and explanations that do not occur out of context. Through the enactment of behaviour, the individual is able to access thoughts and emotions that are not accessible via other research methods. However, it is important to acknowledge that the behaviour is not 'real' since the observer changes the behaviour in some subtle way that is impossible to assess. Good rapport may lead the researcher to discuss the degree to which the individual might be behaving differently for the camera.

'Through the enactment of behaviour, the individual is able to access thoughts and emotions that are not accessible via other research methods.'

The other strength of this approach lies in understanding the in-home repertoire of brands and products used for bathroom and toilet cleaning. The co-existence of own-label and brands allow a comparative discussion of their differences and similarities in terms of usage, perceptions, storage and display.

The group discussion method, not surprisingly, did generate insights into the process of cleaning a toilet – that is, what people actually do. The researcher had to rely on reconstructed memories of behaviour expressed through 'the dense veil of interpretation' – the individual's own projection of how she wanted to be 'seen' by others as well as the researcher's interpretations of 'the consumer' or 'consumer behaviour, attitudes and emotions'.

The main strength of the group discussion methodology lies in the arena of the emotions, which could be placed in the broad social, cultural and psychological values of the target market. Here the use of projective techniques such as thought bubble completion and personification exercises brought into the open the ways in which human beings attach human motivations to inanimate objects.

> *The very fact that women were released from the real context of home and toilet allowed participants to share with each other and bring to the surface feelings that had remained hidden before ... A group discussion that has moved beyond the realm of politeness into a space where there is a willingness to expose, reveal and divulge personal feelings without fear of embarrassment becomes a powerful vehicle through which to gain insight into the dynamics driving the category. This is clearly rich territory sympathetic to marketing and advertising objectives such as understanding the core motivations on which brand positionings and propositions can be built* (2).

The intimacy of the subject matter did not deter the group. Once they had formed and normed, the members of the group became voyeuristically involved in the intimacy of their own behaviour. A side issue was that the group so enjoyed this process of disclosure that they hijacked the agenda and refused to co-operate with what they perceived to be more boring areas of enquiry, i.e brands, packaging.

'A group discussion that has moved into a space where there is a willingness to expose personal feelings without embarrassment becomes a powerful vehicle through which to gain insight into the dynamics driving the category.'

Psychodynamic group discussions, conducted by a researcher highly skilled in the use of projective and enabling techniques, is able in the space of two hours to offer insight into the psychological, social and cultural meanings that underpin human behaviour and actions.
It should perhaps be made clear that, from this experiment, two hours was insufficient time to cover all the research objectives and therefore extended group discussions would have been the preferred choice of group interview variant.

The accompanied shopping interviews, where the researcher accompanied the respondent to two different retail environments after having conducted a brief interview in the home, provided an insight into the

brand-consumer interface that neither of the other methodologies could accomplish.

> *The accompanied shopping method allows researchers to understand real people in real shops at the real brand–consumer interface defined by the chosen retail environment. The cues within the shopping environment serve as stimuli through which the researcher can understand how an individual makes sense of the overwhelming amount of products, brands and information in-store* (2).

'The accompanied shopping method allows researchers to understand real people in real shops at the real brand–consumer interface.'

This method offers a specialised but restricted opportunity to understand how brands operate in the complex competitive environments in which they have to search for competitive advantage.

Again, it is important to emphasise that accompanied shopping (or accompanied trips of any kind) does not demonstrate true behaviour. The respondent acts as co-researcher and through the real-life environment is able to explain how he or she decodes and interprets point of sale, merchandising, packaging, promotion and environmental cues.

The experiment also revealed differences in rapport between the three methodologies. Briefly, the rapport between the researcher and participant was strongest in the ethnographic approach and most superficial in the accompanied shopping method, which was strongly context-bound and rational. The nature of the rapport in the group interview is created between the members of the group, including the moderator, rather than between any one member and the moderator – evidence of the nature of 'the group psyche' discussed in Chapter 4.

Mixed methodologies – a real option

This review has demonstrated that qualitative researchers are in the fortunate position of having a large toolbox from which to select the most effective combination of tools for the job.

Combinations of methodologies add richness of insight and robustness, within the boundaries of the majority of project budgets. When combining methodologies, the whole is more than the sum of its parts and therefore it is not necessary that each approach consist of a 'stand-alone' sample. Each element of the combined method does not have to replicate the sample design for the whole study.

There are many ways of combining methodologies in addition to that described in the experiment:

- people can be interviewed individually or in pairs before attending a group discussion

- groups can be conducted *in situ* such as in a retail shop, a place of work, a restaurant, hotel or leisure club

- participants in research can be set a task prior to the interview or group discussion in order to heighten awareness of the subject to be covered.

It is possible to offset the disadvantages of a 'pure' methodology by incorporating some of the benefits of another approach. A group discussion held in an office at a supermarket which includes a trip around a section is not meant to replicate the real purchase occasion, but does bring to light some of the group responses to the look and feel of the store environment. It jogs people's memories about their behaviour, which is not possible in an off-site group venue.

If the budget does not allow for in-home or in-store individual interviews, then unaccompanied shopping is an option. Here the recruited respondent is asked to visit a number of stores before the group

'Qualitative researchers are in the fortunate position of having a large toolbox from which to select the most effective combination of tools for the job.'

'It is incumbent on buyers and users of qualitative research to find out which of their suppliers have the resources to provide mixed methodology solutions to contemporary problems.'

discussion to observe the fixtures of interest. People are prepared to conduct a great deal of work provided they are given an understanding of the importance of the task. Cupboard, freezer, larder, bathroom, garage and storeroom 'audits' are all ways to understand real-life contexts for brands and products.

The biggest obstacle to the use of combined methodologies, particularly observation and individual interviews, is research practitioner/company profitability. For small companies of qualitative researchers or single-handed practitioners it is far more profitable to conduct eight standard groups (two per night) than to conduct five extended groups or even to combine two extended groups with six accompanied shops and ten individual interviews.

In addition, the smaller research companies tend not to have invested in training and experimentation and therefore lack the skills and resources necessary to conduct participant observation sessions using video. This is more complex than simply wielding the camera reasonably competently; it involves rigour in editing, integrity in acknowledging the presence of the camera and researcher, and authority in presenting the findings to the client.

It is therefore incumbent users of qualitative research to find out which suppliers have the resources, expertise and experience to provide mixed methodology solutions to contemporary problems. Many researchers argue for conventional groups because this is more profitable and easier, not because it is right – a sad observation.

It is also incumbent on all qualitative researchers to provide more extensive training in methods other than the group interview. The alternative methodologies, particularly participant observation and individual interviews, should not be used as initiation rites for untrained young practitioners. Each requires its own particular training 'module' to ensure that it delivers against expectations.

REFERENCES

1. M. Denny, 'Inspiring Details: The Role of Ethnography in a Kaleidoscope Age', ESOMAR Congress, Paris, 1995.
2. R. Pike and W. Gordon, 'Carry on round the "U" bend: an experimental comparison of three qualitative methodologies', ESOMAR Congress, Edinburgh, 1997.
3. W. Gordon and S. Robson, 'Respondent Through the Looking Glass: Towards a Better Understanding of the Qualitative Interviewing Process', MRS Conference, 1982.
4. W. Schlackman, 'A Discussion of the Use of Sensitivity Panels in Market Research', MRS Annual Conference Proceedings, 1984.
5. C. Burns, 'Individual Interviews' in S. Robson and A. Foster, *Qualitative Research in Action*, Edward Arnold, 1989.
6. R. Wynberg and M. Synnivig, 'Watching You, Watching Us, Watching You', MRS Conference, 1986.
7. H. Marianpolski, 'Ethnography as a Market Research Tool' in P. Sampson (ed.), *Qualitative Research Through a Looking Glass*, ESOMAR, 1998.

FURTHER READING

W. Gordon and R. Langmaid, *Qualitative Market Research: A Practitioner's and Buyer's Guide*, Gower, 1988.

AQRP Directory and Handbook of Qualitative Research.

C. A. Restall and R. Auton, 'From Passivity to Interaction? The Future of Qualitative Research', 49th ESOMAR Congress, Changing Business Dynamics: The Challenge to Marketing Research, Sep. 1996.

Annual Study of the Market Research Industry, ESOMAR, 1997.

The Psychology of Small Groups

Chapter four

Group discussions, or 'focus groups' as they are now known, form the backbone of contemporary qualitative research practice and are often synonymous with the discipline itself. A well-run focus group looks incredibly easy – observation shows a relaxed moderator sitting back in his or her chair occasionally rising to write points on a flipchart while the participants are exchanging views with one another in an animated manner. The discussion flows effortlessly across the relevant main topics, highlighted by interesting insights, provoked through the use of projective techniques or responses to material shown to the group. A well-run focus group seems to take place rather like an informal chat with some acquaintances, rather than a process that requires skill and experience to manage.

'A well-run focus group seems to take place rather like an informal chat with some acquaintances, rather than a process that requires skill and experience to manage.'

It is this innocuous ease and seamlessness that seduces many young people or inexperienced older ones into thinking that they can conduct a group discussion and save the costs of employing a trained moderator or qualitative research company. And novices do succeed in running a group – for an hour or two: people are generally polite and willing to co-operate; they may talk a great deal, or at least some of them may do so more than others (but who cares what the 'mice' think anyway?); there may not be any silences (for isn't that how you tell whether a group discussion is good or bad?); participants may be prepared to talk enthusiastically about advertising or a new product in a positive way (isn't that good, you don't want a whole lot of nega-tive criticisms?); everyone goes away saying how interesting it was to contribute to the subject (another sign of a good group discussion).

But what was the nature of the conversation? Was it equivalent to cocktail-party talk – facile, entertaining, socially conformist or posturing – or was it the kind of conversation that one has with people who trust one another and are prepared to reveal things about themselves because they are confident their 'sharing' will be reciprocated?

The facilitation of small groups – known as moderating – is based on sound theoretical principles and learned techniques which have been passed down from the early pioneers of qualitative research, many of whom had psychotherapy or psychological training, to practising researchers who learned by apprenticeship, trial and error.

This chapter tries to make the processes, dynamics and issues clear and provides help to both inexperienced and experienced researchers alike – the former to learn and the latter to help train the younger practitioners with whom they work.

'Novices do succeed in running a group – for an hour or two.'

The nature of groups

Belonging to groups is a condition of being human. From the moment of birth we belong to a number of groups: the nuclear family, extended relatives, work teams, network groups, associations, clubs, communities, towns, cities and nations. Belonging to a group is an active not a passive act. Even if one does not participate in a group event (a Christmas gathering, a farewell party, a team 'away day'), the decision not to do so is an active one and affects both the individual and the group.

'Every single person brings emotional baggage to a group – and lots of it.'

Groups have the potential to be positive or negative. In the context of market research, brainstorming or a meeting, a group will spiral downwards into criticism, defeatism and lack of focus, displaying characteristics of energy loss, withholding or hostility. On the other hand, a group can be uplifting for all its members and be charac-terised by energy, enthusiasm and the exchange of personal feelings and views. A powerful group has synergy – the combined effect of the group exceeds the efforts and contribution of its individual members.

If you plan to run groups of any kind, it is essential to understand the underlying dynamics that drive a group of people towards a positive or negative outcome.

Every single person brings emotional baggage to a group – and lots of it. Ideas about how life was, is or should be, hang-ups and *bêtes noires*, prejudices, tragedies and stories, memories, ways of speaking and ways of learning. If this is not enough, there is more: beliefs about the world and one's place in it, desires, hopes, fears, tolerance or lack of it in others, internal dialogues that play as others are speaking or as events unfold, issues about control, power and fear. All of this has been learned through our interaction with the many groups in which we have participated since the moment of birth. Early expe-riences shape our behaviour in groups when we are adults – the first day of nursery school, the group dynamics within the nuclear and extended family, peer group experiences in adolescence.

In addition to this excess baggage, people who attend market research group discussions bring with them a few more packages and parcels. There is:

- anxiety about meeting strangers and having to spend a few hours with people whom one does not know

- insecurity about the value of one's opinions

- anxiety about how one is being judged and by whom

- lack of confidence in expressing views intelligently

- day-to-day pre-occupations – Are the children all right? Is my partner at home? What shall I buy for dinner? Can we smoke? I wonder how my friend's father is?

Group leaders would do well to understand this hidden baggage and learn how to create an environment in which it does not interfere with the performance of the group.

'Group leaders would do well to understand this hidden baggage.'

Two models of research groups

There are two models of qualitative market research groups – the dependent group and the psychodynamic group. The experience of one or other of these groups is completely different for the observers, for participant members and, naturally, for the moderator.

Figure 1 illustrates a dependent group in action. The moderator sets up a dialogue with each of the participants in turn and, within the first five minutes that the group has been in progress, has trained members – through explicit or implicit reinforcement – to answer questions put to them and to wait until addressed before contributing to the discussion.

Figure 1: A Dependent Group

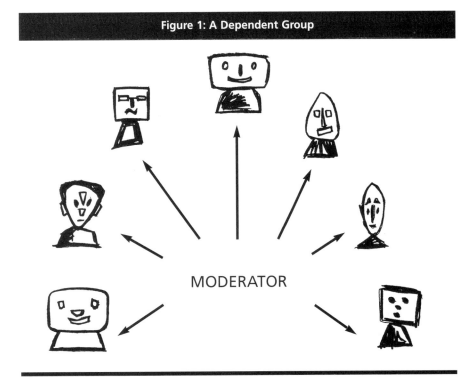

MODERATOR

'There are two models of qualitative market research groups – the dependent group and the psychodynamic group.'

'Dependent groups are often charac- terised by low energy and by silences until someone is asked by name or through body language to contribute.'

This group experience is like eight simultaneous depth interviews orchestrated by the group moderator who separates him/herself, psychologically, from the group and who appears to be in control. This kind of group is parental or authoritarian in nature and is based on the belief that anarchy (or childish misbehaviour) will take place unless discipline is imposed from the start. It also rests on a number of other assumptions:

- a group discussion is a rational forum for debate

- respondents have information the moderator can extract by asking questions

- what people say in group situations is what they mean

- the moderator is in control of the process

- people are able to articulate feelings and emotions when asked to talk about them

- there is a truth (about the market, the brand, behaviour or opinions) that can be found through following an agenda of questions set by the client or research co-ordinator.

Dependent groups are often characterised by low energy and by silences until someone is asked by name or through body language to contribute. These groups lack humour or spontaneity and are exhausting for moderators to lead since, as with the conductor of an orchestra, the musicians do not know what to do or when to play unless they are given the lead to do so.

The psychodynamic group rests on completely different assumptions, the key one being that the moderator is part of the group and that all members are influenced by one another and by the climate of the group. In this type of group, the moderator sets up permission for the group members to address one another directly and to agree or disagree with any point of view being expressed. Members are encouraged to see themselves as part of the group rather than separate from it and to ask for clarification of the moderator if necessary. Sensitivity in relation to other group members is taught through gentle reinforcement.

The assumptions underlying the psychodynamic group are that group processes and group 'baggage' are the bricks and mortar of the group procedure. The content of a group discussion reflects the social and cultural dynamics driving the attitudes and behaviour of the members as a group, rather than reflecting the psychological profile of each individual. In addition:

'The content of a group discussion reflects the social and cultural dynamics driving the attitudes and behaviour of the members as a group.'

- what people say may or may not be what they really think, do or mean

- socially acceptable, politically correct and conformist attitudes will be expressed unless the group is encouraged to share more heartfelt feelings and beliefs

- while direct questions are necessary, it is equally important to ask questions in an indirect and less confrontational way, using projective questioning and enabling techniques (see Chapter 6)

- there is no objective truth that can be extracted from a group of people – all of the contributions are subjective and even when participants agree with one another, this does not mean that their agreement makes the content factually correct

- people who attend group discussions are neither stupid nor intellectually inferior – if they are puzzled by the material shown or seem to have difficulty understanding the questions or what is required, it is the fault of the moderator or the client for not having designed the material well enough or for having presented it in an inappropriate manner.

It is obvious that I am a firm believer in the value of conducting market research group discussions with the psychodynamic model in mind. This is an opinion based on experience but also on background and training. There is no right or wrong way to conduct a group, only that the moderator and clients accept the model in operation, and therefore understand the nature and limitations of the information and insights contributed by the participants.

'There is no right or wrong way to conduct a group, only that the moderator and clients understand the nature and limitations of the information contributed by the participants.'

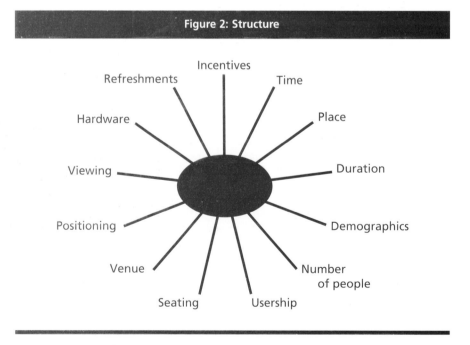

Figure 2: Structure

The components of groups

There are three components of a group discussion: structure, content and process.

Structure

Figure 2 shows some of the structural factors that can influence the success or otherwise of a group discussion. If any one of these aspects is ignored or seriously mismanaged the group may well flounder or have to be aborted.

Many of these structural factors will be well managed by a professional researcher or qualitative research company, both of whom will have local knowledge and experience of a particular demographic, user or gender group and can advise on the best time, place, environment and duration for the group. Professionals can also make decisions about:

- the most appropriate incentive

- the best time to serve refreshments

- whether or not alcoholic beverages are a good idea

- safety issues for participants on their way home after the group is finished

- whether or not the desired respondents will attend a group discussion at all.

Research practice varies between countries and between different research practitioners or companies on issues such as:

- the demographic make-up of the group (homogeneous or heterogeneous)

'Professionals can also make decisions about the most appropriate incentive, the best time to serve refreshments, whether or not alcoholic beverages are a good idea.'

- the mixing of gender in the same group

- the age or life stage range of members of a group

- the number of people who should attend

- whether or not it matters if people have attended group discussion before.

'Photography and video-recording of the group must be decided in the context of the culture.'

In America it is common to invite ten to twelve people to a group discussion, which usually takes place around a board room table. In the United Kingdom it is more common to hold the discussion with six to eight members and to sit on sofas and soft chairs round a coffee table. In the United Kingdom it is still common practice to hold two group discussions in one evening, each lasting about one and a half hours; in other parts of the world, particularly Europe and South America, a four-hour session is not uncommon.

In some countries where qualitative market research is relatively new, video cameras (manned or automatic) are placed in the group discussion room, while in those countries where viewing rooms have become commonplace, such equipment is well hidden. Photography and video-recording of the group must be decided on in the context of the culture – such behaviour on the part of researchers is unacceptable among women participants in Pakistan and is still highly suspicious in countries like Lithuania. It would not worry people in other parts of the world, beyond initial embarrassment.

Countries and researchers differ too in their beliefs about the ethics of viewing group discussions and the degree of transparency shown to participants. In the UK, the Market Research Society Code of Conduct has been expanded to provide guidance on confidentiality, use of video and honesty in communication with participants about the presence and role of observers. In other countries where there is no such code, the goodwill of participants is sometimes abused and the qualitative research process is deceptive.

The AQRP (Association of Qualitative Research Practitioners) publishes a *Directory and Handbook of Qualitative Research*, in which a chapter is devoted to the rights of respondents. The main point made is that qualitative researchers and their clients should not lie nor deceive respondents, should not abuse their confidentiality and should not coerce them into saying or doing anything in a group discussion that makes them feel uncomfortable. A summary of the main recommendations of the MRS Guide to Qualitative Research prepared in consultation with the AQRP states that:

- the rights of respondents take priority over the rights of clients

- an effort should be made to tell respondents as much about the interview or discussion before they come along, particularly if the subject of the discussion is deemed sensitive

- respondents should be told before they come along if the session is to take place in a viewing facility, if it is to be video-recorded and/or audio-recorded

- permission should be gained from respondents for audio- or video-recording the session and, at the same time, they should be told how the tape will subsequently be used

- respondents should be given every opportunity to withdraw from the discussion, not to answer questions and not to participate in projective techniques, if they so wish

'Qualitative researchers should not lie nor deceive respondents, and should not coerce them into saying or doing anything in a group discussion which makes them feel uncomfortable.'

- everything you say to respondents must be correct and honoured, such as the length of the session

- the identity of the client(s) has to be revealed to respondents, whether in a recruiter's home or in a viewing facility, preferably at the beginning of the session or, if there are good reasons to withhold, at the end.

The consequences of deception and economy with the truth are severe; people do not share their more personal or important thoughts and feelings since they are aware of being manipulated and are suspicious about the hidden agenda of the researcher.

'The shift is towards recognising that group discussion participants are human and, if treated as adults with respect and appreciation for their willingness to help, we professionals might learn from listening.'

Voluntary adherence to these recommendations requires a change of attitude towards respondents and to the processes and principles of qualitative research. It means a shift in perception from treating respondents as laboratory experiment 'fodder' or human guinea pigs to consenting adults who have points of view to contribute. It means letting go of the idea that the information the client is looking for can be extracted from respondents whether or not they give permission. It means challenging the view that both client and researcher have the right to be manipulative and controlling because they have paid the respondents to attend the session, or have paid the researcher (or company) a large amount of money to retrieve information to solve a marketing problem.

The shift is towards recognising that group discussion participants are human and, if treated as adults with respect and appreciation for their willingness to help, we professionals might learn from listening. To paraphrase David Ogilvy:

> *The consumer may or may not be your wife, husband, child or parent, but you can be sure that he or she is a*

real living, breathing, thinking and doing human being,
who has as much of a right to their way of life as you
have to yours.

Content

Content refers to all the components that form the subject matter of
the group discussion and that are evidenced in the group discussion
guide: projective techniques, example products, new product, service
or pack concepts, positioning statements, advertising material, other
forms of below-the-line stimuli, products to taste and so on.

It is important to remember that the researcher and client know what
the objectives of the survey are, and how all the material (including
the discussion guide), should be used. Respondents have no idea.
They do not know where the discussion is going, nor how they should
or should not respond to anything that is shown.

These content issues, unless understood and pre-planned, undoubtedly
interfere with the learning from the group and therefore require the
most professional attention prior to the research process. Even the
discussion guide can turn out to be a hindrance rather than a help.

Too many clients and researchers believe that a long and thorough
topic guide (discussion guide) will ensure that all the required information is gathered; this is not so. Moderators become anxious about
remembering to ask all the questions as written and approved by the
client. They forget to listen to respondents, do not follow up interesting insights or leads and become attached to the guide as if it were
a lifeboat and rush over each item in order to get to the next.

The point to bear in mind is that the researcher needs to internalise
the study objectives so as to ask the most relevant questions or introduce topics in a way that makes sense to participants, rather than

*'Too many clients
and researchers
believe that a long
and thorough topic
guide will ensure
that all the required
information is gath-
ered; this is not so.'*

attempt to administer the discussion guide as if it were a long questionnaire. In the latter case, all that is generated in terms of content, is
the same kind of information that could have been gathered from a
telephone or street interview – a waste of qualitative potential.

There are unfortunately no black and white answers. Discussion
guides and stimulus material are essential. For example, a good
discussion guide, which indicates the course of the content to be
covered and the key points at which the stimulus material needs to be
introduced, is helpful in co-ordinating a number of different
researchers working across a project (especially internationally) and
ensures comparability. Like most things it is a question of balance
combined with experience and expertise.

*'All groups work by
proceeding through
a life cycle similar to
the human cycle of
birth and death.'*

Process

All groups work by proceeding through a life cycle similar to the
human cycle of birth and death. Think about a time you joined a new
club, started a new job, went to a different school or changed countries and had to make new contacts and friendships. The relationship
with a new group of people changes and deepens over time. The
stages of group evolution have been cleverly called – forming,
storming, norming, performing and mourning [1].

At the first stage – the birth of a group – people tend to try to include
members of the group. This stage is characterised by introductions,
polite behaviour and an exchange of personal details such as name,
marital status, country or home neighbourhood and reasons for being
at the group, each member tentatively establishing facts in common
with the others. This is called group forming and characterises the
initial stages of group formation.

In the qualitative research group discussion, forming begins to take
place as the group assembles in the waiting room before entering the

discussion room itself. Since the moderator is part of the group, it is necessary to allow a period of forming once the group and the moderator have got together. The way in which this is done sets the pattern for the remainder of the time the group is together, hence it is essential that the moderator think carefully about the first five to ten minutes of the group.

If the moderator asks each individual in turn to introduce themselves by name together with a few details of personal biography and use of a brand or product category, the group quickly learns to talk only when directly addressed. Each member learns to say the same kind of things as the person before. The longer that questions and answers continue, the more difficult it is for the group members to be spontaneous, to enter into dialogue with one another and to develop a climate of their own. A dependent group – like separate spokes of a wheel – is in the making. This group will be leader-centred and will often be compliant but will be unlikely to take any risks in revealing any intimate thoughts or deeply held views.

'In the qualitative research group discussion, forming begins to take place as the group assembles in the waiting room before entering the discussion room itself.'

There are several ways to overcome this and some suggestions are given below.

A well thought-through and rehearsed introduction

The moderator spends up to ten minutes addressing an agenda of explanations:

- who he or she is

- what the survey is about

- who the client is

- why it is taking place in a viewing room

- who is watching

- whether or not it is being filmed or audio-recorded

- how the information will be used

- whether or not smoking is permitted

- how long the discussion will last

- whether or not there will be a 'comfort break'

- not everyone is expected to agree with one another

- different points of view are encouraged

- participants will be asked to think about products, services and brands in a way that they might not have ever done before

- there are no right or wrong answers

- the group members should feel that they can talk directly to any member if they wish

- the moderator's role is to guide the discussion across a number of topics

- the moderator is independent, with no vested interest in the category or brands.

'For new moderators an introduction requires practice, as the tone of voice is also important – not too serious and intimidating and not too frivolous or lacking in sincerity.'

The importance of clarity of communication at this early stage cannot be over-emphasised. For new moderators an introduction requires practice, as the tone of voice is also important – not too serious and intimidating and not too frivolous or lacking in sincerity.

Paired introductions

The next step is to introduce the members to each other and a simple and quick way to do this is to divide the group into pairs (including a trio if the numbers are uneven), asking each pair to introduce themselves to each other. The instruction might go something like this:

> *I'd like you to pair up for a few moments and introduce yourself to your neighbour. Exchange names, anything about yourself that you would like to share and perhaps something about the kind of day you had today – good, bad or neutral. Then, when we've all done that, we will introduce our neighbour to the rest of the group. We all want to remember each others' names.*

For those moderators who feel confident it is often fun and helps set the climate by asking each person to share with their neighbour what kind of an animal or bird they would most like to be and to explain why. This kind of exercise helps to break the ice and energises the group through laughter.

The main purpose of this approach, beyond learning each others' names, is to allow each member to speak in front of the group. Fear of public speaking is one of the most anxiety-provoking actions that people mention and thus a technique that overcomes this fear is enormously helpful. It also teaches people to pay attention to each other, to listen and exchange information without the moderator having to intervene.

Introducing the first topic

The moderator must be aware of time and introduce the first topic as quickly as possible. If the first and second respondents address their comments to the moderator, he or she must establish quickly that individual members should address their comments to the group as a whole and not simply to the moderator. This can be reinforced through body language by not engaging the respondent's eyes or by

'For those moderators who feel confident it is often fun and helps set the climate by asking each person to share with their neighbour what kind of an animal or bird they would most like to be.'

shifting body position towards the group as a whole rather than the person talking. It is surprising how fast a group of people will learn the basic rule – namely that the group exists in some invisible space between them and not in relation to the moderator.

Educating individual members about the importance of group respect

During the forming stage it may be important to guide members so that they learn to listen to the views of other members of the group. If one person interrupts continuously, or is always first to contribute to the discussion, it is important to make some gentle points about etiquette, for example:

> *I know that some of you have really important things you want to say. Can we all try to listen to each other without interrupting? Can we hear from those members of the group that are finding it a little more difficult to get a word in edgeways? Can we avoid speaking in whispers to the person nearest to you? Can we try to find out what conclusions the group would come to after having heard from a number of different people?*

'It is in the space of the first 10 to 15 minutes that a dependent or psychodynamic group is established.'

This emphasis on the group – the invisible matrix – helps to create the culture of exchange and respect that marks a good group discussion.

Remember that it is in the space of the first 10 to 15 minutes that a dependent or psychodynamic group is established.

As members become more comfortable, the storming stage begins. This is similar to teenage rebellion or posturing and is all about power and control. The symptoms vary depending on the nature of the group, but often involve attention-seeking behaviour. The power struggle is between one or two respondents and the moderator, with the remainder of the group becoming participant observers with a strong interest in the outcome. One of the key indicators of storming is that someone makes a strong point about being different from the rest of the group. For example, if the group is discussing advertising on television, one member might announce that he or she never watches television but only reads books. Now what does this mean? It might be true but is unlikely since the recruitment criteria would have precluded this person from attending a group on advertising. It is more likely to be a bid for attention – a way of signalling perceived intellectual superiority and difference from other group members.

Asking questions of the moderator is another sign of storming. Someone challenges the moderator and asks questions about why or how this information is to be used, who is sponsoring the project if it has not been revealed and whether participants will benefit from having 'helped' a company develop its advertising or a new product.

A member of the group may challenge a fellow group member. Here one person strongly objects to another's point of view. The tone of voice is the give-away clue. It is often aggressive and inappropriate for the stage of relationship the group has established.

Someone may try to befriend the moderator. This is the classic 'teacher's pet' strategy. The individual tries really hard to be co-operative, calling the moderator by his or her first name, taking on tasks and attempting to show that he or she is better than the rest of the group. The problem magnifies itself if this is not addressed and the remainder of the group can become hostile.

'Someone may try to befriend the moderator. This is the classic "teacher's pet" strategy.'

Another sign could be physical domination through body language. Examples of this would be standing up in order to reach the refreshments or drinks, leaving the room for a cigarette or comfort break, shifting around in the seat so as to make the neighbours on each side uncomfortable and so on.

Finally, group members may pair off and start a conspiracy. Here two members of the group begin a conversation between themselves, excluding other members of the group and the moderator. This is a form of passive aggression or, using the teenage analogy, is like two naughty children whispering and passing notes in class. The effect can be disruptive and divisive.

Storming creates tension and discomfort, and members of the group react in different ways. Some members may attempt to rescue the group through striving to contribute intelligently to the topic under discussion, using humour to relieve the tension, or pacifying the aggressor. Others tend to opt out and watch from the sidelines. Others may feel drawn to take sides.

The important point to remember is that this is all a fantasy that is going on in the combined mind-space of the group. At the same time, the group is discussing topics on the discussion guide. Storming and the struggle for power are covert – felt rather than explicit.

'The important point to remember is that this is all a fantasy that is going on in the combined mind-space of the group.'

In order for the group not to become stuck at this phase the moderator must be able to recognise storming and know how to deal with it. This can be done in many different ways depending on the way in which the storming is being manifested:

- a gentle reminder that the task of the group is to help the client develop new and relevant advertising (new products, understanding of the category and so on) and that the group needs to move on

- introducing a new subject or task often helps bring an end to storming, such as looking at advertisements or mapping tasks with actual products

- reinforcement that it is safe to disagree, that differences in opinion are really useful to explore and that in a few moments the group will need to come to a view as to what could be concluded from the past ten minutes of conversation

- gentle admonitions that 'pair conversations' are not acceptable and need to be shared with the group.

If the group becomes stuck in storming, all the participants, including the moderator, can become depressed about being unable to achieve what is expected of them. Once it has been handled, the next phase develops. This is called norming: the early adult phase of development.

> When the group has successfully sorted out some of the issues of power and control, it is free to develop trust, cohesion and a degree of intimacy ... group culture emerges. Part of this process is the establishment of norms, or accepted ways of doing things, and agreement about sanctions and where the limits are (1).

'When the group has successfully sorted out some of the issues of power and control, it is free to develop trust, cohesion and a degree of intimacy ... group culture emerges.'

Norming comes as a relief. Some moderators describe it as the moment when the group 'begins to take off, like a jumbo jet gathering speed down the runway'. The group has settled down, participants have learned how to behave in relation to one another, and to the moderator, and it has become clearer which role participants have adopted.

There are a number of different roles relating to the performance of tasks and to the process itself. For example, the group has been asked 'to map a range of products into categories so that those products and brands most similar to each other in some way are placed together'. People adopt different roles: the initiator (the person who begins the task and enrols others to help), the opinion-giver (the person who advises from the sidelines), the builder (the person who constructively develops other people's ideas) and the clarifier (the person who makes sure the task is understood or that what the group is doing is useful).

Then there are process roles – as listed below – some of which are positive and some negative (2).

Tension reliever	Aggressor, negator, blocker
Compromiser	Limelight-hogger, joker
Encourager	Topic jumper
Harmoniser	Devil's advocate

Norming quickly develops into performing – the moment when the group jumbo lifts off into the sky! This is the mature stage:

The point at which group members begin to take responsibility, individually and corporately, for the group and its tasks, is the point where they are ready to perform (1).

'Performing can revert to norming or storming if the moderator introduces a new task or one that is less fun.'

The members of the group will be working well at this stage and are happy to involve themselves in tasks or more complex issues for discussion. It is a good time to introduce projective techniques, particularly those that are more challenging (e.g. guided fantasy, psychodrama, brand personification); it is also a good time to break the group into smaller units to conduct a task or 'brainstorm a problem-solution'. The performing phase is characterised by high energy, full contribution by all members of the group, laughter between members and the moderator, freedom to move around the room, and task orientation. The moderator can often sit back and let the group run without the need to guide and interject other than to encourage and keep an eye on the time.

However, performing can revert to norming or storming if the moderator introduces a new task or one that is less fun. For example, a group may be performing well constructing 'a new advertisement for Bloggo using scrap art from magazines and newspapers' but it may resort to storming when asked to do something else – 'Now I'd like us to look at seven different ways of talking about this new product.

What I have here are four different ways of talking about this product, written by the advertising agency'. A group can hijack the agenda and refuse to participate in what it perceives to be less interesting work.

In this case, the group requires encouragement, gentle reminders about why it has been formed in the first place (to accomplish a task for the client) and time to resettle. It will then start to perform again. Storming, norming and performing can occur several times during the course of a group as is demonstrated in Figure 3.

'Storming, norming and performing can occur several times during the course of a group.'

The final stage is often overlooked by moderators and is called mourning. The moderator may well feel that he or she is in 'injury time', having obtained the kind of information and insights required, but the group may not wish to disband. After all, this has turned out to be entertaining and a different way to spend the afternoon or evening. In order to avoid leaving participants feeling like squeezed oranges, it is important to begin to give some warning bells to the members about the imminent end of the group, some 20 minutes prior to completion. This may take the form of a simple time announcement such as: 'In the last 20 minutes or so I would like the

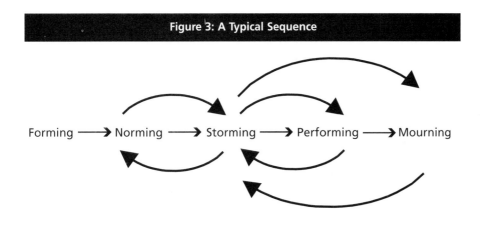

Figure 3: A Typical Sequence

Forming → Norming → Storming → Performing → Mourning

group to consider ...' or moving the group to draw its own conclusions: 'I would like the group to think for a few moments about what I should conclude from this discussion – what do you suggest I tell the client which summarises your points of view?' or 'We will be finishing this discussion in about ten minutes or so, does anyone have any questions they would like to ask or contribute a few final points that might be helpful?'

'Mourning can be acknowledged by thanking the members of the group for their hard work and assuring them that what they have said and done is of real interest and practical application.'

Mourning can be acknowledged and facilitated by thanking the members of the group for their hard work and assuring them that what they have said and done is of real interest and practical application. It is often helpful to heighten awareness that the research process does lead to real products and services in the market-place and that the group members should look out for the new idea in a few months. Of course, the outcome may not be the one they suggested and therefore it is worth saying so by reminding them that the survey involves other people besides themselves.

Group processes take time to understand but are vital for effective group moderation since the introduction of client-relevant stimulus material (new packs, new products, advertising concepts, brand imagery), at the wrong stage of the group can affect the quality of response and the nature of the information generated. A group should be given tasks and discussion topics appropriate to its stage of development and then the discussion flows seamlessly, not jerkily, in response to the moderator imposing his or her agenda at will.

In conclusion, there are the following 20 guidelines to more effective moderating skills.

1. Be 'present' – aware and conscious of what is happening in the group.
2. Be adaptable.
3. If you don't know, say so.

4. Trust the resources of the group.
5. Respect each group member.
6. Be yourself.
7. Develop discernment (the ability to make distinctions).
8. Keep intervention to a minimum.
9. Monitor the energy level and change it if necessary.
10. Remember there is a job to be done.
11. Watch your ego.
12. Everything that occurs is relevant.
13. Improvise – there is no right answer.
14. When in doubt, check it out.
15. Be culturally sensitive.
16. Encourage agreement and disagreement.
17. Start well.
18. Work with conflict – don't run away from it.
19. Acknowledge and affirm.
20. Use humour.

'A group should be given tasks and discussion topics appropriate to its stage of development.'

If you are a learner-driver use these 20 points as a guide. Find out from more experienced moderators exactly how they have learned to do each one. If you are already experienced and are in the position of having to train younger practitioners, think about each of these guidelines and write a number of bullet point explanations under each one.

REFERENCES

1. W. B. Tuckerman, in A. Brown, *Group Work*, Gower, 1986. See also S. Robson and A. Foster, *Qualitative Research in Action*, Edward Arnold, 1989 (Chapter 4).
2. D. Hunter, A. Bailey and B. Taylor, *The Zen of Groups*, Gower, 1992.

Communication and Rapport

Chapter five

Most client buyers and practitioners of research would agree that a good qualitative researcher would have 'excellent communication skills' – they should be someone who enjoys talking to people from all walks of life, a good listener, able to build rapport and engender trust. We take this for granted as if it is a natural process and many of us believe that some people are better at it than others. We rarely think about the process itself and whether or not, by spending some time becoming consciously aware of how we do communicate and create rapport, we might become better at it.

'Every human being selects that part of the world that he or she wishes to experience at any one time.'

Let us begin with *selective perception* – every human being selects that part of the world that he or she wishes to experience at any one time. When walking down the street, for example, we choose what to notice and what to exclude from our consciousness depending on the context. If I have agreed to meet a friend at a particular street corner, I will be scanning the crowd for a familiar face. I might become aware of other people – someone who behaves strangely or is dressed unusually, someone who reminds me of the friend I am going to meet, someone who is wearing something that I would like to own. I am excluding the vast majority of other people, things and events. Two people will not see the same set of things and, even if they do, they might interpret it differently – the meaning alters depending on who, when, why, where and how. Basically, we notice what is relevant to our needs at any one particular time.

One of the deepest insights a qualitative researcher can have concerning the fundamental nature of communication is never to take anything for granted. You may think you are showing a perfectly straightforward description of a new product proposition; the person you have shown it to might interpret it as boring sales information. You might be presenting an advertisement as an example of an effective testimonial campaign; the respondent might dislike the music and fail to recognise the famous personality.

Qualitative researchers are constantly interviewing people who are different from themselves – in terms of gender, socio-economic and educational background, race, religion, culture, sub-group, urban tribe and so on. When interviewing people it is important to remember that they may have been 'taught' to experience things differently from yourself and that the reason for frustration is not to do with basic intelligence or ability but to do with differences in context and experience.

The parable of the blind men and the elephant is very apposite here.

It was six men of Indostan
To learning much inclined,
Who went to see the Elephant
(Though all of them were blind),
That each by observation
Might satisfy his mind.

The first approached the Elephant,
And happening to fall
Against his broad and sturdy side,
At once began to bawl:
'God bless me! But the Elephant is very like a wall!'

The second, feeling of the tusk
Cried: 'Ho! What have we here?
So very round and smooth and sharp?
To me 'tis very clear
This wonder of an Elephant
Is very like a spear!'

The third approached the animal
And happening to take
The squirming trunk within his hands
Thus boldly up he spake:

'I see,' quoth he, 'the Elephant
Is very like a snake.'
The fourth reached out an eager hand,
And felt about the knee:
'What most this wondrous beast is like
Is very plain', quoth he;
'Tis clear enough the Elephant
Is very like a tree!'

The fifth, who chanced to touch the ear,
Said: 'E'n the blindest man
Can tell what this resembles most;
Deny the fact who can
This marvel of an Elephant
Is very like a fan!'

The sixth no sooner had begun
About the beast to grope
Than seizing on the swinging tail
That fell within his scope.
'I see,' quoth he, 'the Elephant
Is very like a rope!'

And so these men of Indostan
Disputed loud and long,
Each in his own opinion
Exceeding stiff and strong
Though each was partly in the right,
They all were in the wrong!

The parable teaches us that each person experiencing the same event
or object can have completely different interpretations and successfully communicate these to one another. However, if each had

'Each person experiencing the same event or object can have completely different interpretations.'

experienced what another had (a different part of the elephant), they would have ultimately agreed a better description of an elephant. If we listen to others and truly accept that their point of view and experience is as valid as our own, we can begin to have a closer understanding about the experience of someone else. And, in the final analysis, this is what qualitative research is all about.

Communication takes place in three principal ways – by physical touch, by visible movements of our bodies and by symbols that stand for something we have experienced (i.e. visible words, images and audible sounds).

'Interpreting body language is something that all human beings do all the time, although not consciously.'

Body language is the term used to describe physical touch (a tap on the shoulder, a pat on the back) and body movement (wagging a finger, winking an eye, yawning, leaning back in the chair, leaning forward with hand cupping chin). It also includes a large number of other signals and cues: voice intonation and volume, appearance and dress, self-presentation. We use non-verbal cues to draw conclusions about other people and make interpretations about character, intentions, feelings, views, thoughts and so on. Body language is both voluntary and involuntary – dress, appearance and voice intonation can be brought under control but facial expressions and body posture are more autonomous.

Blushing is a uniquely human trait and signals discomfort. It is a good example of non-verbal behaviour that is not controllable and is usually accompanied by other signals such as averting the gaze, lack of fluency in speech or movement and self-consciousness. Blushing may be interpreted in a number of ways: it may signal the fact that the person is telling a lie, or performing a task incompetently or it may simply mean that the person feels scrutinised and finds being the centre of attention uncomfortable.

Interpreting body language is something that all human beings do all the time, although not consciously. For researchers, it is important to begin to make distinctions between one kind of body language signal and another, and the only way to do this is to practise. A simple way to do this is to look at a video of a group discussion in progress (or an interview) and turn off the sound. Then try to work out who is going to talk next. Is the group engaged in the subject or not? Who is dominating the discussion? Who is responsive to whom and how is the moderator encouraging or discouraging individual members of the group from contributing to the discussion? None of it is rocket science.

'Withdrawal or boredom is recognisable by: yawning, looking away or up to the ceiling, examining nails or doodling on a piece of paper.'

Some examples are described below (1).

- A desire to speak is indicated by: raising a finger, tapping a foot or a hand, direct eye contact with the moderator or someone else, sitting up or shifting position, leaning forward into the group space, coughing or clearing the throat.

- Withdrawal or boredom is recognisable by: yawning, looking away or up to the ceiling, examining nails or doodling on a piece of paper, repeated gestures (slow foot tapping), low energy, slumping.

- Anger or hostility is indicated by: sudden movement, stiffening of the posture, clutching the fists, tightening lips and jaw, turning away pointedly from someone, expelling air through the nose, tutting, engaging someone in the group in a complicit signal, banging down a cup or glass, flicking away specks of fluff from clothes, head tossing.

- Discomfort signals are many: blushing, hesitancy, shrinking, restlessness, looking at a watch, gaze avoidance.

'*Qualitative
researchers need
to become sensitive
to patterns of
gestures rather than
taking any one
gesture as a definite
sign or meaning.*'

- Arrogance and superiority are signalled by: taking up a large amount of physical space, placing hands behind the head, looking down the nose while talking to someone, helping oneself to food or refreshments in an obvious way, getting up and walking around (to gain attention).

- If someone wishes to interrupt, he or she will often nod vigorously, tap the fingers fast, say words like 'yes, but, well'.

It is important to remember that body language is not only culturally determined but also needs to be checked. If someone scratches his nose, it may mean that he is not telling the truth but it may also mean that he has an itchy nose. Qualitative researchers need to become sensitive to patterns of gestures rather than taking any one gesture as a definite sign or meaning.

Importantly, a researcher needs to become aware of body language contexts – for example, body language, which may indicate the climate of the group as a whole, rather than any one member. This is critical in terms of understanding group process – is the group storming, norming or performing? Then there is body language in response to something that is shown to the group – a new product or an advertisement for example. Here it is important to watch the group while the ad(s) are being shown and also as soon as they are finished. Finally, there is body language in response to other group members and also in response to the moderator.

Some of the more common body language clusters are as follows.

- *Opening up* – moving back into the chair in a more comfortable position, expanding and opening the posture (legs stretched, legs apart, figure-four leg crossing),

engaging other group members in smiles, eye contact
or laughter.

- *Closing down* – shrinking, folding arms or crossing legs,
  stillness, gaze avoidance.

- *Interest* – leaning forward, touching the face, facial
  expressions to match the conversation, spontaneous involuntary movement.

- *Lack of interest* – shrugging shoulders, examining hands,
  clothes, objects, the floor, folding arms, vacant staring,
  yawning, not listening.

- *Evaluation* (undecided) – scratching ear or back of head,
  hand on or around chin or face, frowning, forefinger on
  lips, silence, slow or hesitant speech.

- *Positive evaluation* – leaning forwards, slight head
  nodding, palms turned upwards, slight or full smile.

- *Negative evaluation* – leaning back, side-to-side movements, palms down on lap, folding arms.

'As a moderator there are a number of body language cues that can be used to guide the group without resorting to verbal interference.'

As a moderator there are a number of body language cues that can be
used to guide the group without resorting to verbal interference.
These are as follows.

- *Engaging eye contact* – reinforces behaviour, encourages a
  member to contribute, gently remonstrates if someone is
  being non-compliant, shows openness and interest. This
  can be combined with a 'towards' body movement.

- *Breaking eye contact* – signals to the group member that his or her contribution is not wanted at that point or that it is taking too much of the group time. As above, this can be combined with an 'away' body movement which is an extremely effective way of 'turning off'.

- *Mirroring* – a technique of matching the behaviour patterns of another person in order to establish rapport, i.e. subtly copying gestures, facial expressions as though seen in a mirror. Mirroring the same vocabulary as someone else can be a powerful way of demonstrating empathy.

- *Pacing* – a means of achieving and maintaining rapport on both the conscious and unconscious level, by matching their behaviour both verbally and non-verbally.

'There are two other important silent languages – the language of time and the language of space.'

Mirroring and pacing require practice and need to be executed subliminally otherwise the person becomes conscious of them and interprets them in any one of a number of ways – not always positive.

In addition to non-verbal communication, there are two other important silent languages – the *language of time* and the *language of space*.

Time is culturally determined rather than absolute. Southern Europeans have a completely different concept of 'early' and 'late' than have, for example, Americans. Certain Indian tribes have no word for 'waiting' because there is no limit of time for an event to take place.

Individuals also have different concepts of time. Some of us operate as if time were a signed contract. If I say I will meet you at 5.00 p.m. I mean 5.00 p.m. I might give you five to ten minutes' grace but if you are later than that you have broken an agreed contract and I will interpret your behaviour in a particular way. Others operate as if time is approximate. A 5.00 p.m. meeting could mean a meeting anywhere between 5.00 and 5.45 p.m. without being late.

In the market research context time is contractual. People are invited to a group discussion or interview and are told that it will last x many minutes or hours. If the moderator abuses the contract communication might break down – certainly for some of the respondents and perhaps some of the observers too. Being early, being on time and being late brings either positive or negative interpretations into operation. Like body language, time keeping gives a range of signals and qualitative researchers would do well to devote some time to analysing their own time beliefs and behaviour.

'Personal space is a psychological construct referring to the physical distance or boundary each of us creates to separate ourselves from another person.'

The way we use space is another way of communicating with one another. Personal space is a psychological construct referring to the physical distance or boundary each of us creates to separate ourselves from another person. There are four distances that give clues to the nature of the relationship: an 'intimate distance' reserved for close relationships; 'personal distance' for family and friends (and slightly further away) for business contacts; 'social distance' which determines impersonal transactions; and 'public distance' such as a speaker addressing an audience.

In a conventional group discussion held in a city venue, personal space becomes an issue. In the formal board room environment, business space is comfortably maintained; in the lounge or living room environment of UK qualitative research, where people are forced sometimes to squash on to a sofa, comfortable business space (the contract for the meeting) has become uncomfortable intimate space. Moderators need to be sensitive to space and to think about how to manage the situation so as to reduce initial feelings of tension and embarrassment.

'It has been esti-mated that there are 600,000 words in the English language and that the average person uses about 2,000 in daily conversation.'

The way we distribute ourselves in space also speaks volumes. The moderator at the long end of a board room table may communicate authority and leadership in some cultures and yet not in others. The angle of chairs in relationship to one another in a depth interview can subtly change the nature of rapport, giving strong clues about the power relationship. The separation of the moderator and observer in their own chairs from the sofa seating of the group members gives a message which may or may not make the rapport easy to build and maintain.

So far, we have discussed communication of the silent kind. But what about the meaning of what people say?

There are two issues here. One is that people do not always say what they mean and do not mean what they say. This happens for a number of reasons:

- not *wanting* to tell you

- not *being able* to articulate feelings or thoughts clearly (in words)

- *posturing*.

The second issue is that the symbols (words and images) we use to transfer meaning are very inefficient. It has been estimated that there are 600,000 words in the English language and that the average person uses about 2,000 in daily conversation (excluding work-related or technical terminology). Of these, the 500 most common words have 14,000 dictionary definitions – room for miscommunication (2)!

How do we know what a word means? Usually we have to ask the person who used the word to explain: 'what exactly do you mean by that?'. Some words work perfectly well as labels or technical words (e.g. computer), others can be understood by the context. Others are very ambiguous – the dictionary does not help and neither does the context.

These words can be thought of as 'fat words' – words that carry layers of meaning depending on the individual and the context. In the course of qualitative market research, the definition of fat words is one of the most useful roles for the discipline. Think for a moment of the kinds of words used to describe the characteristics of a brand – words like British, sophisticated, modern, classic, cosmopolitan. Each of these has very different meanings depending on who is using the word and in what context. Britishness may be applauded in America as a sign of control, professionalism and good manners, but reviled in the East as a sign of aloofness, racial insensitivity and arrogance.

The same complexity applies to the multitude of words we use to describe the benefits of brands – refreshing, convenient, relaxing, reliable, good quality and so on.

> Common words do not have meanings –
> Only people do.
> And sometimes they don't either (1).

'Deceptively simple words may not have the same associations and meanings in someone else's mind as they do in ours and the only way to discover this is to ask.'

Deceptively simple words may not have the same associations and meanings in someone else's mind as they do in ours and the only way to discover this is to ask. Good qualitative researchers are aware of fat words and make sure that they do not take their meanings for granted. Simple questions to the group (or individual) like 'You used the word _____ a moment ago, can I ask you to expand a little?' or 'Joe used the word "relaxing" a moment ago to describe the mood of this commercial, what do we understand by that?'.

There is a pitfall here that is worth anticipating. Often, we are so determined to define a fat word (or series of them) that all we succeed in doing is adding more fat synonyms to the layers of meaning. While synonyms are helpful, they do not necessarily add clarity. For example, if we wanted to explain in a little more detail why Mercedes is seen to be a 'classic' brand, we could encourage group members to define what they meant by this word. Soon we would have a number of other words or phrases on the flipchart – 'timeless, contemporary but unchanged, a standard, a prototype, legendary, enduring, first-rate, superior, exemplary'. We might even ask for examples of other classic brands/people: Burberry, Harrods, Colman's Mustard, Heinz Baked Beans, Marks & Spencer, Princess Diana, the Rolling Stones.

'Often we are so determined to define a fat word that all we succeed in doing is adding more fat synonyms to the layers of meaning.'

The problem compounds – what I think and feel about Harrods may or may not be the same as what someone else thinks and feels and therefore opportunities for miscommunication multiply.

One of the ways to deal with the problem of fat words is to draw on one of the fundamental concepts of NLP (neuro-linguistic programming) (see the reference section). There is a model called representational systems which is a foundation stone of NLP and which is very relevant to communication issues such as the problem of definitions.

Representational systems refer to the way in which we code information in our minds through the use of the five senses – sight, hearing, smell, taste and touch – and then make sense of the experience. There are three primary systems – visual, auditory and kinaesthetic (feeling) and two secondary systems, olfactory and gustatory. We use all three systems continuously yet we tend to favour one more than another, especially in conscious thinking. Some people think in terms of pictures (visual) while others think by carrying on an internal dialogue (auditory) and still others 'get a feeling'. No system is better than any other – it is simply that people develop different thinking strategies.

It is relatively easy to notice which lead system someone prefers – a visual person will often draw diagrams while explaining something and use phrases such as the following.

- I see what you mean.

- We see eye to eye.

- Show me what you think.

- It looks like this to me.

- Let's take a view on this.

Someone with a kinaesthetic lead system will use phrases such as the following.

- I will get in touch with you.

- I can grasp that idea.

- Hold on a second.

- I can't put my finger on it.

- I feel comfortable/uncomfortable about this.

The following language betrays an auditory lead system.

'Representational systems refer to the way in which we code information in our minds through the use of the five senses – sight, hearing, smell, taste and touch – and then make sense of the experience.'

- We're on the same wavelength.

- It rings a bell.

- Tell me word for word.

- In a manner of speaking.

- What a lot of mumbo jumbo.

There are also easily noticed olfactory and gustatory phrases such as: smell a rat, a bitter pill, fresh as a daisy, an acid comment, a sweet person. Representational systems are not mutually exclusive. We often use two or three systems simultaneously as input channels but favour one when we want to bring back the information to conscious thought or when trying to describe a thought or experience to someone else.

'Representational systems are not mutually exclusive. We often use two or three systems simultaneously.'

This brings us back to the problem of fat words. Using the concept of representational systems we can encourage group members or an individual to 'go inside their heads' in order to re-experience the word. The instruction might go something like this:

> *We've been talking about whisky as relaxing ... what I want you to do is to shut your eyes for a moment or two and re-experience in your mind's eye yourself drinking your favourite whisky. Without talking, I want you to get in touch with what you can see – colours, images, pictures, people, places. Now listen to what you can hear – sounds or music, loud or soft, fast or slow. What do you feel that you can touch or perhaps feel inside your body? Is there anything you can smell or taste?*

When the group members have shared their internal experiences, the term 'relaxing' will be far easier to pin down – it will have a sensory definition.

Obviously, every word in a conversation cannot be clarified in this way, nor should it be. Only those key terms related to furthering understanding of the brand values, brand essence or brand communications need to be anchored.

'We can encourage group members or an individual to "go inside their heads" in order to re-experience the world.'

What to do when things go wrong

Things do go wrong. No matter how experienced the moderator, human beings are not controllable, especially by such imprecise methods as have been described in this chapter. What follows is a short description of a problem and how the author has responded. This advice may not work for everybody since it depends very much on your personality and status, but it is a starting point.

A respondent is mis-recruited

During the first 20 minutes of the group discussion you realise that someone has been mis-recruited and does not comply with the group specification previously agreed. The seriousness of the problem depends on the nature of the mis-recruitment. Could it be age? Socio-economic group? Creativity profile? Usership details? A marketing or advertising professional? Someone from a competitive company?

The first decision must be made very quickly – how damaging to the group cohesion, confidentiality of the project, or nature of the conversations within the group will this mis-recruited person be? As a rule of thumb, actual age and demographic characteristics are less important than life-stage, lifestyle and mind style (attitude of mind) and therefore if the latter characteristics fit with the group, the respondent is likely to be homogeneous.

Usership mistakes are far more of a problem. If the group is supposed to consist of heavy eaters and buyers of boiled sweets and one person claims only to eat them occasionally if offered, his or her views will be atypical and will not help the objective of trying to understand the nature of heavy users. If someone is a frequent leisure flier but never travels by air on business and the group is focused round the needs and behaviour of business fliers, again the odd person will stand out and have little to contribute.

Confidentiality problems need to be dealt with immediately. No client will appreciate having the objectives of the study (usually not difficult for a professional to determine) fed back to a competitive company or leaked to a trade journal.

The best way to handle an 'unwanted' respondent in a group discussion is tactfully and impersonally. The moderator makes an excuse to leave the room and finds the hostess, recruiter or group organiser for the evening with the instruction to come into the room and ask the respondent to come outside for a few minutes. This same person then explains to the respondent the problem and why the group would be difficult to run if the person remained in it. The respondent is then given the incentive in full together with apologies and any travel expenses incurred. Meantime the moderator explains to the rest of the group the nature of the problem and why it was necessary to ask the individual to leave the group.

'The best way to handle an "unwanted" respondent in a group discussion is tactfully and impersonally.'

Group members always understand if the process is completed calmly and the explanation given openly. The group will work extra hard to mend the breach in its infrastructure.

A respondent is drunk or behaves in an odd manner

Sometimes a respondent arrives at the group venue having spent the past few hours in a bar or having had a few drinks before arriving and is drunk or difficult. Or as the group proceeds it is apparent that one member is drunk or is displaying behaviour that is inappropriate for the meeting. Here again a quick decision is needed and the same procedure as that described above should be followed. The moderator should try to avoid engaging directly with the respondent and requesting that he or she leave the group as this risks alienating the remainder of the group. Usually, the other members feel relieved when the 'odd' person leaves the group and, provided the explanation given was direct and honest, the group members tend to be supportive of both the moderator and each other.

Late respondent

The question of how to deal with a late respondent or two depends on the time beliefs of the moderator. I believe that a time contract has been established and that there is a small window at the beginning of a group when a late entrant will not interfere with the important group dynamics in progress. This is the first five minutes after people have sat down in their chairs. After this time, the late entrant experiences difficulty in becoming an equal group member, requires time from the moderator in order to become comfortable and has missed some of the important information imparted at the introduction of the group.

Silence – a group silence

Most moderators, particularly inexperienced ones, are uncomfortable with silence in the group. If the group model follows the idea of a coffee morning or a cocktail party, then silence is a signal that something is wrong. Silence is certainly a sign that something is happening in the group, but what?

'Silence is certainly a sign that something is happening in the group but what?'

It could be a number of different things: the group is finding the subject difficult and challenging and is thinking; the group is bored with the subject; the group is 'storming' and is withdrawing co-operation; or the group is confused about the question asked or the task requested.

The moderator needs to do what is called an 'ecological' check: to diagnose the problem, if there is one, before continuing. The way to do this is to present the group with the observation about the silence, rather than looking for a rescuer among one of its members. Thus:

> *The group seems to have become silent – is there a reason for this? Can we offer a few suggestions? It is important to all of us that we understand what is happening here.*

Rather than:

Joe I wonder if you would begin – what do you think?

Once the group has been given permission to voice the problem, it takes responsibility for its energy levels and can continue with a good heart.

For example, the difficulty might be expressed in the following ways.

Insurance policies are boring to talk about especially if you haven't bought one for a long time.

I am not sure that I understand what you asked us to do – but maybe it was just me' (looking to rest of the group for support).

I think we need a cigarette break – is that OK?

Dominating respondent

Often the dominating respondent is used to slate the practice of qualitative research as a whole and the use of group discussions in particular. The media, marketing people and, in particular, creative people in advertising and design agencies often use the spectre of the dominating respondent as a reason to invalidate the research study.

A dominating respondent is the fault of the moderator and no one else. What has happened is that the moderator has not allowed the group to form, storm and norm effectively and thus it certainly will not perform. Sometimes a group 'allows' one member to dominate because it is easier. Everyone else can sit back and the 'heat is off'. Sometimes the dominating respondent is insensitive to the needs of the group and has not been given the most appropriate reinforcement by the moderator.

'A dominating respondent is the fault of the moderator and no one else.'

Domination can occur when there are differences in expertise or knowledge. Imagine a group where one individual is an expert DIY person and semi-professional home decorator but the majority are inexperienced. The discussion focuses on hanging wallpaper and painting the woodwork. Most people express how difficult it is. The expert begins to give advice about filling cracks, the differences between matt, emulsion and eggshell, and the pros and cons of different brands. From this point on, the rest of the group is likely to defer to the elected expert on any question that requires some kind of knowledge in order not to appear ignorant or foolish.

'Domination can occur when there are differences in expertise or knowledge.'

There are a number of ways of working with a dominant respondent which escalate in intensity and effect:

- withdrawal of eye contact when the person begins to speak or turning away from the individual when addressing a question to the group

- 'mismatching' by purposely displaying conflicting body language while the dominating respondent is talking

- making a direct request to the person: *'Joe, we know that you have had more experience than anyone else on this subject but it is important to hear from everybody – at whatever stage of experience they have – so do you mind letting the others have a go at thinking about the topic first?'* This kind of intervention usually works so well that Joe may have to be encouraged to contribute again

- handing responsibility for the dominating respondent to the group and letting it deal with him or her. For example, *'we seem to have an issue here which the group might want to deal with – Joe always takes the initiative and contributes first – how does the group feel about this and what would be a fair way to continue so that everyone can contribute?*' This takes the responsibility for a head-on collision with Joe away from the moderator and allows the group to deal with the dynamics.

Pairing

This occurs when two members of the group liaise and begin conversations which either take place while other people are talking or distract the group from the topic being discussed. Again, this may be a signal of storming (a group defensive positioning) or may simply be the result of the moderator having reinforced that this kind of behaviour is acceptable. There are escalating ways of handling this, from using simple body language to interference, either directly or through addressing the group as a matrix or asking them how they feel:

> *I wonder if the two of you would mind sharing your conversation with the rest of us – it might be helpful.*

> *Joe and Jane seem to enjoy having a private conversation with one another every time I show an advertisement on the box. How do we feel about this? Should we all do it or should we try to share our opinions?*

'Were the instructions clear enough? Is the group storming and why now? Is the task too threatening and if so why?'

Fight

This is when a group fights the task rather than doing it. Sometimes this manifests itself in lots of questions from different group members to clarify instructions or persistently cynical, jokey and silly behaviour. The moderator needs to run through the checklist of possible causes. Were the instructions clear enough? Is the group storming and why now? Is the task too threatening and if so why?

There are three ways of handling fight – the first is to acknowledge that the problem might belong to the moderator, who may need to express the task in a different way: *'Perhaps I haven't been clear enough – let me try again – what I want you to think about is …'.*

The second is to give the group the responsibility for the problem and to allow them to express the reasons for this. '*We seem to be having a bit of a problem here – can anyone suggest what the cause is and let's talk about it?*'

The third way is for the group to win and the moderator to try something else that may be less threatening at this point in the group process. Thus: '*I'm having a second thought here – why don't we do something else now – its a different kind of exercise ...*'.

Flight

This is similar to fight in that it is often a manifestation of storming. The group avoids the topic for discussion or avoids the task, usually by diverting the moderator and the rest of the group's attention through anecdotes, interruptions (getting up and offering drinks or food, asking to be excused to go to the bathroom), jokes and other seemingly innocuous behaviour.

'There are no right answers – only a series of initiatives by the moderator, which either succeed or fail.'

The same checking procedure needs to be activated. What could be the problem? Should that subject be introduced later when the group has formed better? Is one member taking on a leading role in the group and becoming its covert representative? Should the problem be overtly expressed by the moderator and presented to the group or should the moderator coast along for a while and let the group pass through this phase? There are no right answers – only a series of initiatives by the moderator, that either succeed or fail.

A quiet respondent

This is one of the most difficult problems to deal with, primarily because clients believe that a group discussion is successful and a moderator is worth his or her salt if every person contributes equally throughout the group. There are many reasons why someone might be a 'mouse' in a group discussion – sometimes he or she feels so threatened that they freeze. This happens because the individual feels out of place – perhaps intellectually, demographically or in usership terms to the remainder of the group members. This is why heterogeneity is important and why a mis-recruited respondent experiences difficulty.

The decision facing the moderator is how to encourage the quiet respondent to participate. Sometimes, the use of encouraging and interested body language can help, accompanied by special gestures such as passing the biscuits or offering refreshment before the rest of the group. This little sign of concern and care may help to relax the person. Addressing the individual by name can work in the same way but can often exacerbate the problem – since the noticeable attention makes a shy respondent even shyer.

Another method is to ask the group to pair up and exchange views about a particular topic. This helps the quiet (shy, embarrassed, unconfident) person to contribute in a less direct and public way and may help to build confidence once he or she realises that his or her contribution is no better or worse than anyone else's.

Flirtation

Flirting with a respondent or, conversely, the flirting with a moderator by a particular respondent, needs to be firmly controlled since it fuels storming and if it continues is likely to annoy the remaining group members who will find a way of punishing the moderator by with-drawing co-operation. The most important advice is simply not to collude. This will happen if the moderator is aware of his or her own behaviour and feelings towards individual members of the group.

It is true in life that each of us is instantly drawn to some people and not to others. This is a fact of human nature. There are those with whom we intuitively feel comfortable and who we find it easy to talk to and others who make us feel uncomfortable. Be aware that this is

'There are many many reasons why someone might be a "mouse" in a group discussion – sometimes he or she feels so threatened that they freeze.'

simply baggage from the past and has nothing to do with the eight people in the room. The advice is to simply stop it – whether it is in you or coming from someone else. It is self-indulgent and manipulative and does not belong in the professional environment of a market research group discussion.

When groups go wrong, it can usually be managed by a good and experienced moderator. The frequent comment that one hears from observers – 'that was a good group' or 'that was a difficult group' (or even 'that was a waste of time') has nothing to do with the participants and everything to do with the skill of the moderator. The majority of human beings are a rich resource for marketing or social problems – those commissioning qualitative focus groups need to know this and learn how to choose the best qualitative professionals to manage the process.

'When groups go wrong, it can usually be managed by a good and experienced moderator.'

Implications for other methodologies

This chapter has discussed selective perception, the languages of body and space, time-keeping and verbal communication or miscommunication, mostly in the context of group discussions. All of these considerations are equally as important in the one-to-one interview and other non-group methodologies. In many cultures, spending time alone with one other person suggests either personal intimacy (with, say, a friend, relative or partner), or an unequal relationship or situation, such as boss/subordinate, teacher/pupil, senior experienced/ younger novice, a job interview or some other encounter with authority. If the interview is to evolve into a richer and more productive experience than a formal question and answer session, the researcher needs to use all possible communication tools to set up an open atmosphere, framed within a different but equal human relationship.

Indeed, it is highly desirable for the researcher to approach the interview in the frame of mind where (s)he feels intrigued and privileged to be allowed a glimpse of another person's life, particularly if it involves talking to them in 'real' environments.

'It is highly desirable for the researcher to approach the interview in the frame of mind where (s)he feels intrigued and privileged to be allowed a glimpse of another person's life.'

Imagine, for a moment, that you have agreed for an unknown 'market researcher' to visit your house and look at the cooking sauces you have in stock. The researcher has also asked you to jot down a couple of your favourite recipes, and has asked to accompany you while you do some shopping in one or two supermarkets. It would be a rare human being that was not at least a little intimidated by such a prospect. Thoughts such as 'my house is messy', 'I'm not an adventurous cook', 'I'm a disorganised shopper', 'will I come across OK?' are entirely reasonable human responses to the situation.

There are other scenarios which, on the surface, look as if they will make the interview easy and yet turn into a situation that can undermine the integrity of the whole research process. Imagine interviewing a married couple about the holiday decision-making process. The interview begins with one member of the couple taking the lead while the other defers. This is very typical. As the interview proceeds, the underlying dynamic of the relationship begins to emerge – perhaps one of competition or passive aggression. Before long, the interviewer is embroiled 'in the game that couples play' – a process not dissimilar to storming. While marriage therapy is obviously out of the question, the interviewer needs to decide how to overcome this problem which will interfere with the nature of the information being learned. There is no one solution to this: awareness and sensitivity to the pitfalls in couple or family interviews helps a great deal.

'Researchers need to be aware of time boundaries when interviewing people on their own or in other combinations, out of the group discussion context.'

Researchers need to be aware of time boundaries when interviewing people on their own or in other combinations, out of the group discussion context. If the researcher is late, or even early, before the inevitable tidying up of the house (in-home interviews) is finished or the babysitter has arrived, then disrespect for the interviewee and his or her way of life can be communicated.

A sensitive individual picks up non-verbal cues extremely easily. The researcher might believe he or she is hiding distaste for the neighbour-hood, judgment about the interior design of the house, disapproving evaluations about tidiness, the way in which the interviewee is dressed or the way in which the parents address their children and so on. All of these bring with them associated judgments, which are communicated amazingly easily if the researcher is unaware of his or her own areas of prejudice.

Accompanying people as they shop, cook, spend a Saturday, go club-bing with the girls, spend the day at a theme park and so on needs to be approached with sensitivity and humility. Over-detailed questions, 'leaked judgements', inappropriate dress, lack of respect for space or time can leave the person (couple, friendship pair, family, social group), feeling abused. They will 'close down' and give you very little of value. Interpreting their behaviour, like the parable of the blind men and the elephant, will be blinkered and partial, and your approach could be described as contempt prior to investigation. A far more productive paradigm is the old Indian proverb: 'To really know a man you must walk five miles in his moccasins'!

One of the main differences between interviewing people in a conventional group discussion (eight to ten people who do not know each other), and interviewing people on their own or in their usual social groupings (partners, friends, families, work groups), is role-playing.

Chrissie Burns (3) writes cogently about the importance of making the distinction between public and private faces. Each of us has many faces – both public and private – and the challenge for the interviewer is to work out which one is being exposed. The mother who expresses concern about the environment and the effect of genetic engineering on the quality of food she gives her family may be showing her public face. This is different from her private face – the mother who buys sweets and chocolate bars as bribe treats for her children and who will not make the effort to return glass bottles to the bottle bank.

Each human being is a bundle of seeming inconsistencies. In individual interviews, people tend to play safe. They come across as logical, rational and composed rather than a heady mixture of the impulsive, irrational and spontaneous combined with the planned and considered. One of the advantages of the individual interview (or variations thereof), is that a detailed 'story' of attitudes and behaviour can be elicited which is very useful when trying to gain insight into decision-making or historical brand relationships. The challenge is to determine whether or not the individual is adopting only one of his or her public faces, striving hard to be consistent with that face throughout the interview. The researcher needs to marshal all his or her observation acuity, indirect or projective forms of questioning and skill in rapport building in order to understand what is going on.

'Each human being is a bundle of seeming inconsistencies.'

Burns points out that one of the most valuable assets of a good researcher is self-awareness. We need to question our integrity continuously. To begin, we can ask the following kinds of questions.

- Am I encouraging role-playing?

- To what extent am I expressing my own needs in the interview situation?

- What game is going on here? Flirtation? Mothering? Surrogate friend?

'One of the most valuable assets of a good researcher is self-awareness.'

One doesn't need to be trained in transactional analysis or indeed in any psychological framework to understand the issues of faces, roles and game playing. We all adopt them and play them. However, to recognise their existence and to work through them in the individual interview situation clearly takes time (3).

The same is true no matter which 'interview unit' has been chosen – individual, pair, family, friendship, mini-group, standard group or large group.

In conclusion, the advice I would give to anyone who wishes to improve his or her interviewing skills is to begin a journey of self-development. This could begin by reading a selection of popular books which explain the fundamental dynamics of human behaviour, particularly the influence of our past experiences on the way we live our present and which determines the framework of our expectations of the future. It might involve enrolling in courses, lectures or further study in contemporary psychology, social anthropology, communications or media studies. It could encompass jumping 'out of the box' and exploring other worlds outside your own discipline. There is no right way – only right intentions. These are to become less insular, to become more aware that other people are both very different and very similar to yourself and a commitment to reduce the arrogance that often breeds unhealthily in the minds of research, advertising and marketing professionals.

REFERENCES

1. W. Gordon and R. Langmaid, *Qualitative Market Research: A Practitioner's and Buyer's Guide*, Gower, 1988.
2. D. Fabun, *Communications: The Transfer of Meaning*, Kaiser Aluminium and Chemical Corporation, reprinted by arrangement with Macmillan Publishing Company, a division of Macmillan, 1968.
3. C. Burns, 'Individual Interviews' in S. Robson and A. Foster, *Qualitative Research in Action*, Edward Arnold, 1989.

FURTHER READING

W. Gordon, 'The Map is not the Territory', ESOMAR Seminar on Qualitative Research, Geneva, 1990.

S. Newman and S. Lonsdale, *Human Jungle*, Ebury Press, 1996.

J. O'Connor and J. Seymour, *Introducing NLP*, Aquarian Press, 1993.

J. Sinclair, *An ABC of NLP*, Container Marketing Limited, under the Aspen imprint, 1992.

Revealing Insight

Chapter six

Introduction

If we accept that qualitative research is fundamentally concerned with understanding the meaning that people bring to 'things' – events, objects, products, brands, places, people and relationships – we need to know how to open the doors to these perceptions. To do this, we must have the co-operation and goodwill of the 'meaning-maker'.

This chapter is concerned with projective and enabling techniques that have become an essential part of qualitative research.

The most commonly used techniques (and some less popular ones) will be reviewed, together with guidance as to how they are best administered and interpreted.

The application of projective and enabling techniques lies primarily in the arena of brand development – understanding the nature of the relationship consumers or customers have with a brand in the past, present or future – domestically and internationally.

> *In an increasingly competitive and complex world, the building of successful brands relies on establishing and nurturing a strong and relevant relationship between the seller and the buyer. More than ever before, the seller needs to truly understand the lives of potential consumers; their behaviour, attitudes, hopes, fears, needs and desires. Only then can the brand be managed and presented in a way that will be attractive to them* (1).

People are not always aware of the nature of the relationship they have with brands and services. They simply feel 'good', 'bad' or 'indifferent' about the myriad of brand and service choices that face them every day. They will give various reasons for choice if asked: price, promotion, value, habit, change, recommendation or reputation. They will not be aware of the deeper emotional ties that have been forged with a brand or the extent to which it has come to have a symbolic value in their lives.

These hidden meanings can be made more explicit through the use of projective and enabling techniques.

What is projection?

The concept of projection derives from the insights of Freud (1856–1939) who may be thought of as the founder of psychoanalysis. The *unconscious* is a central tenet of psychoanalysis and is best understood as a large part of the psyche of which we are unaware. This is in contrast to the pre-conscious and conscious parts that can be brought into awareness. Thoughts, feelings, terrors, impulses and desires that are unacceptable are dumped into the realm of the unconscious, so as not to threaten the comfort level of the conscious life.

When something is relegated to the unconscious, it does not disappear but becomes changed through processes called defence mechanisms. Many of the defence mechanisms described in psychoanalytic literature are fairly common knowledge due perhaps to the popularisation of psychotherapy that has occurred over the past 20 years. Mainstream magazine and newspaper articles regularly cover a multitude of subjects: anorexia, child abuse, serial murder, rape, addictions, stalking and obsessional behaviour.

'When something is relegated to the unconscious, it does not disappear but becomes changed through processes called defence mechanisms.'

A number of terms have become commonplace nowadays:

- repression (forgetting traumatic events)

- denial (placing a block on a facet of reality so that it seems not to exist)

- displacement (instead of targeting an unacceptable emotion at the intended person it is transferred to another)

- rationalisation (legitimising troubling activities or desires on shaky moral or rational grounds).

All of these defence mechanisms occur in the course of qualitative market research interviewing, even in connection with fairly mundane categories and brands, and therefore are worth studying in a little more detail (2).

Projection is yet one more defence mechanism and is defined as:

- 'an attitude or desire that one finds disturbing in oneself is transferred or put into someone else' (2)

- 'the tendency to imbue objects or events with characteristics or meanings that are derived from our subconscious desires, wishes or feelings' (3).

As human beings, we withhold thoughts and feelings from others and we also hide them successfully from ourselves – particularly deeper desires, wishes, fears and emotions that we believe are in some way unacceptable ones to express. Projection wards off these uncomfortable feelings – such as shame, embarrassment, shyness, aggressiveness and anger – emotions that are present for all of us in our day-to-day lives.

Projective techniques consist of a situation or stimulus that encourages a person to project part of him or herself or an idea system on to an external object or to bring it into the interview itself. In the context of qualitative market research projective techniques are designed to enable the individual or group to express these feelings through light-hearted and safe exercises which reveal insight both to the individuals themselves as well as to the researcher.

'Projective techniques consist of a situation or stimulus which encourages a person to project part of him or herself or an idea system onto an external object.'

The basic principle of an enabling technique is 'to create a situation that enables the individual's awareness to be focused on issues with which we may be concerned' (4). For example, we may want to understand automatic behaviour such as shaving or washing hair. We might ask participants in a research study to keep a diary of hair washing: how often; the precise sequence of products and behaviour; thoughts and feelings before, during and after and so on. This raises awareness and makes subsequent discussion in a group interview or individual depth interview more sensitive. Enabling techniques such as this are often called 'heightened sensitivity' techniques.

Other enabling techniques are concerned with raising levels of trust between members of a group and may involve exercises in pairs or small groups designed to facilitate the group dynamics at the early stages of group formation.

'The basic principle of an enabling technique is "to create a situation that enables the individual's awareness to be focused on issues with which we may be concerned".'

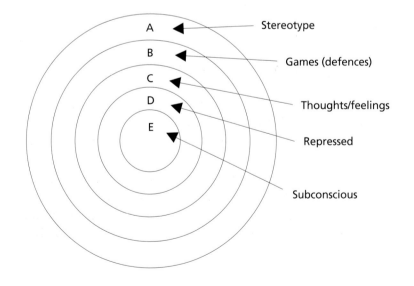

Figure 1: The Structure of Consciousness

A — Stereotype
B — Games (defences)
C
D — Thoughts/feelings
E — Repressed

Subconscious

During the course of quantitative market research and much qualitative research too, people are unwilling to share thoughts and feelings with a stranger, for all kinds of reasons. It may be too bothersome to think about the subject seriously or there may be a desire 'to get the interview over as quickly as possible'. Often people find the questions silly, repetitive or meaningless and the subject boring or embarrassing, or feel anxious about the direction of the questions. The probing nature of the questions can be intrusive, and is not helped by the incomplete understanding of how the information might be used.

In the event that any of these feelings are present, level A and B responses are common (see Figure 1). By stereotypical, we mean conventional or predictable responses – the kind of response that is automatic and unthinking. For example, if someone is stopped at the end of a supermarket aisle and asked why she had put Brand X in her trolley, she is likely to answer: 'It's my usual brand' or 'I felt like a change'. It is highly unlikely that this person will mention brand personality traits or the way in which the brand fits her lifestyle and self-image. This is not to say that stereotypical responses are wrong – it is just that they do not help the process of understanding how to differentiate the brand from its competitors.

Games that people play refer to the first-line defence structure that all human beings are able to raise when desired. We play games like: 'Aren't I clever?', ' I'm just an ordinary bloke', ' I am a reasonable human being' and 'I am a joker'. When pushed or threatened, even moderately, we hide behind our cleverness, ordinariness, reasonableness or jokes – an effective way of keeping the imagined intrusion away.

'During the course of quantitative market research people are unwilling to share thoughts and feelings with a stranger, for all kinds of reasons.'

Qualitative market research is able to tap into level C and this is where much of the useful learning lies about the consumer–brand relationship. For those researchers with a great deal of experience and a psychological background, level D can be made available in high-

*'When pushed or
threatened, even
moderately, we hide
behind our clever-
ness, ordinariness,
reasonableness
or jokes.'*

trust situations and with the use of projective techniques. Level E is
out of reach for the purposes of market research.

Another way of thinking about the layers of consciousness is to think
about the different kind of responses: public versus private, communi-
cable versus non-communicable and aware versus unaware.

Figure 2 illustrates these layers and also indicates the method of questioning on the left and the nature of response on the right.

Figure 2: Layers of Consciousness

Accessibility			Layers of response
P U B L I C	C O M M U N I C A B L E	A W A R E	Spontaneous
			Reasoned, conventional
P R I V A T E			Preconscious, concealed, personal
	N O N C O M M U N I C A B L E		Intuitive, imaginative
		U N A W A R E	Unconscious, repressed

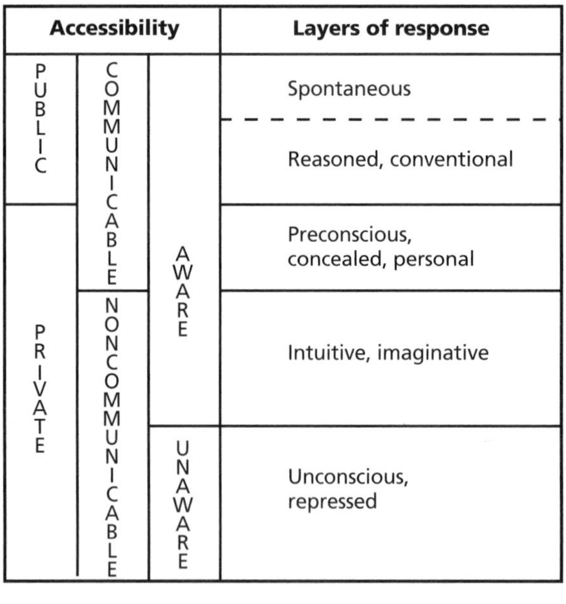

Source: P. Cooper and A. Branthwaite
'Qualitative Technology: New Perspectives on Measurement and Meaning
Through Qualitative Research', Brighton, MRS Conference Proceedings, 1977.

There are different projective techniques that are suitable for the three 'private' layers – they vary in their capabilities of tapping into deeper levels. It could be argued whether it is the subconscious or the unconscious that we access in market research, but this is probably a debate that belongs to those trained in psychotherapy.

In summary, there are a number of indications for using projective and enabling techniques:

- to access experiences without arousing embarrassment or anxiety

- to enable the expression of the deeper levels of response in an indirect way

- to enable researchers to make reality-based interpretations of human behaviour

- to discover new dimensions of meaning in relation to an issue or brand

- to bring the inner world of the brand–consumer relationship vividly to life.

Five main types of projective technique

There are five classes of projective technique:

- association

- completion

- construction

- expressive

- choice ordering.

The single most important 'rule' is that the person must explain his or her response to the projective technique to the interviewer; it is not valid or meaningful for the researcher to proffer interpretations without checking the validity of these with the research participant(s).

Association techniques

The most famous word association technique, much made fun of in cartoons about psychotherapists or psychoanalysts, is the Rorschach ink-blot test which used ten ambiguous shapes (like ink blots) from which the subject was asked to make meaning (i.e. associations). Word association is used in lie-detection tests – a range of words linked and unlinked to the crime are read to the 'suspect' and physio-logical verbal responses recorded.

'Word association is both easy and involving for people. Responses can be written down or spoken out.'

Word association is both easy and involving for people. Responses can be written down or spoken out; they can be owned or disowned thus allowing the individual space to be less inhibited. Association techniques illuminate the range of connections within a group of people to the same stimulus and also allow vernacular or idiomatic expressions and even strong swear words a legitimate role in the discussion.

Figure 3: Thought Bubble Completion – Situation

Figure 4: Thought Bubble Completion – Brand

Thought Bubble Completion (see Figure 3) is a method whereby a simple drawing of a situation is devised with an empty thought or speech bubble. The exercise requires the group participants or individual person to write in 'what you think this person might be thinking/saying in this situation'. Spontaneity and top-of-mind first associations need to be encouraged. Another way to use this simple technique is to draw the thought or speech bubble emanating from the brand and competitive set (see Figure 4). The instruction might be given as follows: 'Imagine that you were walking past a shelf and all these brands decided to attract your attention and persuade you to buy them, what might they say to be different?'

Once the bubbles have been completed, the interviewer can handle them in different ways. Group members can be asked to read them aloud and the whole group encouraged to discuss the range of associations to the situation, or the moderator can keep the identity of the writer anonymous and read out the bubble. The writer then has the choice whether or not to 'own' the thought in front of the group. Subject matter and group dynamics determine which course of action is best.

'One of the biggest errors made by researchers is to take external appearance descriptors as interpretations of brand personality.'

Brand personality is a metaphor for the core character of a brand and is one of the most commonly used techniques in brand development. It is an effective exercise, particularly with groups, where people are asked to imagine the brand as a person coming to life. The instruction might be as follows: 'Imagine that this brand [e.g. Smirnoff vodka] were to turn into a person right in front of our eyes and walk into the room. What sort of a person do you imagine and how might he or she behave?' One of the biggest errors made by researchers is to take external appearance descriptors as interpretations of brand personality. Such imagined characteristics as 'young', 'male', 'professional person', 'affluent' or 'yuppie' are not brand personality descriptors. Traits such as 'confident', 'sophisticated', 'extrovert', 'the life and soul of the party' and 'trustworthy' are expressions of brand character rather than brand lifestyle.

It is usual to repeat this exercise several times for competitive brands within a category (as with the whisky brands below) as it produces sensitive differences to brands that, on the surface, may be fairly similar (in product, price and usage occasion).

Bell's	The Famous Grouse	Teacher's
'An extrovert who has many friends. He loves chatting in his local pub with his mates. A bit of a lad.'	'A Scottish laird walking through the heather. He is polite, reserved and kind. A little removed but not unfriendly.'	'An old-fashioned older man in his sixties. Rather loud and opinionated. He is not politically correct.'

A variation of this technique is to ask the group to imagine a party at which all the key brands are present. The exercise is to imagine how the various brands would behave in relation to one another. Who talks to whom? Who is the centre of attention and who stays on the sidelines? Who would be the most fun to talk to and who the least fun? If the category is rich in imagery and brands, this exercise can be productive and energising. If a category only has one or two strong brands, it is often a waste of time and results in the group members feeling silly.

There are other ways of generating the 'traits' or 'characteristics' of a brand. Some researchers prefer to use animal 'personification': 'if this brand were an animal, insect, reptile or any form of animal life, what would it be?'. Or car metaphors: 'if this brand were a car, what make and model would it be?'. As before it is essential for the group members to explain the reasons for their choices and also to push the explanations towards traits and characteristics. A brand may be a VW Golf or an otter, but this does not lead to enlightenment unless we understand the meanings of the car and the animal to the group ('fast, powerful, quick on its feet, fun, and so on). This is particularly important cross-culturally – animals mean different things in different parts of the world.

'A brand may be a VW Golf or an otter, but this does not lead to enlightenment unless we understand the meanings of the car and the animal to the group.'

The introduction of brand personality projectives is important and needs planning. If the objective is to understand the brand character of the key brands as they exist in the mind-file of an individual labelled 'jumbled impressions about brands' then it is important to use the technique before any of the packs or brand communications are shown. If the objective of the study is communications related, it might be advantageous to do brand personality work after the pack, advertising or promotions have been shown.

Picture association techniques

Pictures often provide the emotional quality and mood that words cannot communicate as vividly. Colours, textures, people, places and occasions all carry meaning for people, which they can articulate. Because 'a picture is worth a thousand words' this technique is both fun and simple to use.

'Pictures often provide the emotional quality and mood that words cannot communicate as vividly.'

The members of a group, or a respondent in an individual interview, are given a set of pictures and asked to select those that fit the brand, product or service. It is advisable for the set to be large and varied. Once the selection is made, it is essential that the individual(s) explain why they chose certain images and discarded others. There is no absolute truth in any image, especially when the sample involves people from different cultures.

To illustrate this point I will use a case history from South Africa in the early 1960s. A campaign was designed to teach the importance of contraception. A poster showing a family round the dinner table was shown – slim-looking parents with one school-age child eating large bowls of food. The campaign researched extremely poorly until we discovered that in the cultural context of black South Africans (at the time) the picture was interpreted very negatively. The woman was considered mean and unattractive (thin was not beautiful at that time). She was believed to be barren (only one child) and this was compounded by the fact that there was no extended family at the meal – a sign of an unhappy relationship.

Collage boards or mood boards (overleaf) are made of scrap art (pictures and words) cut out from magazines or newspapers. They work in the same way as picture association except that they are designed to explore a theme.

The pictures can be selected to represent an abstract concept such as freshness, balance, wisdom or leadership. Collages can be used more simply to explore user image (perceptions about the kind of person who uses or does not use the brand), occasion image (the kind of occasion in which the brand fits best or worst) and mood (the association between the brand and a particular mood or emotional feeling).

The difference between collage boards and picture association is that the boards are prepared prior to the commencement of the research either by the research company or by the pack, advertising or marketing agency involved in the project.

Analogy boards are also picture boards but are a little less literal. A board might show pictures of a comfortable sofa, a balloon, a flower, a pile of coins, an old statue, a grasshopper and so on. These are a simple way of stretching the imagination of people by asking them to choose a picture from the board which in some way can be associated with the brand and to give their reasons for so doing.

The way in which these boards are both designed and introduced to people in research is crucial. While each picture is important, so is the extent of the range, both in terms of number of pictures and content. The more extreme the parameters of the range, the more useful the stimulus.

'When designing user, occasion or mood boards for use in other countries it is important that the photographs chosen match cultural stereotypes.'

Positioning board: Light and chic

Typology board: Food

Collages provided by John Nolan of the Collage Shop.

User lifestyle board: Early Adopter

Meaning collage: Italian-ness

Word list

Words and pictures – Radox

When designing user, occasion or mood boards for use in other countries it is important that the photographs chosen match cultural stereotypes and that advice is taken from the research company as to the appropriateness of the visuals.

Words and pictures is a phrase used to describe consumer or customer-generated collages completed from a deck of images, words and pictures cut from magazines and newspapers. The deck can consist of pictures of people (ordinary and famous), places, objects, colours, phrases, words, brand names, scraps of material of different textures, food pictures to represent a taste spectrum, smells (real or imagined) and so on.

This technique is most helpful in highlighting the complexity of brand images – both established and new ones – or in understanding the nature of the associations generated through positioning a brand in a range of different ways.

Moderators need to be well trained to use this technique since group members require continual encouragement and gentle guidance to be 'creative', 'to think outside the box' and not to be 'too literal'.

In practical terms, it is often worthwhile dividing the group into two teams for this exercise – for time efficiency as well as greater involvement by all the group members. When the team has selected a range of appropriate images, it is asked to lay them out on the table (or a large flipchart sheet of paper), and for one member of the team to explain the collage to the second team. The reverse then occurs and the similarities and differences between the two collages are discussed.

At the end of the study, an amalgam of the collages can be prepared as a presentation aid or those prepared by the participants themselves can be used to illustrate differences in perceptions of the brand, the new product or service, or the positioning.

'Moderators need to be well trained to use this technique since group members require continual encouragement and gentle guidance to be "creative".'

Obituaries are a popular association technique and are particularly valuable for understanding the relationship people have with brands that have a strong heritage. The group (it works best in a group context) is asked to imagine that the company or brand has died and that the funeral is taking place. Various people related to the deceased company or brand give a short speech at the graveside highlighting achievements and characteristics. Why would the company or brand be remembered? What has been the greatest achievement and greatest gift to the next generation? Who will take over the reins?

This technique allows people to express their relationship with a well-known brand in a humorous way while at the same time tapping deeply held emotional feelings.

Completion techniques

Here the research participant is asked to make sense of a stimulus that is incomplete. A sentence is presented that has a stem beginning. Brands are set down in a higgledy-piggledy way and people are asked to put them into meaningful categories. A photograph or drawing which has a few prompt words on it is handed out, the task being to add to it in order for it to appear complete.

The completion is the projected 'element' brought into the context by the individual(s) depending on their experience or perceptions and beliefs about it.

Sentence completion is a simple and foolproof technique often used in semi-structured questionnaires. This involves asking someone (or a group) to complete a sentence. For example:

My greatest fear about the millennium is that ...

> *... the world will end because we continue to abuse its resources.*

... World War 3.

... my children will not have jobs after they have been to university.

I think people who are making a big thing about organic meat nowadays are ...

... a pain in the arse.

... right to take precautions. I don't trust what the government is telling us about BSE.

Often it helps to use the answers as further discussion points for the whole group to debate or, if it is an individual interview, to enter the 'door' indicated and explore some of the attitudes and beliefs connected to the completion in more depth.

Brand mapping (see Figure 5) is one of the most commonly used techniques in qualitative market research today. A wide range of competitive brands (in their packs), brand logos or press advertisements are presented to the group which is then asked to put them into categories in any way it wishes.

This task often energises the group, whose members can physically move from their chairs, talk to one another and involve themselves actively in a task. Once the first pass groupings are completed and explained to the moderator, the task may be repeated by asking the group 'to think about the brands in another way and see if you can find a different way of grouping them'.

This exercise, whether it is completed with brands or other stimuli, clearly shows the key criteria by which a target group segments

'Brand mapping is one of the most commonly used techniques in qualitative market research today.'

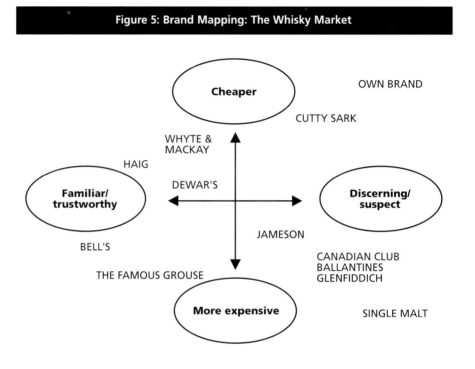

Figure 5: Brand Mapping: The Whisky Market

a product category (by product ingredients, price, quality, communications, packaging, image facets, values, heritage etc.).

Construction techniques

These are more complex techniques and demand more of both parties – moderator/interviewer and participant(s) – since they require the individual to tell a story, imagine a scenario and actively create meaning from a minimal start.

Projective questioning

This is frequently used in market research to encourage someone to 'disown' their thoughts and feelings by attributing them to a hypothetical 'average' person or 'another group of people we talked to', for example:

> *What do you think the average mother might feel if she found out that her daughter was putting on a lot of weight?*

Since there is no such person as 'an average mother', answers to this question will reveal the person's own anxieties about fatness and mothering without causing feelings of embarrassment or discomfort.

Projective questioning is a useful way to challenge a group or a person being interviewed by introducing a hypothetical 'point of view' or to test out hypotheses that might be developed during the course of the research:

> *It is interesting you all feel that this commercial is boring – the group I spoke to last night thought that it was intriguing. Why do you think they might have said that?*

> *People are so different aren't they? I was speaking to some women yesterday and they said that they don't like walking around with an Etam [retail chain] shopping bag. What kind of women do you think they were and why would they say that?*

Projective questioning encourages people to voice beliefs and opinions, that they might have otherwise withheld, in complete safety.

'Projective questioning encourages people to voice beliefs and opinions in complete safety, that they might have otherwise withheld.'

Figure 6: Stereotypes

Paul is 38, married with two children, 10 and 13. He is a financial director of a large multi-national company. His children go to private school. His wife works part-time in a clothes shop. They have a hectic social life and enjoy the theatre, opera and eating out. They go on holiday abroad twice a year.

Laura is a mother and part-time receptionist at a local surgery. She has recently returned to work now that both her children are at school. She attends a keep-fit class once a week but otherwise has little time for herself. Her husband is a bank manager. They take their bottles to the bottle bank every week.

Linda is 29 and a PhD student. She is an active campaigner on all student, political and environmental issues. She enjoys going to marches and is an active NUS member. She sympathises with New Age travellers. She goes to all-night raves and festivals, and drives an old Bedford van.

Marianne has three children and is married to a postman. The children are two, five and seven years old. Funds are limited but until the youngest is older, Marianne will not be able to return to work. They like to have days out as a family during the school holidays.

Stereotypes

This is a useful technique (see Figure 6) for understanding user image – the kind of person (demographic profile), life stage, lifestyle and attitude set (traditional versus modern, conservative versus liberal) who might use the brand or new product.

The group can be encouraged to develop a story about the person and explain how and why the brand does or does not fit into his or her life.

Guided fantasy and brand fingerprint

One of the most common failings of contemporary qualitative moderators is to rush the group or interview because so much has been

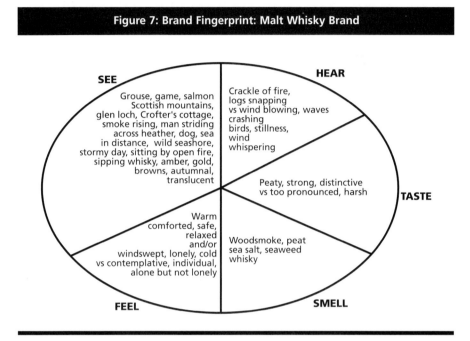

Figure 7: Brand Fingerprint: Malt Whisky Brand

crammed into the allotted time. Question follows question without allowing the participants any time at all to access the rich images and associations that form the jumble of impressions we call a brand.

A guided fantasy may take the following form:

> *Let your mind go back to the last time you cleaned your oven. Put yourself back into the situation and imagine yourself thinking about cleaning it. How does it look? What do you see? Hear? Smell? Feel? What kind of thoughts are you having? Now you are cleaning it – what do you see/hear/feel/smell? What kinds of thoughts run through your mind? Now you have finished it – what do you see, hear, feel and smell? What are your thoughts now?*

While the moderator is talking through this scenario in a slow and measured tone of voice, participants are asked not to talk, but simply to experience whatever images and feelings emerge. These are then 'dumped' on to a flipchart and the main themes discussed.

A guided fantasy is particularly useful for any automatic act of behaviour that has come adrift from the sensory associations and emotional feelings surrounding it.

The brand fingerprint (see Figure 7) uses the same approach but is brand focused. It clearly brings out into the cold light of day the subtle difference between brands and demonstrates their complexity and the sensory anchoring that underpins them. Brand fingerprints are discussed further in Chapter 7 as a useful model of thinking to explore competitive brand differences.

The script below is intended as a guideline for the first-time flyer and shows how three well-known brands can be compared. The tone of delivery should not be too slow nor hypnotic.

'A guided fantasy is particularly useful for any automatic act of behaviour that has come adrift from the sensory associations and emotional feelings surrounding it.'

> *Imagine that you are walking down a grey passage. You are going to come to three doors that lead into three worlds and you are going to visit each one in turn and let whatever is in your head come to the surface. The first door you come to has Coca-Cola on the door. Go inside and take a good look around. What do you see? What kind of colours, what kind of people, what are they doing, what is the scenery like, where is this place? What do you hear? How loud or soft is it? What do you smell? What do you taste? How do you feel in this space – is it a place you feel comfortable in or is it one you want to go away from? What atmosphere and mood does it put you in?*

Now you are going to leave and go to the next door
which has Fanta on the door [repeat prompts].

It is easy for people to keep all three brand images in their minds. The
moderator then writes 'Coke' up on the flipchart and the group shares
its experiences under sensory headings – see, hear, taste, feel, and
smell. Fanta is constructed in the same way, followed by the third
brand. Similarities and differences are compared and discussed.

*'Psychodrawing is a
fun technique to
use and one that
participants enjoy a
great deal even
though they tend to
make excuses and
complain while
doing it.'*

Expressive techniques

All the projective techniques described so far rely on verbal content as
the output – whether in written or spoken form. The emphasis is on
the individual and what he or she produces in response to the stimulus.

Expressive techniques are slightly different in that the emphasis is on
how rather than what is generated by the task set, even though the
output is written, drawn or spoken.

Psychodrawing

This is a fun technique to use and one that participants enjoy a great
deal even though they tend to make excuses and complain while
doing it. The group is provided with many coloured crayons and felt-
tip pens and asked to draw:

- a brand showing its pack and label, e.g. Marmite or
  another brand (see Figure 8)

- a feeling, for example, 'imagine eating the most delicious
  chocolate you have ever eaten. Draw what it feels like'
  (see Figure 9).

- a process, for example, 'draw your mood changes over the
  course of a week from the time you buy a lottery ticket to

Figure 8: Psychodrawing

Dear Joe Bloggs
This is how my asthma feels
if I am having a bad attack,
otherwise I just feel wheezy
& short of breath.

.Maria.

Figure 9: Drawings Expressing Deliciousness

the time after the draw, or draw the course of your relationship with this bank'.

The drawings, in terms of quality, accuracy or artistic merit, are irrelevant. What is extremely important is what the task itself brings into awareness or relief. In the case of a brand, such drawings often reveal the key identity elements (colour, graphics, pack shape and brand icons). Drawing feelings often allows the individual to become aware and then share emotions in a spontaneous, safe and childlike way. Process drawings enable the individual to focus on high and low points in the sequence of events or the history of a relationship and to become aware of the reasons for these.

'The drawings, in terms of quality, accuracy or artistic merit, are irrelevant. What is extremely important is what the task itself brings into awareness.'

Psychodrama (or play-acting) techniques

Psychodrama was developed by J. L. Moreno (1892–1974) and is a technique used with groups to explore interpersonal relationships, feelings and emotional problems through dramatic methods. Moreno is widely believed to have first used the term *group therapy*, which he fused with theatrical processes to explore the way in which human beings play roles. Roles are automatic and observable patterns of social behaviour that occur in particular situations and we are all multi-talented in this respect. We play the roles of mother/father, boss/employee, doctor/patient, priest/congregant, teacher/pupil, leader/follower, victim/aggressor and many others, slipping from one to the other. Sometimes roles are in conflict – a boy may feel compelled to take on the role of high achiever and Wall Street conqueror to compensate for feelings of rejection or the unresolved ambition of his parents.

The conflict of roles is of interest to us in the context of market research. There may be an opposition between the roles of 'business executive' and 'cattle class passenger' imposed by an airline. There are many examples: between 'responsible father and provider' and 'holder of an insignificant bank account', between a 'CEO (who happens to be female)' and a 'dumb woman'. By encouraging members of the group to enact a scenario between 'the protagonist' and the 'other', participants can articulate, through the drama, the intensity and tonality of the conflicting roles.

Play-acting can be constructed in other ways too. One member of the group can volunteer to play a role such as 'a headache' and the others can select to play the part of different remedies. Each volunteer selects a remedy from a list – aromatherapy, acupuncture, aspirin, Panadol Extra and Tyanol (a very strong painkiller) – and spends a few minutes rehearsing the part. The remaining participants are the audience who have to guess which remedy is which from the way in which 'the headache' responds to the different characteristics of each remedy.

Psychodrama is not for the faint-hearted among moderators. It requires experience and a very clear understanding of group dynamics.

'Psychodrama is not for the faint-hearted among moderators. It requires experience and a very clear understanding of group dynamics.'

Choice ordering techniques
These are so commonly used in both qualitative and quantitative research methodologies that most researchers are unaware that, technically, they are projective in nature. Simplicity is their hallmark. Individual interviewees or group members are requested to arrange a number of stimuli in order against a given set of criteria – best to worst quality, most expensive to cheapest, younger to older in appeal and so on.

Timelines
This is a simple and useful way of understanding the image of a brand or company among others in terms of temporality (see Figure 10). The instruction might be as follows.

> *Imagine a time line stretching behind you to the past, through you which is the present, to in front of you which*

is the future. How would you arrange these (brands, services, organisations, ads, pack designs etc.)?

The resulting line-up forms a useful basis for discussion, particularly if the subject of the research has been placed in the past in the sense of 'old-fashioned and out of date' rather than 'nostalgic and/or classic'.

'Timelines are not only useful for ordering competing brands on a continuum but can be used to elicit past, present and projected future brand associations.'

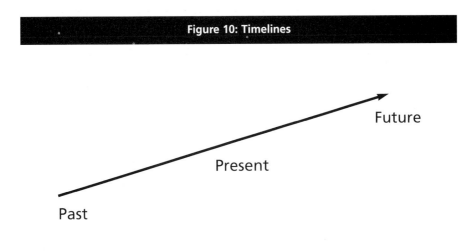

Figure 10: Timelines

Future

Present

Past

Timelines are not only useful for ordering competing brands on a continuum but can be used to elicit past, present and projected future brand associations or worlds. It may be that a brand has changed its image substantially over a period of time because of the change in packaging or advertising communication. This kind of projective technique can help these subtle changes surface more easily.

Choice ordering is useful to introduce as a written exercise within the group. A simple line anchored at both ends can help order responses (in importance, in categories, in ranking) to a range of new product ideas or positionings without treating the results as numerically valid.

The instruction might proceed as follows.

> *We have discussed a number of different new ideas during this session and what I'd like you each to do now is to put them in order by making a cross on the line and writing the number of the idea underneath it.*

No interest--Strong interest

Depending on the number of groups, the results can be used to indicate the broad ranking of stimuli, which helps decision making about the next stages of the brand or product development process.

'There are no hard-and-fast rules as to how to introduce projective and enabling techniques.'

Some practical tips

Here are some practical tips about when to introduce projective techniques and how to design them.

- There are no hard-and-fast rules as to how to introduce projective and enabling techniques other than remembering that the individual or the group must feel relaxed and comfortable in order to 'risk' disclosing heartfelt thoughts and feelings.

- Practise on colleagues if the technique is unfamiliar.

- Use common sense. Keep it simple.

- People generally try to please and to 'do it right' – a legacy from our pasts. A great deal of reassurance is necessary together with light-hearted reminders such as: 'there is no right or wrong'; 'it is not an intelligence test'; 'drawing skills will not get a gold star'; and 'have a go'.

- Be clear about the task, the timing and whether or not you wish the respondents to talk to one another or to do the exercise on their own.

- Be especially aware of body language, particularly signs of anxiety or frustration.

- Watch your own body language. Do not behave like a teacher or the parent of naughty children. Do not peer at the efforts of individuals or walk behind them and look over their shoulders.

- Introduce the projective technique at the right time. There is no point in the group discussing a brand for ten

'Watch your own body language. Do not behave like a teacher or the parent of naughty children.'

minutes and then introducing a projective technique, as the group will be influenced by the previous discussion.

- Be organised yourself – calm, well prepared, with all the necessary utensils to hand.

- Do not 'over-egg the omelette'. Using a huge number of techniques can be inhibiting both for the members of the group and for the nature of the disclosures.

'Do not be disheartened. If there is a poor response the first time ask yourself whether or not you were clear in the task instructions.'

- Do not be disheartened. If there is a poor response the first time ask yourself whether or not you were clear in the task instructions and whether the group dynamics were receptive to the exercise. Then try again a little later using a different technique.

- Give hints that the time is coming to an end ('we only have one minute or so left to do this – don't worry if you haven't quite finished').

- Ask someone in the group to show or read their own projection and explain to the others what it means. Invite the other members of the group to do the same and then ask the group as a whole what conclusions they might draw from their responses.

- Design projective techniques with the research objectives firmly in mind. Care must be taken that the projective techniques – word lists, bubble drawings or guided fantasies – are relevant and germane to a key area of enquiry and that techniques are not selected for their show value (that is, to demonstrate or entertain the observers behind the one-way mirror).

- Try to keep the stimuli 'pure' – that is, free of gender, class or role stereotypes and cues – avoid too much detail and stylisation.

'Care must be taken that the projective techniques are relevant and germane to a key area of enquiry.'

Analysis and interpretation

There is only one way to analyse projective material and that is to encourage the individual who generated it to explain it. In a group structure, it is the projections that the group now 'owns', placed in the metaphorical open space of the group, that form the basis of discussion. This point cannot be made too strongly. It is in the explanations of the output of projectives that we gain the richest insights.

In order to make it clear to people that ownership of the explanation does not lie with the moderator, it is a good idea to encourage the group to make sense of its own output as follows.

> *If you were me what would you conclude about the way this group of people think or feel about (issue/brand/product/problem)?*
>
> *If you were the Managing Director who is looking for a safe solution ...*
>
> *If you had just taken over, and wanted to be different and exciting ...*
>
> *Say you had £1,000 to invest in this idea. Would you do it?*

These 'projections of projections' and the reasoning behind them can produce powerful insights.

At risk of 'over-egging the omelette', it is the descriptions and explanations given by participants themselves in the research process that constitute the 'data bank' which, when integrated with more conventional questioning, informs the interpretation.

The responsibility of the researcher is to be sensitive to patterns and themes of response and in particular to look out for dialogue and language, mood and tone, structure and contexts. Language is the key to understanding and it is often ignored because it is the invisible wall between us all. Yet careful attention and gentle exploration or analysis of the exact words used to describe something can lead to unexpected insights.

'It is the projective mechanism that is powerful rather than the technique per se.'

'The responsibility of the researcher is to be sensitive to patterns and themes of response.'

Conclusions

There are probably many projective techniques that have not been mentioned in this chapter as new ways of eliciting or enabling 'heartfelt' responses in an ongoing act of creativity among research professionals.

The point to bear in mind is that any stimulus can be used to encourage people to project their own values, feelings, thoughts, motivations and behaviours into the context. It is the projective mechanism that is powerful rather than the technique *per se*.

> *The extent to which projective techniques can make a contribution to the market research survey largely depends on the imagination of the practitioner. It is really up to the researcher to see where the opportunities exist and where projection may be a relevant procedure. Once this is recognised, then it is up to the researcher to decide how to tap this potential. Hopefully, something original and appropriate to the situation can be created* (4).

REFERENCES

1. S. Byfield & L. Caller, 'Fitting international brands for consumers: stewarding transnational brands through the consumerisation continuum', *Journal of Brand Management*, Vol. 5 No. 1.
2. B. Avery, *Thorsons Principles of Psychology*, Thorsons, 1996.
3. W. Gordon and R. Langmaid, *Qualitative Market Research: A Practitioner's and Buyer's Guide*, Gower, 1988.
4. W. Schlackman, 'An historical perspective' in S. Robson and A. Foster, *Qualitative Research in Action*, Edward Arnold, 1989.

'The extent to which projective techniques can make a contribution depends on the imagination of the practitioner.'

Models of Thinking

Chapter seven

What are models of thinking?

The word *model* is commonly used in everyday language. Most people define it by thinking of different kinds of model. A model railway or model of a new building is a miniature copy of the real thing – a small-scale representation of the original object. A model of a new mobile telephone or car is a prototype – a pattern or illustration of the intended design. Models like Naomi Campbell or the late Princess Diana are seen to be superior examples of feminine beauty for many women around the world today. A model can also be a map (a simplified representation of something) described verbally or visually.

'Each of us creates a map of reality that allows us to operate automatically and in a particular way.'

Each of us creates a map of reality that allows us to operate automatically and in a particular way. Our unique experiences, culture, language, beliefs, values, interests and assumptions shape our maps. We take this perception of reality for granted and expect others to perceive something in the same way we do, often being surprised that they do not. None of us perceives the 'real' world. We only perceive a representation of it – a model of reality.

There is an expression used by NLP practitioners: 'the map is not the territory'. If one thinks of visiting Africa, one might consult a number of different maps in order to make a decision about where to go. There are physical maps showing the geography of the continent, rainfall and temperature, and political maps, not to mention the number of maps of possible routes that might be in various guidebooks. None of these are the reality of Africa. They are each a valid representation of it. No single map is right and the others wrong – all are useful depending on our purpose and, without the information contained in them, we are truly without guidance.

Because the world around us is so complex, with thousands of stimuli demanding our attention, human beings simplify and select those elements of personal significance or relevance. We notice only a tiny proportion of the world we come into contact with, ignoring much of

'Whatever the role – marketing director, brand manager, advertising planner – we all make assumptions we believe to be correct.'

it. We are often oblivious of the filters or assumptions we impose on the world. This is because they are ingrained in language that represents our thoughts and experiences. Think of the word *British* and what it means to you. You probably have experiences and memories, internal pictures, sounds and feelings that help you to make sense of the word. Someone else will have a completely different set of experiences and sensory images about the word. Neither person is right or wrong.

Our opinions and beliefs also act as filters through which we make assumptions about the world. The trouble is that each of us believes that our own version of reality is right and we will even die for it. History books are full of examples of groups of people or nations who believed their map of the territory was the real one.

Why is all of this relevant to the world of marketing, communications and research? Whatever the role – marketing director, brand manager, advertising planner, creative, qualitative researcher, client researcher – we all make assumptions we believe to be correct. We make assumptions about 'how advertising works', the essence and nature of a brand, consumer and customer motivations and behaviour, managing global brands across borders and so on. We generalise from the particular, we delete those elements that do not fit and thus we create distorted models of reality.

Narrow and limiting models will make the world we are interested in seem predictable, dull and lifeless: the same world can be rich and stimulating. It is not the world that is different but the model.

The answer therefore lies in becoming aware of one's own models of brands, advertising, pack design, below-the-line marketing activity (to mention only a few of the many worlds in which research operates) and then extending one's awareness of possibilities that emerge from the use of other models. As De Bono states in one of his many books on creative and lateral thinking:

You can never prove that your model is the actual one or the only possible one. At best ... the model is comparable with what we know about the subject and the model provides useful results. Another model might do the same. The value arises from the practical use value.

'Narrow and limiting models will make the world we are interested in seem predictable, dull and lifeless.'

Why are models of thinking important?

Why do we need models to help us think in the context of the insights qualitative research is expected to provide? There are four main reasons.

Information overload

There are over two million pieces of information being fed into the human nervous system every second (1) and, unless human beings filter out most of it, we would be swamped by incoming sensory data and unable to function. Giep Franzen in his book *Advertising Effectiveness* (2) describes the extent of information overload. For example, every ten years the quantity of mass-media communication doubles. Since 1960 it has octupled.

'As professionals working in the world of marketing we have to understand how to make our brands and services effective without drowning in the swamp of information.'

It is called 'data smog' by *Inc.* magazine in an article entitled 'Why you feel the way you do' (3). The author, David Shenk, begins by pointing out that one weekday edition of today's *New York Times* contains more information than the average person in 17th-century England was likely to come across in an entire lifetime!

> *Data have become more plentiful, are more speedily processed (computer processing speed has doubled every two years for the last 30 years), and are more dense. (From 1965 to 1995 the average network television advertisement shrank from 53.1 seconds to 25.4 seconds, and the average TV news soundbite shrank from 42.3 seconds to 8.3 seconds; over the same period the number of ads per network TV minute increased from 1.1 to 2.4.)* (3)

And again:

> *In 1971 the average American was targeted by at least 560 daily advertising messages. Twenty years later that number had risen sixfold, to 3,000 messages per day.*

As professionals working in the world of marketing we have to understand how to make our brands and services effective without drowning in the swamp of information.

Complexity of human behaviour

People are not simple to understand. We may wish they were but we know from experience that they do not always say what they mean and they do not always mean what they say. They also behave unpredictably despite our well-thought-out programmes of marketing and advertising through which we hope to influence them. We listen to them in focus groups and they seem unaware of the inconsistencies in their opinions, beliefs or behaviour. We find that quantitative research describes one set of behaviours and yet qualitative research indicates others; we have not yet resolved the debate over whether attitude change precedes behavioural change or whether the act of changed behaviour influences attitudes. We have found difficulty in applying psychological models of the individual to populations surveyed in the aggregate. We pay lip service to the differences in culture of consumers around the world, yet use simplistic measures of commonality such as awareness and response to advertising. We attempt to put bundles of consumers into boxes in order to segment the market and then find that the labels we have given them, and the insights this classification seemed to provide, fail the test of successful marketing.

A common framework

Within a company, and between companies involved on the same project, there is a need for a common framework – a shared model and language of understanding and description. It is in this area that models of thinking can be most valuable. If a team of people drawn from different disciplines and operating within different corporate cultures can agree a common model of investigation or implementation, co-operation increases. Communication and rapport-building result in fewer and fewer opportunities for members of the team to undermine progress through interpreting the information or problem in a different way.

'Within a company, and between companies involved on the same project, there is a need for a common framework – a shared model and language of understanding and description.'

Action standards, timescales and measurement

'We need models of thinking because we are paid to illuminate issues and solve problems.'

The working world of the last decade of this millennium is characterised by the word 'accountability'. What this means in practice is that we have to be effective in what we do in the quickest possible timeframe and at the lowest possible cost. Not only is this essential but we must demonstrate through measurement that our decisions have been 'correct' and have yielded the desired result. We have to implement actions and divide up responsibilities for getting things done.

There are simply too many variables to compute, no matter how powerful the technology has become. Yet as marketers, researchers, brand owners and advertisers we must continue to try to create models of how a particular target market of people behave, think and feel. We constantly need to try different models and select those that provide the most help in dealing with the problem at hand.

Models of thinking are a core component of accountability and it is wise to become aware of the way in which these will influence decision making within the team or company.

As professionals we need models of thinking because we are paid to illuminate issues and solve problems. We are not paid to add clouds of confusion!

Types of models of thinking

There are four types of models of thinking:

- classification

- causative or sequential

- hierarchical or centrifugal

- metaphorical.

Classification models

Classification models are the most commonly used in marketing, research and advertising practice and in other disciplines as well. When there is complexity and chaos, the first step is to simplify, and the way to do that is to divide the observations and information into smaller groupings and sets. This is one of the basic processes of scientific enquiry – observe, classify the observations into similar sets, describe the characteristics and behaviour of each set and then predict behaviour as a result.

Figure 1 shows a classification model that divides brands into sets against two axes.

The authors explain how it works and its value as a simple tool for strategy development as follows.

> *The value consumers place on a brand can be measured in terms of how much it satisfies a functional need (i.e. tangible performance requirement) and a symbolic (representational) need (i.e. the ability to say something about the consumer in a particular situational context).*

'When there is complexity and chaos, the first step is to simplify, and the way to do that is to divide the observations and information into smaller groupings and sets.'

Figure 1: Example – De Chernatony-McDonald Brand Matrix

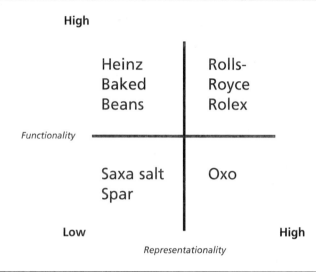

Source: De Chernatony & McDonald (4).

Once the marketer is aware, from consumer interviews, of the extent to which the brand is perceived on these two dimensions, the brand can be plotted on to the matrix (as shown).

If the marketer is satisfied with the quadrant within which the brand is located, (as would be Rolls-Royce in the high representational–high functional quadrant), then the brand strategy needs reinforcement.

If, though, the brand is not perceived by consumers in the quadrant desired by the marketer, a new brand strategy is required. (4)

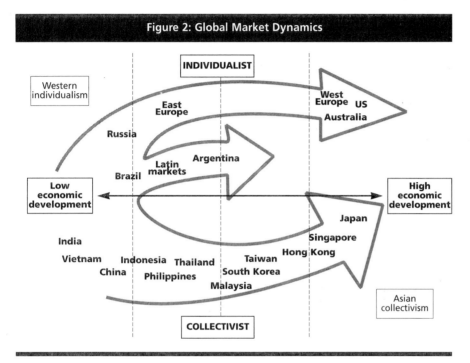

Figure 2: Global Market Dynamics

Source: Peter Cooper, 'Western at the weekends', *Admap*, Oct 1997.

'Segmentation is a contemporary term for a very old concept.'

The classification model lies at the heart of market research. It is a very useful tool for describing complex dynamics. Figure 2, developed by Peter Cooper of CRAM International, is an excellent illustration of how a simple four-quadrant classification model can make immediate sense of the world stage of brand relationships.

Another major use of a classification model of thinking is usually referred to as *segmentation*. Segmentation is a contemporary term for a very old concept. Wendell Smith wrote the first pioneering article on segmentation in 1956 and, since then, it has permeated the thinking of marketing people and researchers alike. It has led to a voluminous body of literature and is loved by journalists who took to sloane rangers, yuppies, dinkies and crusties as proverbial ducks to water.

At the most basic level, we classify human beings by demographic criteria such as age, sex, education, employment and income, in order to determine whether or not behaviour and attitudes differ between groups. But there are many other segmentation models in use today.

There are those borrowed from clinical psychology, which uses the Introversion–Extroversion scale, and others based on Jungian archetypes – these models were popular in the 1960s and are still in currency today in certain countries of the world, notably New Zealand and Australia where the Heylen model is common (5). From the 1970s to the end of the 1980s, lifestyle and value segmentations multiplied. Nowadays these have come under a great deal of criticism primarily because the generalisations and deletions inherent to model making prove ill equipped to explain and predict subtle differences in brand behaviour. More importantly perhaps, attitudes to life (politics, religion, hobbies and the environment) do not necessarily relate to brand choice. Even strong agreement on the importance of environmental conservation does not necessarily correlate with the use of Body Shop products or the purchase of brands that have not been tested on animals.

'Many of the early models of how advertising works were sequential in nature – a model of thinking whereby each event causes the next to happen.'

Nowadays, the emphasis is on tailor-made segmentations for very specific product categories incorporating a range of variables that are strongly linked to brand behaviour. All over the world consumers are becoming increasingly sophisticated as they are exposed to more and more advertising. Many are able to see through transparent marketing ploys and strongly resent being stereotyped. This is particularly so for women who still form the main target market for so many grocery and household brands. In Asia, advertisers are beginning to realise that by addressing women in their external roles as housewives, mothers or wives they are missing the opportunity of touching the hearts of female consumers through acknowledgement of inner values (rebelliousness, female friendships, self-indulgence etc.) which cut across role.

The classification model in Figure 2 not only segments countries in terms of economic development and orientation (collective versus individual), but is dynamic in that it suggests direction of change.

Causative–sequential models

Many of the early models of how advertising works were sequential in nature – a model of thinking whereby each event causes the next to happen. In the late 1950s the SLAB effect was a common way of understanding how people responded to advertising and therefore how it should be designed. First, an audience Sat, then Listened, then Absorbed and then Bought. The most widely known acronym for this model of thinking was AIDA. In order for advertising to work effectively the advertisement had to demand Attention, create Interest, stimulate Desire and lead to Action. In the 1960s the DAGMAR (Defining Advertising Goals for Measured Advertising Results) model of thinking, a similar sequential model, was common. Here the task of advertising was to lead a person from a state of Unawareness through to Awareness then Comprehension then Communication and finally Action.

The point to make about causative–sequential models of thinking is that they still exist today even though the acronyms may no longer be used. In 1991 Hall and Maclay delivered a paper to the Market Research Society Conference in the UK (6) based on a study among marketing directors to find how they believed advertising worked. They found that many subscribed to causative–sequential models of thinking with their in-built assumptions about rational persuasion and conversion. Their belief system was that advertisements must move people along a continuum from awareness to conviction to action and that each step is a 'necessary condition' (7) that must take place before the next can occur. This model of thinking perceives human beings as passive players in their relationship to brands and that also the target consumer is open to persuasion if given a strong and rational reason

'The point to make about causative–sequential models of thinking is that they still exist today even though the acronyms may no longer be used.'

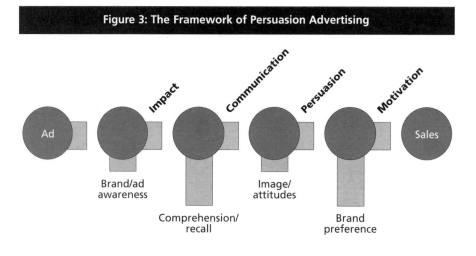

Figure 3: The Framework of Persuasion Advertising

Ad — Impact — Brand/ad awareness — Communication — Comprehension/recall — Persuasion — Image/attitudes — Motivation — Brand preference — Sales

Source: Mike Hall, 'Using advertising frameworks', *Admap*, March 1992.

why. By providing someone with information, this model of thinking creates the expectation that people will convert from their current brand to Brand X.

'Motivation to act is measured by brand preference, brand purchase or purchase predisposition questions.'

Those who assume that advertisements work in this way are responsive to research methods which are congruent. Figure 3 shows the nature of research measures for each stage of the sequence. This research model of measurement can be used qualitatively or quantitatively in advertising development, pre-testing and advertising tracking.

The advertisement is exposed during the process of research, usually embedded in a competitive context, followed by a series of questions on brand and/or advertising awareness. The next series of questions taps recall of the content of the advertisement, main message playback and comprehension. The research then moves into brand image and attitudes designed to measure the degree of shift created by exposure to the advertisement or simply to obtain a profile against key brand differentiating attributes. Finally, motivation to act is measured by brand preference, brand purchase or purchase predisposition questions.

Causative–sequential models are attractive because they seem to explain confusion and complexity. However, they tend to be abandoned as explanations of situations in general because experience proves that many cases do not conform to the logical sequence. This model is used in direct response advertising and also for categories where purchase involves rational, informed decision making.

Hierarchical and centrifugal models

These models of thinking are based on the assumption that some elements of the observed phenomena are more important than others and that, therefore, there is a hierarchy of effects.

Figure 4: Maslow's Hierarchy of Needs

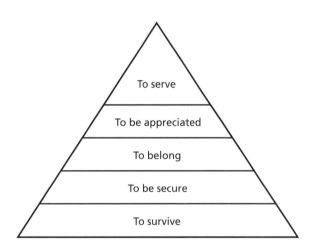

To serve

To be appreciated

To belong

To be secure

To survive

'Causative–sequential models are attractive because they seem to explain confusion and complexity.'

A famous example is Maslow's pyramid of psychological needs (see Figure 4). The underlying assumption is that people progress through basic needs to spiritual ones. Although this did, and does, apply to many societies, it is far too simple for marketers in Western countries of the world.

Another simple model is one developed by Valentine and Gordon (8) to explain that each brand exists in the centre of a number of contexts. Shoppers respond to the covert communication embedded in each context (see Figure 5).

Figure 5: Point of Choice

'Retail outlets have cultural meanings that differ. Supermarkets, corner stores, garage forecourt shops and off-licences are not just different retailing operations.'

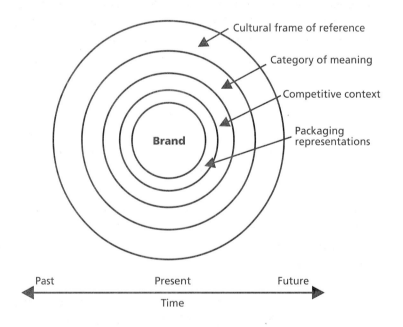

The usefulness of this model is that it reduces brand myopia – the tendency that many of us have to concentrate on the brand in isolation. Instead it enables the brand owner, through the process of research, to understand how to leverage the brand to its full potential. It can do this not only through conventional tools of advertising and below-the-line promotions, merchandising, packaging and pricing, but through understanding more subtle ways in which to influence the consumer–brand relationship at the point of choice. The model works by analysis of the brand from the outer ring to the inner heart.

Retail outlets have cultural meanings that differ. Supermarkets, corner stores, garage forecourt shops and off-licences are not just different retailing operations. They mean different things in the UK and communicate these meanings through their semiotics of design and merchandising. The ordered aisles of the supermarket carry different meanings in the West from the higgledy-piggledy arrangement of goods in corner stores (owner-managed shops, not chains), which have different connotations from petrol-dominated forecourt shops.

'All brands exist also in a competitive context – not simply the brands directly competing for share but in terms of the dynamic or static nature of the category.'

The next concentric circle refers to the cultural meanings of the category – beer for example, with its codes of laddish humour (in many Western advertisements), compared to the codes of feminine beauty in shampoo or cosmetics advertising.

All brands exist also in a competitive context – not simply the brands directly competing for share but in terms of the dynamic or static nature of the category. This in itself frames the way in which a particular brand is perceived.

Then there are the codes of packaging that are sometimes rule-bound within a category. The extent to which a brand conforms to the rules or breaks the mould says something to shoppers about its positioning and proposition.

Finally, at the heart of the concentric circles lives the brand – its purpose, essence, fundamental nature, heritage and values as understood by all those involved with it.

Centrifugal and hierarchical models are useful for explaining complicated dynamics. By virtue of the fact that the model orders the elements into levels of increasing importance (or complexity or essence), the model helps guide analysis and thinking towards a direction.

Metaphorical models

A metaphor is a figure of speech that describes the application of a name or phrase to an object or action when it is not literally applicable, e.g. 'he made a glaring error' or 'she is a tower of strength'. Metaphors bring descriptions to life and thus have more impact.

A metaphorical model of thinking can be a powerful tool in communication. Many advertising agencies have such models about the relationship between brands, consumers and creativity. For example, brand architecture, brand DNA, brand stewardship.

'Smirnoff is a badge brand that reflects certain characteristics of the individual such as confidence, adulthood and self-expression.'

Kapferer (9) uses the metaphor of a prism to describe the identity of a brand (see Chapter 8). It is easier to work with the model by using an example. Smirnoff in the UK is clearly identified by the shape of its bottle, its logo and colours. This forms its *physique*. Its *brand personality* is 'edgy', modern, assertive and surprising – the result of long-term communication, particularly via cinema and, more recently, TV advertising. The brand reflects the *culture* of streetwise, 'cool', younger drinkers who are highly literate in terms of marketing communications. Smirnoff is a badge brand that reflects certain characteristics of the individual such as confidence, adulthood and self-expression (*self-image*).

Figure 6: The Prism Model

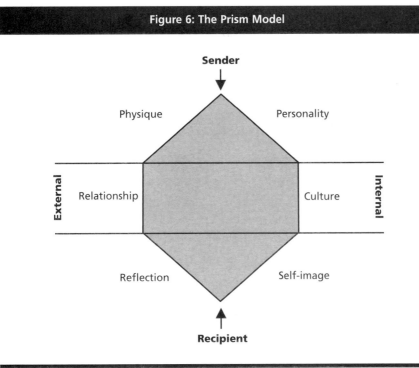

Source: J. N. Kapferer, *Strategic Brand Management.*

There is also a *reflected image* (often termed 'user image') that can be understood through qualitative research. The question 'what kind of person would drink Smirnoff vodka?' would generate the characteristics Kapferer refers to as reflected image. Finally, there is the identity facet of *relationship*. People have connections with brands just as they do with human beings. Some relationships are equal while others, such as parent-child or teacher-student, imply authority differences. In the case of Smirnoff, the relationship is like two friends – one brave and extrovert (Smirnoff) and the other in need of some encouragement (the drinker).

Figure 7: The Iceberg Model

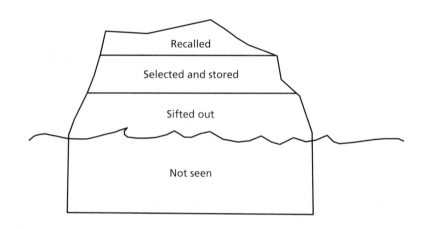

Recalled

Selected and stored

Sifted out

Not seen

Source: The Research Business *International*

'Someone who has recently bought a car tends to notice car advertisements in order to reinforce their choice of marque.'

Using this model, the brand team is able to design a research project to explore each facet of the prism and then draw conclusions as to which of the facets are flawed or perfect.

Another metaphorical model is the iceberg model of print advertising. The assumption here, based on studies designed to understand and measure the effectiveness of a print campaign, is that, like an iceberg, the majority of people do not get the opportunity to see the advertisement when it appears. Either that copy of the magazine or newspaper is not read or, through poor coverage and frequency of exposure, the chances of seeing the advertisement are minimal. Alternatively, the advertisement can be overshadowed by the activity of a competitor.

Above the water line, a large number of advertisements are seen (in the sense of being recognised if shown again) but are filtered out of

consciousness for many different reasons: aesthetic; low impact; rejection of the product category, brand or message; offensiveness or
simply lack of relevance. Many financial advertisements suffer from
this problem.

A smaller number of advertisements is noticed, selected and stored for
future reference. Again there are many reasons: rewarding creativity;
familiarity; impact; relevant to the past or future behaviour. Someone
who has recently bought a car tends to notice car advertisements in
order to reinforce their choice of marque; someone buying a house
will notice advertisements to do with furnishing, house removals,
loans and so on.

At the tip of the iceberg is the tiny minority able to recall the advertisement spontaneously. Relevance is the usual reason for recall, but
advertisements are also remembered because they have adopted a
consistent theme, are topical or have a high media spend.

As with other models of thinking discussed in this chapter, this one
enables the brand team to design research to understand and *measure*
in which cross-section of the iceberg the advertisement is likely to
be embedded.

'Relevance is the usual reason for recall.'

Some useful examples of models of thinking

This section offers a few examples of models of thinking that have stood the test of time or have proved useful across many different brands and problems. Three were developed by myself and have been tried and tested by many researchers and clients over the years. The models are the brand fingerprint, brand diamond and brand communication hierarchy. Another model called brand essence is in circulation but its originator is unknown.

This section describes the assumptions underlying each model, indicates the problems for which each is most suited and the nature of the research input required in order to use the model effectively.

Brand fingerprint

'Brands exist as a jumble of images in people's heads.'

Brands exist as a jumble of images in people's heads and one of the most useful roles of qualitative research is to describe this unique fingerprint – this swirl of lines and patterns – to those responsible for the welfare of the brand. Only when the pattern is understood can decisions be made about what to do.

There is a theoretical foundation to the brand fingerprint that derives from neuro-linguistic programming (as discussed in Chapter 2). All human beings experience the world through the five senses – visual (sight), auditory (sound), olfactory (smell), gustatory (taste) and kinaesthetic (touch and feelings) – which code, sort and file the information in the mind. This information can be obtained externally from the world outside, or internally through emotional feelings.

Each person tends to give greater weight to one or two of the senses. In response to an invitation to go out and have a tandoori, I may see the deep-red colour of the wallpaper in my favourite Indian restaurant, followed by seeing in my mind's eye the red-yellow colour of the tandoori mixed grill on a black steaming grill plate. I can also hear the sound of sizzling. My partner, however, begins to salivate and can taste in his mind's eye the dish of tandoori prawns and feels at ease and relaxed. In NLP terms, my dominant representational system is visual and his is gustatory–kinaesthetic.

When this is applied to brands, there are some interesting findings. All established brands, particularly those that have been advertised for a number of years, are absorbed, stored and coded in the mind in terms of the five senses. This pattern of impressions is the brand fingerprint and it can be revealed through a particular form of qualitative questioning (see Chapter 6 – projective techniques). Competitive brands have quite clear brand fingerprints: British Airways is distinctly different from American Airlines; Smirnoff Vodka from Absolut; The Famous Grouse from Bell's and Teacher's whisky.

'All established brands, particularly those that have been advertised for a number of years, are absorbed, stored and coded in the mind in terms of the five senses.'

The power of this model in brand investigation studies is that it makes explicit those aspects of the brand that explain the relationship consumers have with it. A brand fingerprint also demonstrates the influence of previous advertising, packaging icons, dominant colours or patterns core to the brand identity.

Elicitation of brand fingerprints has to be learned. It requires skill as a qualitative moderator (for it is best elicited in group discussions) and it also needs experience in the interpretation of the impressions generated by different members of the group. The brand fingerprint forms part of a toolkit of models that help to understand brands.

The brand diamond
Like the brand fingerprint this is a metaphorical model that is used to explore the fundamental nature of the brand–consumer relationship in a competitive context. While the brand fingerprint is like looking at a photograph, the brand diamond model allows the viewer to concentrate on details of different parts of the photograph using a magnifying glass.

Figure 8: Brand FIngerprint – Private Health Insurance Brand

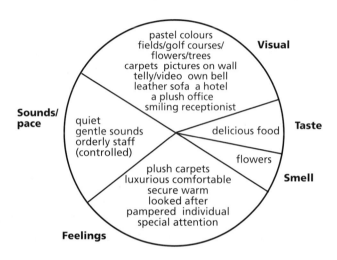

pastel colours
fields/golf courses/
flowers/trees
carpets pictures on wall
telly/video own bell
leather sofa a hotel
a plush office
smiling receptionist

Visual

Sounds/pace

quiet
gentle sounds
orderly staff
(controlled)

delicious food

Taste

flowers

Smell

plush carpets
luxurious comfortable
secure warm
looked after
pampered individual
special attention

Feelings

Source: The Research Business *International*

Figure 9: Example – BrandWorks™

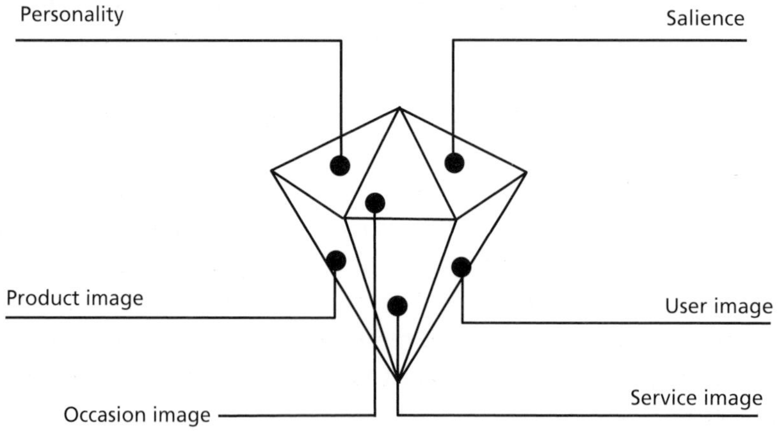

Personality

Salience

Product image

User image

Occasion image

Service image

Source: The Research Business *International*

The underlying assumption is that a brand is like a diamond that has many different facets. As flaws are not visible to the naked eye, the diamond can only be valued by looking through a number of facets in turn. There are five or six facets depending on the brand category: user image; occasion image; service image; product image; brand personality; closeness or distance of the relationship. Each facet is defined as follows.

User image – the kinds of people believed to be the most likely buyers (eaters, drinkers, users, consumers) of the brand. This facet explains the marketing relationship between a brand and its consumers. The brand owner has defined the target market and a member of this target market recognises that he is or is not the addressee of the brand communication. His beliefs about who is the likely consumer of the brand may or may not mirror the intention of the brand owner.

If there is congruity then consumers tend to respond to the user image in terms such as 'people like me' (use, buy the brand), but if there is dissonance then the user image offers no point of identification. Sometimes the user image can be aspirational, i.e. a businessperson, a mother who has broader interests than the children and her husband. Here again the interpretative skills and experience of a qualitative researcher in understanding aspirational responses is essential.

Occasion image – the belief consumers hold about the times, occasions or moods when the brand is most appropriate. Brandy is believed by many to be an after-dinner drink when relaxing or unwinding whereas vodka is an upbeat party or pub drink in the UK. Direct questions designed to understand the occasion image could produce very literal and rational responses (in the evening, in a restaurant, on a picnic) that do not differentiate between brands within a category. It is therefore important that indirect methods of exploring this facet are used.

'As flaws are not visible to the naked eye, the diamond can only be valued by looking through a number of facets in turn.'

Service image – this is a crucial facet for service brands such as banks, insurance companies, airlines, utility companies and so on. It encompasses the beliefs customers hold about the way in which the brand (company) delivers service. For example, a direct insurance company is imagined to have a building full of telephone operators frenetically answering telephones and responding to enquiries by asking questions that come up on their computers. The staff are imagined to be young and inexperienced although well trained in telephone skills. A problem is thought likely to be too difficult for them to handle with the result that the caller will be shunted on to a supervisor to explain the problem all over again!

Care needs to be taken in eliciting service image traits. For example, if the service is described as 'friendly' it is important to understand how friendliness manifests itself in the course of the customer dealing with the company. Specific examples are needed.

Product image – this is the most frequently used image facet and is often equated with brand image, to the detriment of understanding the emotional richness of the brand–consumer relationship. People have beliefs about the physical or functional characteristics of a product or service that may or may not reflect its true performance. In a blind product test, Brand A performs as well as Brand B in terms of authenticity of flavour, richness of taste, quality and colour but, in a branded preference test, Brand A outperforms Brand B on taste, colour appeal and quality attributes.

Typical product image attributes include good quality, good value for money, cheap and expensive as well as specific characteristics of the category such as crunchy, sweet, cloying, dark, bitter and so on.

Brand owners respond well to product image feedback because it seems to offer the opportunity for remedial action. If the brand is

'People have beliefs about the physical or functional characteristics of a product or service that may or may not reflect its true performance.'

perceived to be poor value for money, then the packaging design, size and price relationship can be restructured; if the product is perceived to be too dark then it can be lightened. The problem is that product image is only one facet and it relates to all the others. Years ago British Rail ran advertisements in the press showing that 99% of trains on a certain day left and arrived on time. This rational information did not change the attitudes and beliefs of the target market, that persisted in the view that British Rail was inefficient, based on years of poor service.

Brand personality – this is a metaphor for the emotional relationship that exists between a consumer and a brand. It is a shorthand way of describing the nature and quality of the relationship. Understanding that Domestos is like 'a knight on a white horse coming to save me from evil' (or 'a good policeman chasing the baddies from the world', 'a nurse in a starched white uniform who does not stand any nonsense at all') clearly explains the relationship. The brand is a supremely effective saviour. This information alone is insufficient since different users of household cleaning brands respond to the character of a saviour in various ways. Domestos users respond with affection, gratitude and relief while those using a competitive brand respond with hostility to the paternalistic and old-fashioned authoritarianism of the brand.

'The most common pitfall for qualitative researchers is to elicit superficial descriptions of the brand personality that are confused with user image.'

The most common pitfall for qualitative researchers is to elicit superficial descriptions of the brand personality that are confused with user image. Thus describing The Famous Grouse as a Scottish laird striding through the heather with a dog bounding next to him does not tell us much about the brand relationship. It is only when consumers describe the character of the laird – 'reserved, quiet, polite, gentle, showing respect to those he meets no matter what their background' – does the researcher begin to understand the nature and quality of the brand relationship.

Emotional closeness or distance – this is the linchpin that holds the other components of the total brand image in place. It refers to the importance of the brand for different groups of consumers. You either feel distant to or close to a brand and your feelings are a complex mix of past, present and future (anticipated) experiences of the brand, which are felt with different levels of intensity. Some brands are stored in our minds in the past but evoke strong feelings of closeness; others can be stored in the past and almost forgotten. Some brands are positioned on a time line in the here and now and yet are experienced as distant (perhaps because of the user image or a perceived faddishness). Other brands are positioned in the future, sometimes drawing consumers towards them and sometimes being perceived to be out of reach.

'Some brands are stored in our minds in the past but evoke strong feelings of closeness; others can be stored in the past and almost forgotten.'

Temporal information of this kind requires the use of sensitive projective techniques such as the brand fingerprint and the time line, both of which are models of thinking as well as techniques, to reveal greater insight.

The brand diamond has intrinsic flexibility and can include even more facets depending on the research objectives. The retail environment image is one such facet. A particular brand may bring to mind an aspirational delicatessen or authentic chef even though it is available in every supermarket. Conversely, another brand may be associated with the retail environment of a small, overpriced 'late-night' store, even though it is a mainstream supermarket brand.

Another facet is the packaging image. This is useful when conducting packaging research, especially when it is elicited early in the interview along with the other brand facets. It generates the main parameters before exploring the pack in detail, often a highly contrived exercise in group discussions or depth interviews.

The brand diamond model demonstrates to the research buyer and
end user of the study how the brand image is constructed and how
the different facets interrelate, thus indicating which aspects of
the brand offer the most competitive edge and which require
re-engineering.

Use of this model involves highly developed qualitative research skills,
both to elicit the detail and emotional nature of the information, but
also to make relevant interpretation and actionable recommendations.
(Some of the techniques for eliciting brand image information are
described more fully in Chapter 6.)

Hierarchy of communication model

This is a difficult model to work with but one that can bring
rewarding insights to a problem of communication. Mass communication, particularly television advertising, can be understood in the same
way as individual communication – the levels are similar.

*'Mass communica-
tion, particularly
television adver-
tising, can be
understood in
the same way
as individual
communication.'*

I can communicate about myself in a number of different ways:

Vision (I promise ...)	e.g. creative problem solving and breaking the mould suggestions
Identity (I am ...)	e.g. innovative, intelligent, responsible
Belief (I believe in ...)	e.g. the power of ordinary people
Capability (I can)	e.g. qualitative expertise and craft skills
Behaviour (I do ...)	e.g. consultancy and training
Environment (where)	e.g. London

The higher up the scale (top three), the more intimate, the more
revealing and the more emotionally loaded the communication.
Cocktail party or conference tea break conversations usually take
place at the bottom two or three levels. All of the levels operate
consistently rather like a nest of tables or a Russian doll – one fitting
neatly within the bigger one above it.

Figure 10: Communication Hierarchy

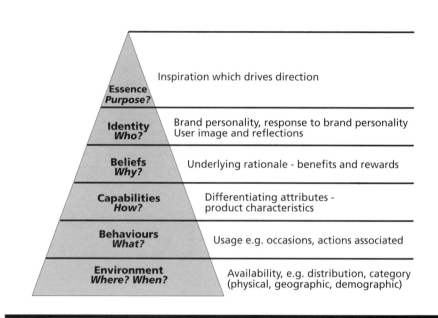

Source: The Research Business *International*

'The brand essence model is hierarchical in that it assumes that the most important brand values lie in the centre and the least important on the outside.'

This model can be used to analyse the different ways in which advertising for brands within a sector are communicating. The model is most useful as an interpretative framework or stimulus for team brainstorming.

Brand essence

The brand essence model is hierarchical in that it assumes that the most important brand values lie in the centre and the least important on the outside. Importance, in this case, refers to the power to differentiate from competitors.

Figure 11: Brand Essence Model

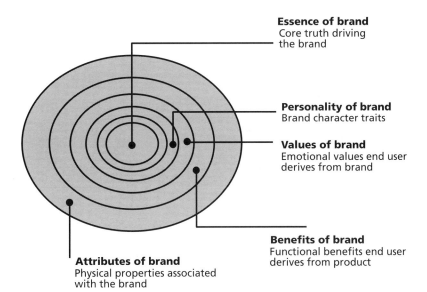

Essence of brand
Core truth driving
the brand

Personality of brand
Brand character traits

Values of brand
Emotional values end user
derives from brand

Benefits of brand
Functional benefits end user
derives from product

Attributes of brand
Physical properties associated
with the brand

*'The team begins
by individually
completing each
ring of the model
based on their
understanding of
consumer response
to the brand.'*

The model is valuable when it comes to instilling intellectual rigour at the end of a qualitative brand study. The findings of the study must be debriefed and the brand team given time to digest them and challenge any inconsistencies. Then the brand essence model can be used to create a brand template against which all future NPD, communications and below-the-line activity can be checked.

The team members begin by individually completing each ring of the model based on their understanding of consumer response to the brand. The facilitator then encourages people to share their perceptions of the attributes, which can be positioned at the outermost level. Usually many different physical properties of the brand find their way into the discussion. The challenge is to agree which are critical in differentiating the brand. Often these are to do with the product and brand 'idents' – colour, symbols, graphic style, product appearance and so on.

The group then works through each level in turn, debating the team contributions and agreeing a smaller set of descriptors at each level. Finding a way to encapsulate the essence of the brand is the hardest part: an exciting phrase is the goal rather than a set of adjectives which run the risk of meaning different things to different people.

The brand essence model can be one of the most dangerous to use without a deep understanding of its strengths and weaknesses. Because it reduces a brand to a series of words, even though these are organised into concentric circles, they will mean different things to different people. There are enormous problems in using brand essence diagrams such as this to brief those who will implement the brand communications through different channels. It is like the game of Chinese whispers where each person along the chain slightly mishears the intended communication. In connection with this, the problem of 'fat words' is discussed in Chapter 5.

___

'The brand essence model can be one of the most dangerous to use.'

What are the dangers?

The models explained here are only the tiniest sample of those that exist 'out there'. One can find many more by reading other books and articles. They are fun to collect and fun to experiment with since this process itself expands thinking and creates new opportunities for insight. The point to remember is that they are only as useful as the user finds them to be! It also takes practice. Some of the models require effort and time, and need to be applied across a number of different brands and categories in order to determine their usefulness.

Try them out, but remember that models can also interfere with thinking. They can be 'models of not thinking'.

This is because inexperienced or overly enthusiastic researchers or buyers can be tempted into using a series of models for no particular purpose other than that they appear to make sense and look good as presentation charts. The research findings are shoehorned into the model whether or not they fit. This means that a great deal of information is ignored (consciously or subconsciously) in order to make the model work.

'Some of the models require effort and time, and need to be applied across a number of different brands and categories.'

Models of thinking are presented in research proposals in two ways. First, some researchers or research companies develop branded models to differentiate their approach from that of competitors. There are many of these, which are given brand names and advertised frequently in the research trade press. A few examples are given below.

Millward Brown International has two well-known worldwide models – LINK (a qualitative pre-testing model) and ATP (Advanced Tracking Programmes). Research International advertises MicroTest (product development and sales forecasting), Locator (brand image modelling), SMART (customer satisfaction) and many others. Each of the major research companies and many of the medium-sized and smaller ones have developed acronyms that describe a research service. These

'Use of another
model could create
a completely
different perspective
and hence lead to
radically different
decisions.'

services are nothing more than models of thinking and are therefore only as valuable or 'right' as their users find them to be.

The danger of these models, and others like them, is that they can be simplistic. While they do describe human behaviour to some extent, *use of another model could create a completely different perspective and hence lead to radically different decisions.*

There is no certainty of cause and effect. There are patterns, possibilities and relationships. In order to understand this as best we can, we need to draw on a wide repertoire of models in a creative and flexible way to challenge our thinking, to reveal other solutions and to avoid the concrete mind-set of those who believe the world is flat.

REFERENCES

1. J. Sinclair, *An ABC of NLP*, Container Marketing Limited, 1992.
2. G. Franzen, *Advertising Effectiveness*, NTC Publications Ltd, 1994.
3. D. Shenk, 'Why You Feel the Way You Do', *Inc.*, January 1999.
4. L. De Chernatony and M. H. B. McDonald, *Creating Powerful Brands*, Butterworth Heinemann, 1992.
5. J. P. Heylen, 'Towards an Implicit Psychoanalytic Model ("Libido Model") of Consumer Behaviour', Copenhagen EMAC/ESOMAR Symposium on Methodological Advance in Marketing Research in Theory and Practice, October 1984.
6. M. Hall and D. Maclay, 'Science and Art. How Does Research Practice Match Advertising Theory?', The Market Research Society Conference, 1991.
7. C. McDonald, *How Advertising Works: A Review of Current Thinking*, the Advertising Association in association with NTC Publications Ltd, 1992.
8. W. Gordon, and V. Valentine, 'Buying the Brand at Point of Choice', MRS Conference, 1996.
9. J. N. Kapferer, *Strategic Brand Management*, Kogan Page, 1997.

'The danger of these models is that they can be simplistic … use of another model could create a completely different perspective.'

Fuzzy
Thinking

Chapter eight

Introduction

Useful guidebooks point out areas in a city or country where it is prudent to be aware and to take care. This chapter attempts to do the same thing. The areas that deserve special attention are:

- researching positioning and propositions

- designing stimulus material.

This chapter highlights the key issues that can change fuzzy thinking into clear thinking.

Positioning and propositions

When developing a strategy for a company, brand, product, service, team of people or an individual, we attempt to 'nail it down' by using either a positioning or a proposition or both. Definitions may be helpful here.

A *positioning* can be equated with the compass points or parameters by which a territory is defined compared with competitors. These compass points can be delineated in down-to-earth terms such as the target market or audience (for whom?), the key competitor(s) (against whom?), the specific differentiating benefit (why? when? for what?), or it can be described in terms of an emotional arena, e.g. caring, leadership, inspiration.

A positioning can be used for countries, states, companies, brands, products, services or individuals. For example, individual states in America position themselves in different ways – the Sunshine State (Florida), the Golden State (California) – and today countries are beginning to think the same way too. The Blair government has begun to think about 'Britain Inc.' as a brand (often referred to as Cool Britannia), in order to increase its stature and appeal to a wide range of parties – internal and external investors, manufacturers, importers/exporters, tourists, the British people and so on.

'When developing a strategy for a company, brand or an individual, we attempt to "nail it down" by using either a positioning or a proposition.'

In a brand context, companies expend an enormous amount of effort in clarifying the positioning of their brands, not only against competitors but also within their own portfolios. This facilitates the management of the brands and reduces the chances of cannibalisation (in the case of a company that has a number of different brands within its portfolio). Allied Domecq has two major brands of whisky – Ballantines and Teacher's – clearly differentiated so as to appeal to different whisky drinkers, with different emotional benefits. Mars takes great care to position its brands of chocolate differently, not only against competitors but also against each other. A Mars Bar has come to mean something different from a Bounty or Snickers.

'Companies expend an enormous amount of effort in clarifying the positioning of their brands, not only against competitors but also within their own portfolios.'

Jean-Noel Kapferer in his book *Strategic Brand Management* considers positioning a crucial concept (1):

> *It reminds us that all consumer choices are made on the basis of comparison. Thus, a product will only be considered if it is clearly part of a selection process ... Positioning is a two-stage process:*
>
> *First, indicate to what category the brand should be associated and compared.*
>
> *Second, indicate what the brand's essential difference and raison d'être is in comparison to the other products and brands of that category* (p. 96).

This second element of the positioning – the *raison d'être* – is often referred to as the *proposition*. It is the brand benefit, the USP (unique selling proposition), or the ESP (emotional selling proposition), whichever is the terminology preferred by the brand or service owner. These are all different semantic expressions of the unique advantage of the brand – its value over its competitors. Sometimes this is encapsulated into a single sentence or phrase which serves to focus attention on the key differentiator, e.g. a brand with technical superiority, a service which guarantees next-day delivery, a product that deodorises as well as cleans. Sometimes it is incorporated into an endline that becomes part of the communication and indeed may become the 'brand mantra', e.g. 'The world's favourite airline' (British Airways) or 'Just do it' (Nike). Sometimes it is defined as a set of emotions – caring (Persil) or rebellious (Virgin).

Both terms – positioning and proposition – have limitations, particularly in sophisticated markets.

Choosing the category to which a brand (service, product, company etc.) belongs is not always simple. Disneyland, as a holiday destination, belongs in many overlapping categories: fun for children, educational, sun and sports, sophisticated entertainment etc. As such it competes in many categories, each of which has many competitors. The same is true of a new snackfood product or brand – it may compete with potato crisps, nuts, chocolate bars and healthy snacks. Each of these categories is full of competitors offering a similar repertoire of added-value brand benefits (hunger busters, healthy lightness, vitamins and goodness, quality, taste and so on).

How can the questions 'against whom?', 'for whom?', 'why?', 'when?', 'what?' easily be answered when so many brands and products are essentially competing in the same arena? It is hard to define the competitive positioning when the answers are 'everybody' or 'all people who buy and eat snacks'.

Defining the proposition is one of the most difficult tasks for managers of brands. This is due to a number of factors, none of which may be obvious at the time.

'Choosing the category to which a brand belongs is not always simple. Disneyland, as a holiday destination, belongs in many overlapping categories.'

The team responsible for defining the proposition may be using different definitions of the term. One might be thinking that the proposition has to be rationally supportable and unique and another that it is has to have the power to differentiate the brand in terms of emotional values. Another member of the team may believe that the term is synonymous with 'positioning'. This nightmare scenario of miscommunication is very common and leads to frustration, misunderstandings and wasted research.

An established brand in a well-developed market has a complex 'inner substance' (1) that cannot easily be summed up by a single sentence or territory. Kapferer uses the concept of brand identity, which he

'An established brand in a well-developed market has a complex "inner substance" that cannot easily be summed up by a single sentence.'

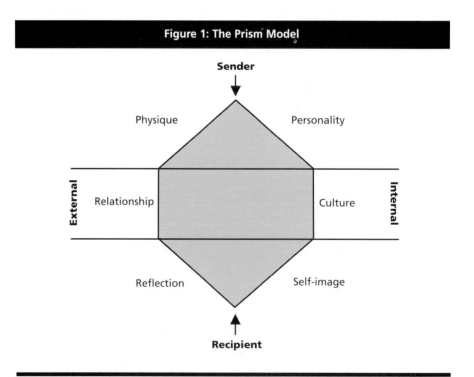

Figure 1: The Prism Model

Source: J. N. Kapferer, *Strategic Brand Management.*

represents as a hexagonal prism, each facet of which is unique and which relates to the others.

Briefly, a strong brand has a unique physical attribute (Orangina's bottle shape, Apple's apple logo) and a set of character or personality traits that describe its style of communication. It also has a distinctive culture that stems from its heritage and that of the company to which it belongs, as well as a relationship with its customers (a love affair, parent–child, best friends). Finally, it has a symbolic meaning for the individual (self-image e.g. Porsche = 'I've made it') and offers a reflected image of whom the buyer wishes to be (e.g. Coca-Cola reflects youth and yet is bought by people of all ages).

This model is one of many that are in use today. There are others that are equally useful such as the core essence model or the brand diamond (see Chapter 6). All have come into existence in order to help the process of defining a strong proposition that differentiates from other brands in the minds of the consumer and that helps to drive a coherent strategy of brand development and brand management for the long term.

'The determination of positioning and proposition as possibilities presents a huge challenge for the discipline of qualitative research and its practitioners.'

The determination of positioning and proposition as possibilities presents a huge challenge for the discipline of qualitative research and its practitioners. It can either be a potential minefield for the unwary and inexperienced or it can be the route to creating today, the competitive high ground for tomorrow. Some of the problems that are frequently experienced are as follows.

- Qualitative muddle and overload – the researcher fails to present the findings of the research with rigour. It is then difficult to prioritise which elements of the current brand perceptions are most significant, which are merely interesting and which are irrelevant to the future development of the brand.

- Cynicism and rejection by research participants of the proposition statements (especially when a verbal expression of the added value or advantage is written). This is because these fail to recognise that, for many brands in many markets, the propositions that are differentiating are emotional – felt and experienced by the consumers through every possible communication avenue – rather than understood and believed rationally.

- The belief by both researchers and brand management that there is one right positioning and proposition and that ordinary people who constitute the potential market or audience will be able to tell us what it is.

'The propositions that are differentiating are emotional – felt and experienced by the consumers through every possible communication avenue – rather than understood and believed rationally.'

Positioning and proposition development require research flying time with consumers in the form of extended group discussions, interactive workshops or mixed methodologies. People need time to engage with the problem so that they can be catapulted into an unfamiliar future scenario. This requires the skilled facilitation of group dynamics and the confident use of projective techniques and stimulus material.

Successful proposition development requires openness on the part of the research buyer. There must be a willingness to share the brand problem with a wide range of stakeholders, including consumers, so that the best possible brand landscapes for the future can be generated and expressed. This leads to the important issue of stimulus material.

Stimulus material that is clearly thought out in terms of both content and form is essential. A brand or corporate positioning comes alive through its people, its products and services, its environment and its communications (see Figure 2). A toolkit of stimulus material needs to be designed to reflect all four of these areas. This can be a mixed-media presentation – words, pictures and moving images.

Figure 2: A Living Brand

Source: The Fourth Room.

'The role of stimulus material is to enable people to indicate how they might respond to the idea when it becomes a reality in the future.'

Stimulus material

Stimulus material can be defined as:

> *Anything used (a) to communicate an idea to consumers or (b) to trigger responses to a particular area of enquiry.*

New product concepts, prototype commercials for TV, 'rough' (as opposed to 'finished') press advertisements, proposition statements and pack visualisations are all examples of stimulus material. The role of this material is to enable people to indicate how they might respond to the idea when it becomes a reality in the future. In other words, today's responses of today's consumers or potential consumers are used to predict how tomorrow's consumers or potential consumers might react to the new product, ad, pack, proposition or corporate identity. Stimulus material is firmly centred in the realm of possibility rather than reality.

Since the late-1970s the range of different types of stimulus material for different purposes has broadened. We now have so much choice that it is very confusing. For advertising strategy development, we can choose between concepts, adcepts, collage boards, stealomatics and video-collages. For advertising development we can use narrative tapes, key frames, scripts read by actors, animatics, admatics (computer-generated images) and so on. All of this can be supplemented by material to help convey style, tone and mood. For new product development, brand repositioning or proposition development, there is a repertoire of different types of material, the final choice depending on client culture and the personal preferences and theories of the researcher. (See the reference section for definitions of these different kinds of stimulus material.)

'It is common nowadays to use a number of different stimuli to convey the complexity of an idea.'

It is common nowadays to use a number of different stimuli to convey the complexity of an idea – one element to communicate the core idea, another for the executional style and another for mood or brand personality. In a new product context, the elements might be the consumer benefit, different pack formats, ingredient variations, brand name options and pack designs.

No matter how much careful thought is given to the design and production of the stimulus materials, the following responses frequently occur:

- people respond to the executional details of the stimulus rather than the core idea, no matter how clear the interviewer appears to be in how it is introduced

- there is a misunderstanding of the role of the stimulus material and therefore a tendency to treat it as an advertisement (final pack design, new corporate logo, detailed service concept), when it has been clearly explained that it is not

- people are confused – jokey responses, repetitive questions to the moderator, silence and defensive body language are the results

- comparisons are made with the existing competitors, anchoring the discussion firmly in the present rather than the future

- boredom frequently occurs

- there are problems when the stimulus material crosses borders or continents – the same stimulus means something different when presented in a different cultural context

- the stimulus elicits irrelevant responses because it is abstracted from an appropriate context (e.g. a magazine ad is displayed on a board eight times the size of the real advertisement and without any editorial or advertising to create a context)

- the 'receivers' of the stimulus material do not receive the same message as was intended by those who designed it! There is often a large gap between stimulus intention and stimulus reality.

'The "receivers" of the stimulus material do not receive the same message as was intended by those who designed it! There is often a large gap between stimulus intention and stimulus reality.'

We need to think afresh about stimulus material and this begins with a new definition.

Roget's Thesaurus uses synonyms for stimulus such as 'energiser', 'activator', 'booster', 'fillip', 'shot in the arm', while material is explained in words such as 'real', 'substantial', 'commodity', 'thing', 'item'. Stimulus material is therefore a thing, or set of items, that energises or activates. Its role is to elicit an active and constructive response which helps us to understand whether or not we have succeeded in stimulating a relevant chord with the consumer. All too often the item(s) we show elicit no response at all or a completely different one from that intended.

The reasons for this are that we fall into the trap of paying far too much attention to the execution and production of the materials and far too little to assessing the effectiveness of the material in creating the desired response. We believe erroneously that if we can only 'get the stimulus material right' we will be well on the way to producing a successful advertising campaign, new brand or repositioned old brand. This is simply not true. Stimulus material is not the same as the real thing, hence the surprise when a finished ad fails to live up to the enthusiasm generated by the narrative tape, or when a repositioning fails to cause consumers to re-evaluate a brand.

The answer is to change our approach to stimulus material by thinking about it in a different way.

Say, for example, you wanted to check out the response of your colleagues to an important new idea you have in mind. What would you do? You might adopt any of the following strategies.

Defining the desired outcome – what do you want your colleagues to say or do? Is there a decision you require (encouragement to continue? Money? Increased stature?)

Be provocative – unless you are brave, challenging and provocative (stimulating), you may not command attention or involvement.

'Stimulus material is not the same as the real thing, hence the surprise when a finished ad fails to live up to the enthusiasm generated by the narrative tape.'

Understand your audience – who are they? What beliefs do they hold? How prejudiced are they or how open-minded? How should you present your case – cool and logical? Stylish? Hot-blooded passion? Flirty?

Practise on a few friends beforehand – how do they respond? Confused? Clear? Excited? Bored?

Use metaphors – explain your idea vividly through analogies and metaphors to help your colleagues lift themselves out of their predictable response pattern.

Stimulus material is no different – although the final material will depend on the brand in question and the stage of development in the process, in terms of both content and format, the same rules apply.

Interrogate yourself and the team about the desired outcome – what specific response do you want from the audience? Who is the audience?

Be different – bland stimulus material, which communicates in stereotypes, is a waste of time and money.

Understand your target consumer's relationship with the brand – are they closed or open-minded? Is the brand in need of light-heartedness or authority? Execute the material in the right way.

Pilot the material first – do this among appropriate people (not professionals in advertising, marketing or research). Allow time to modify or completely rethink.

'Be different – bland stimulus material, which communicates in stereotypes, is a waste of time and money.'

Use analogies and metaphors so that the positioning (repositioning) or benefits can be lifted above the mundane to the arena of emotional rewards.

Unfortunately there is no easy answer. Stimulus material is an attitude of mind not a full wheelbarrow of boards, collages, scripts and videos.

Here are some practical suggestions.

1. Begin by thinking about the objectives of the study in terms of the planning cycle (see Chapter 9). Are the objectives exploratory or concerned with testing two alternatives? The role and execution of the stimulus material will differ depending on where you are in the cycle.

2. Be honest. Although the overt objectives might be phrased as exploratory the hidden agenda might be concerned with choosing and testing rather than developing. Become a sleuth and work out what is going on beneath the surface of the brief.

'Stimulus material is an attitude of mind not a full wheelbarrow of boards, collages, scripts and videos.'

3. A hidden testing agenda is usually indicated when the project is under an exceptionally tight deadline and there is no time for stages of development. A clue is when only one or two 'feasible' executions are considered for research rather than many, or when there is an emphasis on consistency and comparing like with like. If the quantitative stage of research has already been booked and the material is professionally produced and well finished, then you can be sure that the underlying agenda is evaluative rather than developmental.

4. If there is a testing agenda then questions should be asked about methodology – semi-structured individual interviews, sensitive quantitative pre-testing or full-scale quantitative research is far more appropriate than qualitative group discussions or depth interviews.

5. Show the ideas in a realistic context. For posters, magazine ads, newspaper ads, TV commercials and radio commercials create a relevant context through the use of slides, mock-ups, short extracts of programming or editorial to frame the stimulus and other competitive stimuli ('typical' advertisement, promotional material, pack designs and so on).

'For posters, magazine ads, newspaper ads, TV commercials and radio commercials create a relevant context.'

6. Think about how real people come across new products, services or brands. Think about the competitive environment – is it dynamic or stable? Think about point of sale – promotions, signage, pricing conventions. What about merchandising – facings, gondolas, special display units? Finally, ask yourself questions about the retail outlet and how this might impinge upon the idea – a small corner shop, a petrol garage and a supermarket?

7. Make a distinction between the structure and form of the stimulus material. If the stimulus material is designed to communicate an idea for a new television commercial, separate the structural elements – such as sequence of scenes, time period, place, characters and script – from the executional elements – such as mood, photographic style, director's style, character's personalities, type of humour and environment. Design a stimulus material kit that will enable you to explore both.

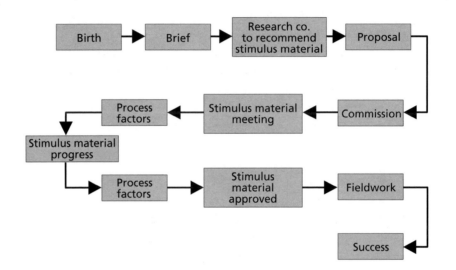

Figure 3: Think Before You Leap!

'It is easy to be ethno-centric and to believe that what seems to work in one country will work in another.'

8. Think before you leap. Figure 3 illustrates that stimulus material must be on the agenda as soon as the project is commissioned, if not before. It can form part of the brief to the researcher or research company requesting that part of the decision as to whom to use on the project will rest on their understanding of the role of stimulus material and their suggestions for what might be appropriate.

9. Take advice cross-culturally. It is easy to be ethno-centric and to believe that what seems to work in one country will work in another. Sometimes it does and sometimes it does not! There are a number of warning signs to observe. Translations require back translations to ensure that the

subtleties of meaning have been correctly conveyed. Image
collages require checking since symbols, colours, people
and environments mean very different things in different
parts of the world. Aim for simplicity and clarity to cope
with moderator variation in expertise or differences in
research culture and practice. Create a core stimulus set
and then encourage local moderators to add to it using
their own experience and knowledge. Above all consult
moderators, local offices and anyone who has some
understanding of the country in which the research is
taking place.

10. There is a moderator effect that is not easy to control. It
therefore needs to be anticipated and understood. Most
stimuli work in the same way with most human beings
most of the time. It is not the consumer who makes the
difference, it is usually the moderator.

Figure 4: A Portfolio of Research Material

DIRECT	INDIRECT
Advertising-related	Projective
Brand strategy propositions	Video collages
Adcepts	Visual collages
Animatics	Vocabulary boards
Storyboards	Talkie tapes
Flip-over boards	Thought tapes
Admatics	Mood boards
Narrative tapes	Music
Photomatic	Scrap art
	Analogy boards
	Vocabulary scatter boards

'It is not the consumer who makes the difference, it is usually the moderator.'

'The adage "rubbish in, rubbish out" is worth keeping in mind.'

11. Make a distinction between direct and indirect stimulus material. Direct stimulus material bears a strong resemblance to marketing tools – advertising, products, services, brands, etc. Indirect stimulus material is projective in nature and designed to stimulate feelings. Figure 4 illustrates both kinds. Descriptions of each can be found in the reference section.

12. Try to design a toolkit of stimuli – think laterally, think open and think approximate. Remember that there are limitations with any one item and separate the material in terms of its purpose: core idea vs execution; structure vs form; rational vs emotional; inner vs outer parameters.

13. There is one minefield that almost all of us fall into at one time or another. We run the risk of recommending a weak strategy because the stimulus material was effective or conversely losing a strong and effective strategy because the stimulus material was weak. There is no way round this other than awareness of the potential danger.

14. A final word on stimulus material – consult an expert. Researchers and planners who work with material across a wide range of projects know which kind of material will work best for a particular research objective. Although the material may look simple, effective stimulus material cannot be thrown together at the last minute. The adage 'rubbish in, rubbish out' is worth keeping in mind.

REFERENCE

1. J. N. Kapferer, *Strategic Brand Management*, Kogan Page, 1997.

'Try to design a toolkit of stimuli – think laterally, think open and think approximate.'

Breaking the Mould

Chapter nine

The purpose of this chapter is to give practical guidance about lateral ways of dealing with brand development. This is necessary because brand teams sometimes become gridlocked and are unable to agree how to move forwards. Power games and politics between different people within the company or between the marketing team and the external agencies (design, advertising, corporate identity) interfere with clarity of thinking and therefore participation in a process. If the process is managed by someone outside the system, these problems can be resolved.

The term brand development includes any problem with service, retail or fmcg brands, with corporate, company or product brands and with any area of development – new product development, communications, below-the-line, promotions, sponsorship, merchandising, packaging and identity.

There are four sections to this chapter:

- Start with the problem

- Set up a fact-finding mission

- Set up a BrandStorming day

- Moving onwards (preparation, after the BrandStorming).

'Brand teams sometimes become gridlocked and are unable to agree how to move forwards.'

Start with the problem

What is the problem? These are four simple words that can send a group of people into debate for hours! We often spend a great deal of energy and time attempting to solve a problem only to find that what we solved was not the heart of the problem at all. Or, even worse, we thought we had solved the problem only to find that we had not, because the other person's definition of the problem was different.

Defining the problem takes effort. It also takes wisdom and maturity because it is often about seeing the issues from another point of view – a position that can be difficult if a stance of 'I'm right' and 'you're wrong' has entered the frame.

A group or an individual with a problem is stuck. There is no other word for it. There is no possibility for movement forwards or backwards and no easy exit from the repetitive statement of assumptions and beliefs. A problem can become a tool of domination in meetings. How many times have you heard the expression 'I have a problem with this'? What this means is that the person disagrees strongly and is unable to provide sufficient evidence to persuade others that he or she is correct.

When a problem within a group of people (or an individual's problem) becomes persistent and repetitive, accompanied by rejection and hostility to suggestions, then group dynamics are the problem rather than how the problem is being expressed. Storming (see Chapter 4) is often characterised by a group becoming argumentative and taking rigid points of view in relation to an expressed problem.

Sometimes the problem is not tainted by the inhibiting nature of group dynamics and simply exists. The brand is showing decline, the market is changing, new developments in technology have created new opportunities and trends are emerging. These kinds of dynamics can create brand problems that need resolution.

The first step is to recognise that the team or the individual is in a hole (i.e. has a problem). What often happens in working groups is that the problem gets talked about a lot until everyone becomes confused by the amount of information surrounding the problem and de-energised by conversations that do not lead to resolution or change. This is like everyone climbing into the hole to keep the problem-owner(s) comfortable but is disempowering for all.

The problem has to be defined rigorously and there are many ways to accomplish this. Timothy Foster in *101 Ways to Generate Great Ideas* (1) and the processes involved in synectics (2) both begin with problem definition.

The approach is to define the problem-owner, to administer a 'problem definition questionnaire' and to resolve the situation if there are multiple problem-owners. The person in a company or team who is the problem-owner is the one who has power to affect the outcome or take responsibility for direction. This person is usually the one accountable to senior management and who will take the rap if the problem remains unsolved. The problem-owner can also be someone who has a genuine need to solve a problem.

'Flushing out the problem-owner can be difficult in hierarchical organisations with a blame culture or a risk-averse company or department.'

Flushing out the problem-owner can be difficult in hierarchical organisations with a blame culture or a risk-averse company or department. No one really wishes to own the problem. It is not wise to choose the CEO to be problem-owner. Although at the final day of reckoning, he or she is the person who is accountable, he or she is not likely to be able to devote the necessary time and energy to solving the problem. If there is no obvious problem-owner who can effect change, then one must be elected by the team for the purpose of that project.

Assuming that it is relatively easy to agree the problem-owner, the next step is to define the problem.

The planning cycle model below can be adapted to problem definition. It begins with defining the current situation – 'where are we now?' – 'we' referring to the brand, team or organisation. It then moves on to 'where could we be?' and following that 'how are we going to get there?'. Expanding the analysis of the current situation by such questions as 'why are we there now?' helps to define the starting point.

Figure 1: Think Planning Cycle

'A SWOT analysis is a good way of defining the current position.'

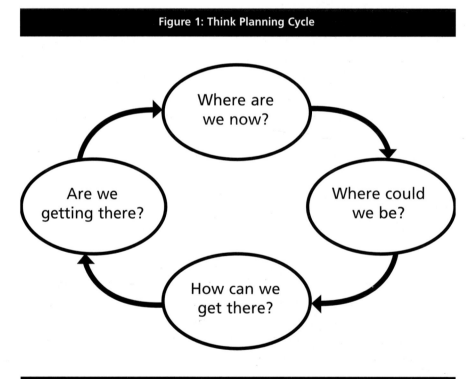

Foster (1) recommends analysis of the current situation using cards or flipcharts under headings such as: background, need, geographical/physical parameters, time parameters, competitive position, financial position, resources available and resources not available.

Alternatively a SWOT analysis is a good way of defining the current position. SWOT stands for Strengths, Weaknesses, Opportunities and Threats and involves a group of people sharing views of the brand or subject under each heading in turn.

Any model of thinking can be used to clarify the present situation – the brand diamond works well for brands and services – as do some of the other models explained in Chapter 7. Management books are awash with models that can be used to add rigour to the definition of the problem. The actual model chosen does not matter so much as the fact that a group of people are focused on applying it to their own problem with good intentions of moving onward.

The next step of the planning cycle refers to the future expressed as a goal – 'where could we be?'. This must be expressed clearly as a measurable achievement, otherwise the team will not know that the goal has been met. Woolly goals add to problem confusion.

'Management books are awash with models that can be used to add rigour to the definition of the problem.'

By comparing the current position with the desired outcome across relevant dimensions, it becomes crystal clear where the heart of the problem lies. This needs to be clearly articulated so that everyone involved with the problem-solving effort has the same expression of the problem on which to focus.

Synectics training provides very useful guidelines on how to define the problem and how to present it to a team of people gathered to begin the process of resolution. There are five parts to this process:

'By talking through the background in a personal way there is a greater likelihood of the problem owner acting on the outcome.'

1. task headline
2. background
3. opportunity
4. tried before
5. ideal solution.

First, the way in which the problem is expressed is critical. Instead of articulating the problem of Brand X as follows:

> *... the problem is that Brand X is underperforming in sales terms compared both to other brands in the portfolio and to the category in total, noticeably in the last quarter of the year ...*

it is more energising and exciting to express it as a task using the phrase *'How to ...'* or *'I wish ...'* which will focus on the future and generate ideas almost immediately:

> *I wish that Brand X could become as common a purchase for Christmas and New Year as Christmas cake!*

or

> *How to make Brand X glow in the dark of winter.*

Expressing the problem headline in this way focuses attention on the core problem (namely that Brand X was underperforming at only one point in the year), inspires, challenges and creates possibilities.

Second, the problem-owner writes down the background to the problem and talks it through – briefly – for the assembled team members who are not allowed to ask questions. The purpose of this step is not to give an overwhelming amount of information but to generate starting points for problem solution.

Third, by talking through the background in a personal way – 'the opportunity for me in solving this problem'– there is a greater likelihood of the problem-owner acting on the outcome.

The fourth element – 'what has been tried before?' – helps define the nature of the problem by indicating to the team whether the problem-owner is looking for new thinking or simply adjusting existing solutions.

Finally, the expression of an ideal solution makes clear the gap between 'now' and 'I wish ...'. It is stimulating to express the ideal as a metaphor or an unreasonable demand, for example:

> *I want to invent a tamogochi that will constantly nag its owner.*

> *I want to be written up in* Marketing Week *as the person who masterminded the revitalisation of Brand X.*

All of the ideas suggested here need to be tried and tested on real problems. Skill in using them also develops over time so it is best to begin in a safe place with colleagues with whom you feel comfortable.

'Woolly goals add to problem confusion.'

Set up a fact-finding mission

In order to *break the mould* or *get out of the box* (or whatever cliché has currency within the team), it is essential to know as much about the shape and nature of the mould as possible, hence a fact-finding mission.

Best current thinking

This could begin with a meeting designed to share BCT (Best Current Thinking) about the problem. Participants agree to present a short summary based on experience, recent research, general information or consultations with others about the brand problem. There is an advantage in inviting people with different areas of expertise or responsibility, i.e. the key stakeholders. The meeting might consist of the following representatives: advertising, packaging design, below-the-line, trade or retail, R&D, research, PR, marketing, production, service, quality etc., depending on the nature of the problem.

'In order to break the mould or get out of the box, it is essential to know as much about the shape and nature of the mould as possible.'

This meeting needs to be planned and well facilitated so that the summaries are concise and built around an agreed format. The role of the facilitator is to distil BCT for reference and stimulus at a later date.

A research macro-view

As part of BCT, or in preparation for it, it is worth reviewing all the past research reports for the previous year or two that are relevant to the problem. Often research is acted upon immediately and not completely squeezed dry in terms of longer-term learning. A macro-view of the learning across a range of projects (and other brands) can be extremely useful – there are often trends and common themes that only become obvious when the body of research is re-examined as if it were one study. It quickly becomes apparent then whether or not there are any gaps in the research.

This takes time and a small budget. It is most useful when the analysis is completed by an experienced qualitative researcher or independent planner, not necessarily the person who has conducted the work or been involved closely with it. Qualitative researchers and planners are used to dealing with multiple sources of information, whether these are qualitative or quantitative. Because their experience covers other brands and categories, they are often able to gain insight through comparison.

An internal brand audit

There are an increasing number of terms and concepts that have currency nowadays in relation to understanding brands and communications. Often, problems within a team occur because key members are using the same term to mean different things. The advertising agency may be using the term 'brand essence' to mean the heart of the brand, the core values that define it and remain constant over time, whereas the marketing manager may use the term to define core functional attributes that differentiate the brand from competitors. In this case, the two people cannot agree on how to move forward since they seem to be at metaphorical or literal loggerheads. This miscommunication multiplies within and across the organisations and departments involved with the brand.

A short exercise might illustrate this point. Take a minute to write down the definitions for the following terms as if you were explaining them to a new member of staff who had recently joined your department. If you wish, give the same list to a number of colleagues and then compare results. The similarities and differences might surprise you. If you were to extrapolate this exercise to members of other organisations or departments with whom you work (advertising, marketing, new product development, research, packaging, promotion, PR, 'the board', sales), you would understand with blinding clarity why so many problems of communication occur.

The terms are: positioning, proposition, personality, brand and brand essence (or any other that seems to have currency in your organisa-

'Qualitative researchers and planners are used to dealing with multiple sources of information, whether these are qualitative or quantitative.'

tion). Definitions of these are included in the reference section at the end of this book.

The way to free this tangle of miscommunication is to explore the models of brand thinking that currently exist. A short questionnaire can be faxed to key departments, functions and suppliers asking for feedback about the brand across a number of headings. For example:

- what are the strengths, weaknesses, opportunities and threats facing the brand over the next three years? (a short SWOT analysis)

- how would you describe the brand positioning?

- describe the essence of the brand in a short phrase

- what makes the brand different from its competitors?

- if you could wave a magic wand and guarantee the brand's success, what would you wish?

'A simple analysis of the range of interpretations of these commonplace brand concepts is a salutary place to start thinking more rigorously about the brand.'

A simple analysis of the range of interpretations of these commonplace brand concepts, together with a sense of ambition for the future, is a salutary place to start thinking more rigorously about the brand.

Set up a BrandStorming day

This is a special event that is well planned and productive. It is not an excuse for a day away from the office, an expensive lunch in a country hotel and drinks and dinner afterwards. While this kind of away day can and does achieve much in terms of team building, it may not solve the pressing problems facing the brand.

What is brainstorming and what is BrandStorming?

Brainstorming is a term that has been in use since the 1940s. It refers to the idea-generation phase of problem solving. A group of people are encouraged to contribute ideas, deferring judgment of each idea until later. The facilitator ensures that all areas are captured, that the main themes are linked, that members build on each others' contributions and finally, but not always, that the group agrees on a resolution.

There are many books and technique 'toolkits' nowadays to help generate creative thinking. Roger von Oech's *Creative Whack Pack – 64 Creative Thinking Strategies* (3) gives some brilliant ideas. There are many paperbacks in the business section of mainstream book stores that offer interesting food for thought. The Internet also details articles and companies specialising in brainstorming.

The use of brainstorming in business is very developed in the US. In recent years, major organisations have been wrestling with the concept of 'innovation'. It is well accepted today that in order to succeed, grow, become profitable and sustain profitability in an increasingly competitive global market-place, it is essential to innovate. Innovation must be continuous – not a stop-and-start love affair with the idea. But how does this happen? Is it the responsibility of a crack team of innovators within a special unit or is it part of the genetic code of the organisation?

Just as organisations became obsessed with continuous quality (Total Quality Management – TQM) and customer satisfaction in

'Innovation must be continuous – not a stop-and-start love affair with the idea.'

the early 1990s as answers to problems within organisations (or their products, services and brands), the current focus of attention is on creativity, innovation and actionability (implementation) of new ideas.

'Brainstorming is enjoying unprecedented popularity and has become legitimised as a powerful tool to offer people within companies as an expression of the commitment to innovation.'

Brainstorming is enjoying unprecedented popularity and has become legitimised as a powerful tool to offer people within companies as an expression of the commitment to innovation. In the US, far more so than the UK, there are thousands of consultants who specialise in running brainstorming sessions for companies. Like qualitative researchers, each has his or her own toolbox of techniques, games and toys to encourage lateral thinking and an environment that is empathetic to playful inventiveness and freedom of expression. There are courses to attend, institutes that train trainers, books, videos and mail-order products to aid brainstorming.

In the US there are a large number of organisations that offer 'branded' innovation or creativity services – possibly as many as there are qualitative research companies in the UK. (Reference is made in the final section of this book to some key e-mail addresses for those who wish to pursue this.)

There is general agreement about the basic rules for successful brainstorming. These read like the bible – the cardinal commandments.

- No criticisms or evaluations – no one should judge, mock, put people down, ask questions or in any way criticise what anyone else contributes.

- Freewheel – no one should hold back, everyone should be encouraged to say whatever comes to mind. The wilder the idea, the better. Crazy ideas often trigger useful ones.

- Quantity – the more ideas the better. It is easier later to cut down a long list than to puff up a short one.

- Combine, change and improve – add to, modify, build on each others' ideas. Can someone else's contribution be magnified, minimised, substituted, rearranged, reversed or adapted?

- Relax, play and have fun – there needs to be a feeling of relaxation, mutual help and friendly competition.

- Silence is OK – good things often materialise after a silence.

'In my view, brainstorming methods and practices, as well as practitioners and companies, will multiply over the next five years.'

Particular facilitators have rules that have developed over time and also particular techniques to encourage left-brain (logical, deductive, analytical, judgmental) and right-brain (visual, spatial, metaphorical, sensory-based) creative thinking. Logic, intelligence, information and assumptions all have a place, but not in innovative idea generation.

After the idea-generation phase of brainstorming comes the evaluative phase – which avenues and directions seem to offer potential? Which are high priorities and which low? What is practical now and what is not? If one looks three years ahead, which are the most exciting ideas even if they are not practical now?

Evaluation requires a process and a set of criteria. Synectics uses NAF (New Appealing and Feasible) ratings to evaluate new ideas and ask three questions: How new? How appealing? How feasible? Other criteria can be developed depending on the problem. A process must be set up so that the whole group takes responsibility for weeding out the quantity of ideas, leaving only those that the group agrees are worth pursuing.

In my view, brainstorming methods and practices, as well as practitioners and companies, will multiply over the next five years. There will be variations in quality – from the excellent to the charlatans.

Buyers will need to be thorough in the way in which they assess the credentials of would-be suppliers. Those who wish to begin offering this kind of service to clients need to be aware that it takes years of experience to become good at something. It cannot be learned from a book or a three-day course over a weekend, just as qualitative researchers cannot be cloned overnight.

BrandStorming is a personal term, invented and applied at The Research Business *International*. It is defined thus:

> *... to encourage a group of people involved with the brand (or whom have brand expertise) to listen to objective facts, to separate these from opinion, to apply creative techniques to break the mould of thinking and to agree a direction and outcome.*

As with brainstorming there are a number of steps and also a great range of techniques that can be used.

The principles offered here are eclectic. They have been borrowed from others and particularly from the creative projective techniques used in conventional qualitative projects.

If this is an area of service that interests you, then it is important to develop a programme and style that fits your own 'personality' or the culture within your company.

There are five guidelines.

1. *Prepare* – a great deal of organisation and planning is required for successful BrandStorming. Participants need to understand what is expected of them, both practically and emotionally. It is therefore important to ensure that the structural arrangements for the day are well planned (venue, seating, catering, telephone messages, timing) as

well as state of mind. It is easiest to communicate these expectations through a written letter of invitation including details of where, when, why and how. The organiser asks participants to do a series of tasks beforehand. These serve as stimuli on the day but also help everyone to understand the desired mind-set.

2. *Experience* – the emphasis is on participation and experiential interaction rather than conventional business meeting discussion. Only through doing tasks and exercises, rather than opinionating about issues and points of view, can the team gain insight and move forwards.

3. *Facilitation* – clear guidance and control from the BrandStorming leader are important. The facilitator needs to create an atmosphere of trust and openness and this is only possible with training and experience.

4. *Enable* – this means using indirect forms of eliciting contributions from all the participants. Projective techniques adapted from the qualitative armoury, in addition to other tools for idea generation used in conventional brainstorming, are very useful.

5. *Outcome* – evaluation, prioritisation, actions, plans and responsibilities are all critical for successful BrandStorming.

'Experience – *the emphasis is on participation and experiential interaction rather than conventional business meeting discussion.'*

Preparation – some approaches that work

There are a number of tasks that can be set as a price of entry for participation. Given that people are busy and time-stressed, the tasks must be easy to do. Here are some suggestions.

Supermarket observation – ask participants to go to the supermarket and analyse two unrelated brands or categories. A prompt list can be provided such as the following.

> *What did you notice on your first scan of the fixture? What stood out? Which brands have presence and which do not? What are the reasons for stand-out? How does packaging work in this category? Are there rules and who is breaking them? How do you know whether the category is active or passive? What is the logic of the fixture from the consumer point of view? Is the fixture easy to shop or not? How are people shopping the fixture – on automatic pilot, browsing or involved? What do you notice about interesting promotions or ways of merchandising brands? What about premium, standard and own-label dynamics? How does the fixture fit into the route within the supermarket and does this make sense? What would you do if you had a free hand to re-order the fixture?*

'Audit a storage space by taking a photograph and writing down names of brands.'

These are just a few of the questions that can be used as prompts.

Audit a storage space by taking a photograph and writing down names of brands – a fun and easy preparatory task. Each participant is asked to photograph brands in the home – the way that they are stored in the fridge, freezer, bathroom cabinet, under the sink cupboards, in dry grocery cupboards and so on. The exercise must be relevant to the brand problem. It is useful to set cupboard audits of categories both outside and within the brand arena. Participants are encouraged to complete audits of this kind with a friend or relative of a different life stage. This yields interesting insights.

Interview a real person – how many people working on a brand truly understand the person at whom the brand is directed, other than by statistics or brief exposure through a viewing room mirror? Participants are asked to interview or simply 'hang about' with someone from the target group – a child of ten, a 16-year-old teenager, a streetwise style leader, a housewife with four children, an empty nester. Friends of friends or relatives can be the contacts for informal sessions that are about trying to experience the flavour of the target group, rather than formal interviewing.

Keep a diary of behaviour – this is a way of heightening sensitivity around areas of day-to-day life that we all take for granted. What does it really feel like to clean the toilet and the bathroom, to shave every day, to go into a DIY store or gardening centre on a Sunday, to paint the house, to go to the bank? Through becoming aware of the experience as it is happening, the emotional feelings and external influences become apparent.

Take off your marketing hat – watch a reel of ads, read magazines, go to the cinema and then think about trends in communications. Which ads stand out and why? What do other people in the household think? How do ads work at different times of the day or evening and in different breaks? What is creativity in communication?

Select a thing (an object, picture or music) that represents a 'big wish' for the future. This exercise is useful in exploring the aspirations and values that the brand team members believe to be important in their lives and which they would like to see integrated with the brand or the organisation in the future.

Stop a routine act of brand behaviour and start another. Exercises such as this heighten awareness of behaviour and attitudes that are taken for granted and help to expand thinking. At one BrandStorming session, everyone was asked not to drink tea for the week prior to the

'"Hang about" with someone from the target group – a child of ten, a 16-year-old teenager, a street-wise style leader.'

away day. As this took place in England, the insights into tea drinking compared to other hot and cold beverages formed a backdrop to the day's work on the brand.

Visit a shop or place that is unusual and bring something that intrigues you. Encouraging people to visit unusual art galleries, New Age shops, markets, 'innovation' stores, highly specialised shops or delicatessens provides interesting starting points for creative thinking.

The purpose of encouraging a team of people to engage in one or more of these exercises before attending the BrandStorming session is to remove blinkers and open the mind to possibilities. The perspective changes from 'what is going on in here?' (here being the company, the problem, the team, the brand) to 'what is going on out there?'. 'Out there' includes the realities of human behaviour, broader social and world trends, other impressive companies and brands and the nature of the particular set of people in which we are interested.

'Many people believe that someone is or is not born creative. Experience suggests that this is untrue.'

Many people believe that someone is or is not born creative. Experience suggests that this is untrue, particularly when it comes to BrandStorming. Thinking up 20 uses for a brick (or a hedgehog or bookends) in five minutes is not a test of ability as a creative brand thinker.

The *Oxford Thesaurus* comes up with the following synonyms for the word 'creative': fantasy, imagination, ingenuity, originality, inventiveness. Everybody has these aspects of creativity within themselves. We often surprise ourselves by causing things to come into existence, discovering, devising or fabricating in our minds or resolving a problem in an original way and yet we do not call ourselves creative thinkers.

The secret of creative thinking is to design the opportunities for it to arise – BrandStorming is such an opportunity.

BrandStorming – an away day

What happens on the day?

Now that everyone has completed the tasks, the structure of the event is well organised and the facilitator experienced, what does everyone do?

Obviously, there is not one method or set of techniques since it depends both on the problem and also the culture of the team or organisation. Some companies are sophisticated users of brain-storming processes and techniques and have a roster of facilitators they can call upon. These organisations can either be easy or difficult to work with. Their exposure to brainstorming techniques makes the participants either jaded and hard to stimulate (the 'I've done this before' mental set) or quick and efficient, suspending judgment, contributing and obeying the basic rules without coaxing.

'What is important is that the facilitator chooses the appropriate tool from the toolbox at the right moment in time.'

Other companies are unsophisticated and arrive on the day with a high level of scepticism. The further the facilitator moves away from the problem and uses exercises which are based on metaphor, analogy and absurdity, the greater the discomfort and resistance. Many people do not understand that the human brain works by connections. By encouraging someone to connect a completely irrelevant object, thought, picture or ambivalent stimulus to the brand or the problem, new thinking emerges.

What is important is that the facilitator chooses the appropriate tool from the toolbox at the right moment. The wrong one can throw the team into problems of group dynamics as outlined in Chapter 4.

So the question 'but what do you do?' still remains unanswered. Here are some suggestions.

- Ask a number of facilitators to come and tell you how they might run a BrandStorming day and then choose the one who seems most likely to work well with the team.

- If you are determined to do it yourself and you have never done it before, go for training. There are organisations that offer basic courses in creative thinking and brainstorming from which you can adapt techniques to suit you. The Internet is a good place to start. The Creative Problem Solving Group (CPS-B) at Buffalo University (www.cpsb.com) offers courses twice a year and its philosophy and processes have been tested within companies of many different types over the past 50 years.

- If you have had some experience, but lack confidence, convene a practice session with some colleagues and try out some of the ideas and processes you have developed.

'It is not important whose definition is right; only that everyone agrees to use the same definition for the brand problem being discussed.'

Qualitative research offers fertile ground for developing skills in BrandStorming. Practise more unusual projective techniques (Chapter 6), become more sophisticated about group dynamics (Chapter 4) and learn how to use models of thinking (Chapter 7) interactively with other people.

Brand problems often involve issues of positioning, brand image, brand personality, brand essence and brand identity. It is therefore very important that everyone agrees what these terms mean or will mean from this day into the future. Definitions are given in the reference section that can be used as stimuli for clarification. It is not important whose definition is right, only that everyone agrees to use the same definition for the brand problem being discussed.

A good place to start, after the initial sharing of insights gained from the preparatory exercises is to do some BHAG thinking. BHAG (Big Hairy Audacious Goal) is a concept used by Collins & Porras in their book *Built to Last: Successful Habits of Visionary Companies* (4).

Visionary is not a spiritual or New Age concept. The authors use it to describe those companies that have two main characteristics in common. The first is rather like DNA – embedded in the genetic make-up of the organisation – and which they call core ideology.

> *Core ideology is the enduring character of the organisation, a consistent identity that transcends product or market lifecycles, technological breakthroughs, management fads and individual leaders.*

The core ideologies of a company consist of its core values – its essential tenets that it holds dear – and core *purpose* – its reason for being. The core ideology of an organisation cannot be created or manufactured (as so often happens with many mission, value and goal statements that decorate the walls of large companies). Core ideology can only be revealed and discovered from the inside. It exists in the hearts of all the people who have pride in their work and in the achievements of the organisation, it is authentic and emotionally important.

'Core ideology can only be revealed and discovered from the inside.'

The second characteristic of visionary organisations is their ability to create an 'envisioned future – a 10-to-30-year audacious goal plus vivid descriptions of what it will be like to achieve the goal'. This kind of goal unites people. It creates the impetus that inspires and challenges. It is a daunting goal that seems almost out of reach and yet everyone wants it to happen so badly that they strive for it. The goal must be expressed in a way that ordinary people can understand – not distanced through financial language or corporate-speak.

Collins and Porras invented the term BHAG (pronounced BeeHag) to describe this goal. BHAGs fall into four groups.

1. *Target BHAG* – a measurable goal that can be set quantitatively or qualitatively, e.g. to be a company worth £10 million by the year

2000, to be the most innovative player in the field (the number one company when the word innovative is mentioned).

2. *David and Goliath BHAG* – a goal set competitively, e.g. to crush X, to knock Y off its position as number one.

3. *Role-model BHAG* – to emulate the performance of another successful brand, e.g. to become the Microsoft of the industry, to gain the respect that Virgin has today.

4. *Transformation BHAG* – to use the brand to change the way in which the company is perceived, e.g. to become the number one or number two in every market in which it operates.

Another might be to revolutionise the company so that it has the strengths of a big player but the agility of a smaller one. Yet another might be to transform this company from makers of widgets to the best-diversified high-technology company in the world.

This is an effective way of enabling a team of people to find common goals for an organisation or brand. It is often far more powerful to express ambitions for the future in this way than to talk in the language of business finance – not that the latter is unimportant, only that it does not have a place on a BrandStorming day.

BrandStorming can be made part of an integrated research project. For example, participants could be asked to attend a focus group the evening before, so that they can experience the ways in which the target market (or potential market) relates to the brand or service. For many people, this might be the first time they have seen or heard 'consumers' first hand, and therefore the experience can be impactful.

'BrandStorming can be made part of an integrated research project.'

BrandStorming can be included at any stage of a qualitative (or quantitative) research project, at a point when there is a need to assimilate, explore, develop hypotheses, evaluate or decide on next directions. It provides a way in which a team of stakeholders, who might have little to do with one another in the normal course of day-to-day work, can unite around a common project in which they are all involved and build the foundations of a united team effort.

'A successful BrandStoming day generates the need for decisions and actions.'

After the BrandStorming – then what?

'If there is a funda-mental belief that "nothing ever changes" then the team is unlikely to succeed.'

One of the biggest problems of brainstorming or BrandStorming sessions comes after they have finished. Often those involved have had a very stimulating and exciting experience. The process has allowed frustrations to be expressed, ideas to be shared and a common purpose to be agreed. Everyone leaves the day thanking the facilitator profusely and sharing with each other how useful a day it has been. Expectations for both change and action are high.

Then nothing happens. The day is forgotten in the busy schedules of day-to-day work. Disillusionment and cynicism set in. The facilitator, the process or the problem-owner becomes tainted with criticism. Next time someone suggests a similar exercise, there is considerably more apathy and resentful participation.

What can be done to stop this happening?

It is a simple idea but very difficult to achieve. A successful BrandStoming day generates the need for decisions and actions. Someone needs to champion these through the complex web of an organisation and not be content that the day itself was sufficient to demonstrate commitment to change. That person also needs to enrol the others, or perhaps people who did not attend the event, to help push brand change through the organisation. I use the term brand change advisedly. It is unlikely that a BrandStoming event results in a decision to do nothing at all and to maintain the status quo. These events are born out of a belief that something is not right and needs to be assessed and changed.

At the end of the session, the need for the allocation of responsibilities, actions and a timetable for completion of these, is a simple hygiene factor that ensures that there is no loss of momentum. Ways to keep the team motivated and involved must be discussed openly and the possibility of failure examined with the same degree of honesty.

It sounds so easy and yet this is the hardest part of breaking out of the mould. It is not that creativity or intention is lacking but that action and consistency of follow-through is weak. Often the problem lies deeply embedded in the culture of the organisation and the ways in which people are motivated. If there is a fundamental belief that 'nothing ever changes' then the team is unlikely to succeed. If, on the other hand, innovation, experimentation and failure are all seen as essential to change and growth, then the team is likely to succeed.

For consultants operating outside the culture of an organisation, there is often a point at which one gives up. Nothing one says or does can make an impression on the organisation – it is simply too 'closed', no matter how much it expresses the desire to be 'open' and take risks.

There is a much-used saying in management – 'you have to walk the talk' (*be* the desired behaviour and not simply talk about it) in order to create change. Breaking the mould is no different.

REFERENCES

1. T. R. V. Foster, *101 Ways to Generate Great Ideas*, Kogan Page, 1994.
2. J. Cesarani and P. Greenwood, *Innovation and Creativity*, Kogan Page, 1995.
3. R. von Oech, *Creative Whack Pack*, Creative Think, Menlo Park, California, 1992.
4. J. C. Collins, and J. I. Porras, *Built to Last: Successful Habits of Visionary Companies*, Century Ltd, 1996.

FURTHER READING

E. De Bono, *Serious Creativity*, HarperCollins, London, 1993.

E. De Bono, *I Am Right – You Are Wrong*, Viking, London, 1990.

E. De Bono, *Six Thinking Hats*, Viking, London, 1986.

R. Gibson (ed.), *Rethinking the Future*, Nicholas Brealey, London, 1997.

D. Hall, *Jump Start Your Brain*, Warner Books, 1996.

G. Hamel and C. K. Prahalad, *Competing for the Future*, Harvard Business School Press, Boston, 1994.

J. Henry and D. Walker (eds), *Managing Innovation*, Sage Publications, California, 1991.

Kleiman, *Get Innovative or Get Dead*, Douglas & McIntyre, 1995.

A. Koestler, *The Act of Creation*, Hutchinson & Co, London, 1964.

M. Michalko, *Thinkertoys: Handbook of Business Creativity for the 90s*, Ten Speed, 1991.

P. Senge, *The Fifth Discipline*, Doubleday, New York, 1990.

D. Sherwood, *Unlock Your Mind*, Gower, 1998.

R. von Oech, *Creative Whack Pack*, Creative Think, Menlo Park, California, 1992.

R. von Oech, *A Whack on the Side of the Head*, Creative Think, Menlo Park, California, 1992.

'There is a saying in management – "you have to walk the talk" to create change. Breaking the mould is no different.'

Researching the Future

Chapter ten

Introduction

One of the harshest criticisms levelled at market research, both qualitative and quantitative, is that it is based on the past. Someone once said that using market research to navigate the uncharted and unknown territory of the future is 'like driving into oncoming traffic in the centre of New York, using a rear view mirror'.

And it is true. Most market research attempts to understand the past and, by so doing, predicts the future. Questions or topic areas ask people what they bought (ate, drank, did) last week, last month or in the last six months. Reels of commercials, examples of current press advertisements, current products and services are shown and discussed in depth in order to understand how a particular set of human beings created meaning in the past. We accept nowadays that brand images are created over time into a complex amalgamation of impressions. *Past* activities create the *current* image – direct and indirect experience with the brand, above- and below-the-line communications and the retail context in which the brand is framed.

'Using market research to navigate the uncharted and unknown territory of the future is "like driving into oncoming traffic in the centre of New York, using a rear-view mirror".'

Few would seriously argue with the fact that the past informs how we behave, think, feel and respond to new events in the present. This is not the issue. More important is the fundamental assumption that there is a linear relationship between past, present and future. If we can understand the influences of the past in causing the patterns of the present, then all we have to do is to extend the understanding of the present into the future and we have the answers.

A non-linear relationship between past and future

There is a great line, attributed to Woody Allen: 'Do you know how to make God laugh? Tell him your future plans!' When market research attempts to establish what people *will do in the future*, the results are rarely accurate, for the simple reason that people do not know what they will do until the reality of the product, service, new commercial or new identity meets them head on in the future. Only then do they respond to it in the context of a particular set of circumstances and needs at the time.

There are some wonderful examples of people getting it wrong [1].

> *In 1893 a group of 74 social commentators met at the Chicago World's Fair to discuss the future. And looking ahead 100 years to 1993, they concluded that many people would live to be 150.*

> *In 1949, the prediction was made and quoted in Popular Mechanics – 'Computers in the future may perhaps only weigh ... 1.5 tons.'*

> *In 1962 Decca Recordings said of the Beatles: 'We do not like their sound, and anyway guitar music is on the way out.'*

> *In 1977, Ken Olsen, president and founder of Digital Equipment Corporation predicted: 'There is no reason why anyone would want a computer in their home.'*

'In 1962 Decca Recordings said of the Beatles: "We do not like their sound, and anyway guitar music is on the way out."'

Watts Wacker and Jim Taylor's book *The 500-Year Delta* has a bright-yellow jacket with the lines 'what happens next after what happens next' repeated over and over [2]. The first chapter challenges 'rules of thumb', one of which is that experience is the best teacher.

> *When a paradigm shifts as is now happening, experience is quite possibly the worst teacher in town. Why? Because in the reason age now ending, experience has been built on a knowledge of causal relationships – if a, then b; if sales spiked, the reason is that prices rose; if productivity increased, the reason is that flexi-time was instituted; if 1.2 million people showed up at major-league ballparks last Sunday, 1.2 million will show up this Sunday. In a reason-based world, the relationship is as plain as the nose on your face. But in the Chaos Age now forming,*

causality, like linear logic, has been summarily deposed.
Those 1.2 million people may or may not show up at ball-
parks on Sunday, but chaos theory says that we cannot
predict a single one of them will arrive without knowing
he or she has bought a ticket and is moving through the
turnstile.

Change moves too fast, time is too compressed to draw
any link with experience, rational connections have been
routed by connectivity. In the world as it now is, you can
no longer discern the cause or the effect of any action.
You cannot control the relationship or even the moment
when the relationship might be valid. All you can know
about any action, any effect, is that it happened. The
more you search for causality, the further behind you will
fall. The more successful you have been in a reason-based
world, the harder it will be for you to leave it (pp. 16–17).

> *'In the world as it*
> *now is, you can no*
> *longer discern the*
> *cause or effect of*
> *any action.'*

The future does not yet exist

The successful development for the future of new products or services, brands, advertising, packs and promotions is difficult and emotionally charged for those given the responsibility for trying. Even more difficult is the problem of devising long-term strategies for re-framing (re-positioning) brands, services and companies or indeed creating new frames of reference, positioning or values for *a future context that does not yet exist.*

For example, how can a multi-utility company create a corporate brand positioning and values when deregulation is not yet complete? Ordinary people are unused to a market in which gas, water, electricity, telecommunications networks, cable television and Internet service providers can (a) be bought from one single company and (b) will be as active a market-place as airlines competing for travellers. So how can they know how they will behave in five years time when the market is a different place and operating with different rules?

How can major multinationals invent successful global brands when human beings do not know what they want and need because they already have an overwhelming number of choices? In sophisticated branded markets, people do not believe they have unfulfilled needs, wants and desires for yet more brands and brand extensions, differentiated only through marketing positioning or product tweaks and twirls. They might respond enthusiastically to a well-marketed and well-positioned new brand (or re-framed 'old brand'), but in advance of the brand existing as a reality, they will more often than not show a lukewarm response to a concept of it. We are still deeply stuck in the mire of reason-based thinking.

'How can major multinationals invent successful global brands when human beings do not know what they want and need?'

More and more client companies know from past experience that qualitative research provides essential information and understanding to enable the short-term management of the business. What is more troublesome is that it has rarely been successful in predicting the future performance of a new brand, a new campaign or a newly designed positioning for an existing brand. Even if it is thought that it might be, quantitative research is nearly always employed as a safety check. Even this reason-based precaution does not necessarily lead to success in the long term.

Qualitative researchers, however, persist in promising clients that their methods and techniques will overcome the client's doubts and scepticism about the outcome. Researchers promise that their particular toolkit of techniques (whether stimulus material, projective and enabling techniques, methods of interviewing customers and consumers or models of thinking), will provide the answer to the core question 'What must I do today to occupy the competitive high ground of tomorrow?'

And it is a seductive promise, which both parties believe at the time. But it is a story – clearly articulated by Wacker and Taylor (2).

> *In story books – and undoubtedly still in some graduate courses in basic management practices – the 'true' condition is easy to describe. Challenges arrive sequentially. Information is gathered. Wise heads are consulted. A plan is formed. Contingencies are pondered and provided for. Ducks are lined up. The big guns are pulled out. And finally the solution is executed.*

But we also know this to be a fantasy – the real world is complicated and the amount of information we have to deal with is overwhelming – variables interact, surprising events occur, time compresses and before the plan is executed, the target has changed its shape, colour and position.

The age of chaos

Contemporary writers about the age of chaos describe a terrifying world in some respects but they also offer solace in the form of intuition and trust. If cause is no longer connected to effect, and if experience no longer guarantees a successful outcome, then there is no right way of doing something. There is only a way that *feels* right, a way that acknowledges that the future cannot be guaranteed and that we have to *own* responsibility for the choices we make.

'The real world is complicated and the amount of information we have to deal with is overwhelming.'

This does not mean making arbitrary choices based on hunches or consultations with astrologers and psychics. However, these may well have a contribution to make in making sense of the huge pile of jigsaw pieces we have in front of us and with which we are attempting to make a coherent whole. What it means is working *with* chaos and not against it. It means accepting that there are no rules, there is no absolute truth out there. All there is is a range of possibilities – one or more of which are to be owned if you so wish.

...There is no mass reality any more, that reality is anything you make it, that you can construct the reality of each moment as you move through it ... There is only the Freedom to Be whatever you want to be and the ironclad necessity to exercise it ... welcome to the Age of Possibility (2).

The age of possibility

The word *possibility* is synonymous with words such as chance, odds, prospect, feasibility, plausibility, likelihood, opportunity and promise. It has been argued that qualitative research is unable to promise the delivery of reliable prediction about the future, so what can it do?

'There is no mass reality any more, that reality is anything you make it.'

It can deliver a number of alternative possibilities about the future. These possibilities illuminate potential threats and opportunities that enable decision makers to rehearse different responses, thus being more prepared, whichever possibility or combination thereof becomes a reality.

Creating possibilities (assumptions, probabilities) relies on good thinking, which is strategic, future-focused, analytical, imaginative and qualitative. It is an attitude of mind developed through experience rather than a set of processes and rules of engagement. We can make the distinction between qualitative research and qualitative thinking as follows.

Qualitative research
Specialist, methodology, techniques, sample, consumers, respondents, practitioners, codes, precedent, practices, industry, qualifications, short-term problems

Qualitative thinking
Expansive, holistic, synergistic, hypothetical, challenges, assumptions, re-frames, mind-sets, generalist, open-ended, individual, intelligent, 'the long view' (3)

Qualitative thinking is able to identify and describe a number of possibilities for an organisation, company, brand, product or service. In this way, it is like water divining – as the diviner crosses the territory, the sticks will bend wherever there is water, even if it is deep down. Within the parameters of the search, the water diviner may indicate two or three places where water may be found – it is then up to the individual to make a decision as to whether to bore in those places or not. Instead of crossed sticks made of willow, the skills of the qualitative diviner of the future are more complicated. They are:

- fingers on the pulse of change – spotting trends

- facilitating innovation – applying qualitative expertise to the field of innovation

- designing possibility scenarios – exploring 'what ifs' with stakeholders of the future

- the power of intuition – the characteristics of qualitative thinking.

'Instead of crossed sticks made of willow, the skills of the qualitative diviner of the future are more complicated.'

Spotting trends

As we reach the end of this millennium, trend-spotting has become very fashionable. A new breed of specialist 'futurologists' has come to the fore – some have been active in this arena for many years. Others have seen an opportunity to position themselves as specialists in the diagnosis and cure of 'millennium fever' and have become either famous or rich, or both, in the process.

In particular the business bookshelf of the world is now overflowing with the predictions, beliefs, views and opinions by an army of worldwide management gurus who have written extensively on organisational change for the future.

The list of the famous is extensive. In *Rethinking the Future*, edited by Rowan Gibson (1), there are chapters by: Charles Handy, Stephen Covey, Michael Porter, C K Prahalad, Gary Hamel, Michael Hammer, Eli Goldratt, Peter Senge, Warren Bennis, John Kotter, Al Ries and Jack Trout, Philip Kotler, John Naisbitt, Lester Thurow and Kevin Kelly.

These authors (and others not represented in the book) have been thinking for many years about the changing landscape of business and the increasing uncertainty in which the nature of work, of organisations and of economics is changing. The cover of the book promises:

> Rethinking the Future *examines the changing role of the leader and the powerful influence of corporate culture. And it probes the universal principles and values that ultimately govern the success of any leader or organisation. It also looks at strategies for creating tomorrow's competitive advantages and tomorrow's markets, which will be driven by new demographics, new global structures and new technology.*

'Cool advisers are becoming valuable to advertising, design and other creative agencies, whose business it is to be one step ahead of the game.'

In addition to the management and business school gurus there is another category of trend-spotters. These people are relatively unknown. They have been called 'the cool sleuths' by the media. Essentially, they are young people at the cutting edge of fashion and trends who are able to translate what is happening on the street for companies whose business it is to know. Levi's, Nike, Coca-Cola and Sony are a few companies that spring to mind immediately. Cool advisers are also becoming valuable to advertising, design and other creative agencies, whose business it is to be one step ahead of the game.

This new discipline of trend-spotting is difficult to penetrate if you have not yet started. For the buyer or user of such advice or expertise, there is a high chance of getting it wrong. This happens because there are many opportunists who claim expertise on the back of very little experience or depth of information. Or because it looks easier to distil information from a wide range of sources than it is in practice.

As with most decisions in life, it is wise to consult with others, to make background enquiries and to check credentials.

There are two types of trend-spotting – hard and soft. The skill of synthesising the quantitative nature of hard trends with the 'touch-feel' qualitative nature of emerging ones is one of the greatest strengths of a serious futurist.

'For the buyer or user of such advice or expertise, there is a high chance of getting it wrong.'

Hard trend-spotting

This section describes a number of companies or types of information about the future, which are very important materials for building the foundations of future thinking and strategy development. The list is by no means conclusive and there are probably many other reputable organisations. A search on the Internet yielded the following list:

- consultants and think-tanks
- college and university centres
- associations and foundations
- government
- corporations
- people
- publications
- models and methods
- education, training and conferences.

This list is updated regularly and is provided by Strategic Futures International (www.sfutures.com).

The names alone indicate the range of interests or the focus.

United Kingdom think-tanks

- Adam Smith Institute
- Institute of Economic Affairs
- New Economics Foundation
- Institute for Public Policy Research
- Social and Community Planning Research
- Henley Centre
- Institute for Fiscal Studies
- Chartered Institute of Public Finance Accountants
- Royal Institute of International Affairs
- Institute for Strategic Studies
- Centre for Policy on Ageing
- Family Policy Studies Centre
- Public Net

'The best search engines find for you what you want to know, quickly and easily.'

Future institutes and think-tanks

- Strategic Futures International
- The Futures Group International
- Futuribles
- Global Business Network
- Institute for Alternative Futures
- Institute for Technology Assessment
- Millennium Institute
- SRI International

- Center for Policy Analysis
- Copenhagen Institute for Futures Studies
- Finnish Futures Research Centre
- Henley Management Centre
- Henley Management College
- Institute for Futures Research (Stellenbosch University)

- Association for Public Policy Analysis and Management
- Global Futures
- Greater Boston Chapter of the World Future Society
- Institute of Business Forecasting
- International Association for Technology Assessment and Forecasting
- Police Futurists International
- The Strategic Leadership Forum
- Technology and Innovation Management
- World Future Society

- Army Environmental Policy Institute
- British Millennium Commission
- Future Technologies Institute (US Army)
- National Air & Space Museum, Future Studies

'Qualitative research methods create the possibility of synthesising and making accessible the wide range of different sources and types of knowledge.'

Publications

- *Millennium*
- *21st C Magazine*
- *Futures Research Quarterly*
- *The Futurist*
- *Global Futures Bulletin* (e-mail)
- *International Journal of Futures Studies*
- *Journal of Strategic Management*
- *On the Horizon*
- *Technological Forecasting and Social Change*
- *Vision of the Future*
- *World Futures*

The vast amount of information is overwhelming. The challenge is how to use qualitative methods of content analysis and models of thinking so as to become a human search engine. The best search engines find for you what you want to know, quickly and easily.

Qualitative research methods create the possibility of synthesising and making accessible the wide range of different sources and types of knowledge. There is no 'right way' to do this. No short-cut or step-by-step guidance can be given. It requires a large dose of intelligence applied in a common-sense way with good intentions and integrity.

Soft trend-spotting

'Spotting emerging trends is not difficult for practising qualitative researchers who have their fingers on the pulse of human behaviour.'

Spotting emerging trends is not difficult for practising qualitative researchers who have their fingers on the pulse of human behaviour and attitudes. It requires a certain amount of sensitivity, awareness and synthesis across a range of studies in different product and service categories. Qualitative researchers are skilled at spotting patterns and shapes in the contextual fabric of their fields of study. For example, long before Tesco showed the strength of its muscle to challenge Sainsbury, qualitative research antennae picked up the vibrations of discontent among its customers. This was expressed as exasperation with the lack of choice in the stores, particularly the predominance of own-label, combined with an over-clinical in-store environment and the inflexibility of staff service.

Human beings respond to change instinctively. We often behave in a new way without conscious recognition that we have done so and are therefore unable to articulate or express through language the underlying reasons for new behaviour. Because qualitative researchers are in constant contact with ordinary human beings (as opposed to advertising, marketing, design and research, corporate), they notice the big wave on the horizon.

In the early 1980s The Research Business *International* wrote several papers presented at conferences, which made little impact at the time, but which proved two to three years later to have described accurately a new phenomenon. One described the way in which UK consumers were becoming increasingly sophisticated about advertising and had begun 'to consume' the form of the advertising as well as the message

(4). This preceded the great years of advertising in the UK that resulted in campaigns that made case history material around the world.

The second soft trend-spotting example is drawn from a similar period. Many qualitative researchers within the company began to notice that consumers had become aware of ingredients in food products. Preservatives, E numbers, artificial additives and chemical-sounding names were mentioned with increasing frequency, leading to an emerging awareness of fat content and healthy eating. While this seems part of everyday life now, it was not so in the latter years of the 1970s.

Although there is no scientific proof of this next statement, my view as a practising qualitative researcher is that good researchers who work together, rather than in isolation, are able to spot trends at least a year before they are noticed by the media or by brand-owning organisations. Often the lead time is even longer.

Facilitating innovation

Innovation is now big news, especially in the United States. For the past two decades, specialists in creativity and innovation have been meeting at conferences and exchanging knowledge about best innovation principles and practice. The body of literature and the number of specialist companies and individual consultants is surprisingly large – especially when viewed from the perspective of the United Kingdom and Europe.

Again, the Internet provides a rich source of Web addresses of people and organisations that specialise in this arena of innovation – one of the most important factors in gaining competitive advantage.

So where do qualitative researchers fit in?

'Good researchers who work together are able to spot trends at least a year before they are noticed by the media.'

The skills employed in innovation brainstorming processes are very similar to those used by experienced qualitative researchers. It is essential to have the expertise and confidence to manage group dynamics so as to create a safe environment of trust. It is also a necessary skill to have at one's fingertips a wide range of projective techniques to help people break free from their normal patterns of thinking. The next most important ingredient is an exuberant and energetic personality, since success often rests on the session being entertaining, fun, free-wheeling, non-judgmental and open. Not every qualitative researcher has this kind of personality.

Innovation principles and practices can be learned. Many courses and training seminars are held in the United States. A good place to start is with the Innovation Network (www.thinksmart.com) which is based in Santa Barbara, California, and provides unique access to a wide and varied range of articles, conference information, a newsletter, e-mail discussions, people and organisations.

'The skills employed in innovation brainstorming processes are very similar to those used by experienced qualitative researchers.'

Designing possibility scenarios

The age of possibility is not a new concept. It has been the central idea at the core of many popular self-development books and teachings and indeed is the underlying assumption beneath scenario planning and processes.

Peter Schwartz, President of Global Business Network, in his book *The Art of the Long View* (3) considers scenarios a tool to enable us to see into a future world of uncertainty. The term 'scenario' generally refers to a script or play. Scenarios in this context are stories about the way the future *might be*. Schwartz defines the scenario as:

> *... a tool for ordering one's perceptions about alternative future environments in which one's decisions might be played out. Alternatively, a set of organised ways for us to dream effectively about our own future.*

Scenarios, like film scripts, are carefully planned and internally consistent. Film or play scenarios are written around characters, events, contexts and interactions. So too are scenarios used by businesses and institutions. Certain elements are highlighted, contexts described, interactions imagined and events (both known and unknown) made to take place. A scenario is like a wind tunnel, allowing a team to test the aerodynamics of their models of thinking, including the important decisions that must be made. It enables people to change their mindsets so that they can anticipate futures and prepare for them.

'Scenarios, like film scripts, are carefully planned and internally consistent.'

Scenarios are not predictions of the future but tools to encourage learning and to arrive at more innovative decisions through practice.

Just as qualitative research has a history of development with highs and lows in its credibility, so too has scenario planning. Scenario planning began during World War 2 when multi-disciplinary academics (physicists, social scientists, psychologists, mathematicians) and military strategists worked on problems beyond the range of any one discipline. After the war, Herman Kahn pioneered the technique of 'future-now' thinking, aiming to produce realistic reports, through rigorous quantitative analysis plus imagination, as if they had been written by people living in the future.

Scenarios became popular in the 1970s when Pierre Wack, a planner at Royal Dutch/Shell, experienced a breakthrough in his own thinking. He and other planners at Shell were exploring events that might affect the price of oil. His team prepared two descriptions of possible futures, one where oil prices held steady as they had since the war, and another which imagined an oil price crisis. The second took into account an unexpected event – a shock that might upset the trend (5).

Although these 'stories' were considered carefully by senior management at Shell, no change in behaviour occurred. Pierre Wack arrived at the view that in order for scenarios to be effective, they had to 'change our managers view of reality' (5, p. 8). The next generation of scenarios was vivid, powerful and interactive, requiring managers to make decisions as if the stories were real. As a result, when the energy crisis following the Yom Kippur war in the Middle East began to unfold across the world, managers at Shell were able to respond quickly to the change. From being one of the weaker players in the global world oil league, Shell became one of the strongest and most profitable.

Wack pioneered the use of scenarios as a method of changing the mind-sets of those who have to make far-reaching decisions. The articles he wrote in 1985 in the *Harvard Business Review* (5) about scenarios showed a change of focus from 'future prediction' to 're-perceiving'.

Gill Ringland's book *Scenario Planning: Managing for the Future* (6) is a comprehensive guide to the art and science of building scenarios. There are many case histories for reference, including ICL, British Airways and United Distillers.

'Wack pioneered the use of scenarios as a method of changing the mind-sets of those who have to make far-reaching decisions.'

One of the points she makes in discussing ICL's experience with this tool is the importance of naming the scenario outcome. The name summarises the essence of the scenario thus helping members of the organisation to grasp the implications immediately. She describes the name as 'an evocative shortcut' and gives examples of two scenarios developed for the information market in 2005 – 'Coral Reef' and 'Deep Sea'. A coral reef has many diverse life forms, a complex ecosystem, many small fish and highly visible activity whereas deep sea has fewer life forms, a simpler ecosystem, bigger fish and less visible activity. However, both can be dangerous. The sea-life metaphor described two scenarios for the future of the information industry which enabled the scenario team to communicate clearly with different groups inside ICL, including the board.

For a qualitative researcher, some of the concepts underpinning scenario planning and the skills used seem second nature. Successful scenarios require careful definition of the objectives, interviews with a wide range of internal and external specialists, brainstorming workshops with key members of the company to write the scenarios, enriching them through a consultative process and finally communication of the 'essence' and implications.

'Intuition is not a magical process but something beyond conscious control.'

The power of intuition – the characteristics of qualitative thinking

The word 'intuition' has no place in the scientific paradigm. Yet in each of the areas described in this chapter it is mentioned often. It helps hard and soft trend-spotters *know* when they find something significant; it is mentioned frequently by those who are directly involved in innovation practice and it is mentioned as one of the key ingredients in successful scenario planning.

Intuition is defined as 'knowledge or perception not gained by reasoning and intelligence; instinctive knowledge or insight' (*Collins English Dictionary*).

Nancy Rosanoff, a pioneer in the field of intuition in personal and business decision-making defines intuition pragmatically: 'Intuition is when we know, but we don't know how we know. Going a little deeper, it is an inner knowing, or knowledge that comes from within.' (7).

Intuition is not a magical process but something beyond conscious control. Hence a strong feeling of intuition is experienced as mystical or magical and not always to be trusted. It 'speaks' through the senses – through images and symbols, through feelings and emotions and through physical sensations. Language betrays this: 'I've got a strong hunch', 'I feel it in my bones', 'I heard warning bells', 'I have a gut feeling about this', 'I smell a rat', 'I don't feel comfortable here' and so on.

Intuition is located deep within each of us. We can either learn how to access it, learn to listen to it or ignore it. It requires acknowledgement and encouragement to become part of everyday life rather than being subjected to judgment and cynicism every time it tries to surface.

Qualitative researchers frequently talk about 'insight' in the same way as intuition. The 'eureka' moment during a research project when all the patterns of thread, juxtaposition of colour and highlights of texture make the picture meaningful, is undoubtedly one of the big buzzes that we all enjoy. This flash of insight, or strong feeling that the problem lies here and not there, cannot be predicted nor called upon at will. Yet it is this mysterious internal process that is most valuable to those end users of the qualitative process.

The two quotes below illustrate the way in which two good qualitative thinkers (and practitioners) describe intuition.

'The "eureka" moment during a research project is undoubtedly one of the big buzzes that we all enjoy.'

> *I think intuition occurs when your beliefs, attitudes and past experiences come together subconsciously and become more than the sum of the parts. The various premises, hypotheses and creative thoughts (probably from areas other than the one under consideration), fit together so well that it feels like a seamless thought or idea. Maybe it even causes some chemical reaction that generates an actual sensation, which would explain why people use expressions such as 'a gut feeling, it feels right, I can feel it in my bones' (Colleen Ryan e-mail, 9 May 1998).*

> *For me, intuition is a mix of 'remembering', 'feeling' and 'internal dialogue'. I find that intuition is frequently involved in research design, analysis and interpretation. Early on in most projects I 'get a feel' for where it's headed. Ask any experienced, successful creative person or*

qualitative researcher. You can't know everything and sometimes you work on a thread of evidence which 'produces' something really useful (Stephen McKernon, e-mail, 7 May, 1998).

Intuitive people often have some of these characteristics:

- good listening skills

- the integration and synthesis of information obtained in different forms from different sources

- awareness of the limitations of models of thinking

- good communication concepts (planning, 'envisioning', bringing to life) and ideas through the use of metaphor and symbols

- the ability to embrace complexity and change

- the intelligence to select and simplify without being facile or naïve

- sensitivity and empathy

- good powers of observation.

This list could be a skeleton recruitment advertisement for a good qualitative thinker!

Concluding thoughts
Neil Postman in his book *Technopoly – The Surrender of Culture to Technology* (8) writes provocatively about the future, warning us all of the tyranny of sophisticated machines over man. The book describes

'You can't know everything and sometimes you work on a thread of evidence which "produces" something really useful.'

the extent to which we 20th-century humans worship technology, how it has entered our language and how it shapes our world view.

He points out that we have hundreds of new words to use. Re-programming, information byte, Internet, software, computer viruses, VCR and digital are all obvious examples. But technology has also changed the meaning of many other words that already existed: information, news, public opinion, political debate. These have all changed through technology and no longer mean the same as they did 50 years ago. These shifts and nuances are silent and less obvious as are indeed the changes in meaning of words such as fact, truth, intelligence, freedom, memory.

The message of the book is that technology in its broadest sense can distance us from the human values that drive our day-to-day lives, cutting us adrift from the meaningfulness of authentic relationships. These relationships, whether intimate, personal, social, public, organisational, national or global, create an 'open system' with multiple communities, identities and boundaries. We as individuals manage somehow to make sense of it all and to find a way of being that is important to us. It seems though that many organisations, companies, brands, products and services have lost the plot and look vainly towards technological breakthrough to create and sustain a long-term future. Instead the opportunities lie with ordinary people and how they relate to the world around them.

It is this message that is relevant to those of us involved in helping organisations prepare themselves for the unknown surprises of the future. It is (relatively) easy to paint vivid scenarios of possible futures using examples of new technology, environmental facts and predictions, economic factors and demographic trends. It is far harder to imagine how human beings will behave towards each other, towards organisations, institutions, governments and nations.

We professionals need to spend more time and effort creating psychological and cultural scenarios for the future, to add credibility to the technological, financial, environmental and demographic ones which characterise much future thinking nowadays. We are responsible for shifting the emphasis of scenarios from aggregate generalisations about 'society', 'markets' and 'consumers' to the likely behaviour, attitudes and decisions of ordinary, individual human beings. A move from 'supply-driven' to 'customer-need' thinking.

'We professionals need to spend more time and effort creating psychological and cultural scenarios for the future.'

REFERENCES

1. R. Gibson (ed.), *Rethinking the Future*, Nicholas Brealey Publishing, 1997.
2. J. Taylor and W. Wacker, with H. Means, *The 500-Year Delta*, HarperCollins, 1997.
3. P. Schwartz, *The Art of the Long View – Planning for the Future in an Uncertain World*, Wiley, 1996.
4. C. Ryan and W. Gordon, 'Consumer Trends in Advertising', MRS Conference 1983.
5. P. Wack, 'Scenarios: Uncharted Waters Ahead', *Harvard Business Review*, 1 September 1985 and 'Scenarios: Shooting the Rapids', *Harvard Business Review*, 1 November 1985.
6. G. Ringland, *Scenario Planning: Managing for the Future*, Wiley, 1997.
7. N. Rosanoff, *Intuition Workout: A Practical Guide to Discovering and Developing your Inner Knowing*, Aslan Publications, 1991.
8. N. Postman, *Technopoly – the Surrender of Culture to Technology*, Vintage Books, 1993.Barker, J.A. (1992) Paradigms The Business of Discovering the Future, William Morrow & Co Inc.

FURTHER READING

S. Adams, The Dilbert Principle, HarperCollins, 1997.

K. Blanchard, Mission Possible, McGraw-Hill, 1997.

J. M. Dru, Disruption, John Wiley & Sons, 1996.

D. Firth and A. Leighy, *The Corporate Fool*, Capstone Publishing Ltd, 1998.

R. Gibson (ed.), *Rethinking the Future*, Nicholas Brealey, 1997.

G. Hamel and C. K. Prahalad, *Competing for the Future*, Harvard Business School Press, Boston, 1994.

J. Naisbitt, Global Paradox, Nicholas Brealey Publishing, 1995.

F. Popcorn and L. Marigold, Clicking, HarperCollins, 1996.

Epilogue

And so to bed...
It is difficult to finish a book! How to end it? Some profound and clever thought to ensure that it ends with a bang? A summary of all the chapters in case anyone wants to read only the last few pages? One possibility is to return to the first chapter to demonstrate that the book has been well thought through. I could end by reminding readers that one of the over-arching themes of this book is the eclectic nature of modern qualitative enquiry. The term 'bricolage' was used to describe this new direction of qualitative thinking both in the halls of academia and the market-places of business.

All I can say is that I seem to have said all that I wanted to say. And I only learned what I wanted to say in the process of saying it!

Throughout the book, I believe I have said five things, in essence.

1. There is no single truth 'out there' waiting to be discovered about the past, present or future. There is only a set of possibilities.

2. There is no 'right way' of doing qualitative research. There are many different approaches and methods – a combination of which is more likely to yield insight than a monolithic approach.

3. Qualitative research as we know it is in danger of having its territory occupied by a number of more adaptable 'experts' – scenario story tellers, futurists, trend-spotters and strategy thinkers. Traditional qualitative research, together with those who practise and those who commission it, will move further and further downstream, away from the heart of decision-making, unless it changes its focus.

4. There is an overwhelming amount of information that threatens to drown us all unless we learn to trust our ability to search and use only the relevant bits and bytes. The search engine is called 'goodthinking' and combines rigorous analysis of the *known* with creative expeditions into the *unknown*, using intuition as the guide.

5. Finally, the future. With the access to information we now have, we find it relatively easy to imagine futures that are driven by technological, political, economic, environmental or demographic changes. But what about psychological and cultural changes? It is far more difficult to create scenarios about how human beings will think, feel and behave in the future, than technocentric stories that ignore they way in which we as flesh-and-blood individuals will engage with the new. This is the most serious challenge for those of us who offer advice to organisations about their 'consumers', markets, brands, products and services.

And do I have a few last words? Yes I do!

Use your heart as well as your head. Let it guide you to be authentic and well intentioned towards those who open the door to invite you into their real and imagined worlds. And remember that qualitative research (whatever your relationship with it) is about sharing who we are as human beings, recognising our similarities and differences, and being aware at all times that our own map of the world is simply an interpretation.

Reference section

Cabbages and Kings

A reference to things important

This reference section is written with a view to helping the reader understand some of the terms, concepts and issues debated regularly by marketing, research, advertising and media professionals. It includes summaries of guidelines for best practice in relation to recruitment of participants to qualitative research, the Code of Conduct developed by the Market Research Society and the *MRS Guide to Qualitative Research*.

Code of Conduct (a summary of key principles)

The key principles of professional market research have been taken from the full text of the Code of Conduct drawn up by the Market Research Society (MRS). These summarised key principles cannot be taken as a substitute for the full Code of Conduct, which is binding on members, as is the Data Protection Act.

Responsibilities to informants
An informant's identity must not be revealed without their consent to anyone not directly involved in the research, nor used for any other than research purposes. *(Code reference A2)*

Nobody shall be adversely affected or embarrassed as a direct result of participating in a research study. *(Code reference A7)*

Interviewers must always show proof of identity to informants, giving the name, address and telephone number of the research agency conducting the study. *(Code reference A9/10)*

Informants must not be coerced or subjected to unwelcome intrusion and must have the rights both to respected privacy and to withdraw their co-operation at any time. *(Code reference A13/17/18)*

No child under 14 shall be interviewed without parent's/guardian's/responsible adult's consent, nor any young person aged 14–17, if the subject of the interview is sensitive. *(Code reference A20/21/22)*

Responsibilities to the general public and business community
Other activities (e.g. selling, opinion polling and collection of personal data) shall not under any circumstances be misrepresented as market research. *(Code reference B2)*

Market research shall be honest and objective and neither research methods nor findings may be used to mislead. *(Code reference B3)*

Responsibilities to clients

A client's identity, information about their business and their commissioned market research data and findings shall remain confidential to the clients unless both client and agency agree details of any publications. *(Code C5/15/17)*

Full methodological details of each project undertaken must be supplied to the client. *(Code reference C10)*

General

All written or verbal assurances made by anyone involved with or commissioning or conducting a study must be factually correct and honoured.

Everyone subject to the Code of Conduct must adhere to its full provisions, protect and enhance the ethical and professional reputation of market research and ensure, whenever possible, that all others connected with studies are aware of, and abide by, the provisions of the full Code.

If in doubt ...

If you are in any doubt, check the full Code of Conduct. Copies are available from the MRS. Practitioners, research buyers and users, and interested members of the general public are urged to become conversant with its provisions. Reference to the full Code is shown beside each of the key principles listed above.

An abbreviated version of the Code (the 'key principles') is available in an A4, A3 or A2 poster format (framed or unframed) from the MRS Membership Department (Tel: +44 (0) 171 490 4911).

It is worth contacting your local market research professional or trade organisation to ensure that you adhere to the guidelines laid down for your country.

A European perspective – facts

The ESOMAR annual study of the Market Research Industry shows that in Europe, on average, 52% of the research expenditure is ad hoc and 48% continuous. The ad hoc total is made up of 42% quantitative and 10% qualitative methods. The differences between the main countries in Europe are marked.

Types of Research – Expenditure 1996

	Total ad hoc %	Quantitative %	Qualitative %
France	46	34	12
Germany	38	34	4
Italy	72	57	15
Netherlands	58	40	18
Spain	61	46	15
UK	55	47	8

Base: Total research expenditure
Source: ESOMAR

The information for qualitative data collection methods clearly shows the predominance of the group discussion over in-depth interviews and any other methods.

Qualitative Data Collection Methods – Expenditure 1996

	Total Qualitative %	Group Discussions %	Depths %	Other %
France	12	7	2	3
Germany	4	1	2	*
Italy	15	11	4	0
Netherlands	18	5	13	0
Spain	15	10	4	1
UK	8	6	2	0

Base: Total research turnover
Source: ESOMAR

It is highly likely, based on my experience, that the picture will be similar in other parts of the world too (US, Australia, New Zealand, South Africa, Asia and South America).

MRS Guide to Qualitative Research

The full text is available from the AQRP or MRS. The main recommendations are as follows.

- The rights of respondents take priority over the rights of our clients.

- Make an effort to tell respondents as much about the interview or discussion before they come along, particularly if the subject of the discussion is deemed sensitive.

- Tell respondents before they come along if the session is to take place in a viewing facility, if it is to be video-recorded and/or audio-recorded.

- Gain permission from respondents for audio- or video-recording the session and at the same time tell them how the tape will subsequently be used.

- Make sure respondents are given every opportunity to withdraw from the discussion, not to answer questions and not to participate in projective techniques, if they so wish.

- Everything you say to respondents must be correct and honoured, such as the length of the session.

- The identity of the client(s) has to be revealed to respondents, whether in a recruiter's home or in a viewing facility, preferably at the beginning of the session or, if there are good reasons to withhold, at the end.

- Behind these guidelines is a more important attitudinal change. There is a tradition in the UK of treating respondents like 'guinea pigs' in a social experiment. Hence they are categorised into certain groups, given certain information and observed in viewing 'laboratories'. Generally they are treated on a 'need to know' basis: anything they do not need to know they are not told. Essentially, they are being asked to respond, not to participate.

- In the case of revealing the identity of a client observer to respondents, for example, respondents wonder who they really are, despite the usually vague introduction, and will be busy making up reasons why they have not been told the truth. 'Oh, I thought you were the man from Acme,' is often the respondent's first words after being told who the silent observer is in the corner. If respondents are told that the observer genuinely wants to hear their views, both negative and positive, it is not beyond the wit of respondents to understand the agenda and co-operate accordingly. Clients will feel more comfortable, too, at being themselves, rather than a 'colleague' or 'researcher'.

- Another harmful tradition is the law-court or police interrogation where the 'witness' is assumed to be hiding the truth which will only be revealed under the pressure of relentless questioning. That may be true in *LA Law*, but it forms a bad precedent for qualitative research.

Qualitative recruitment guidelines

Recruitment is the term given to the processes involved in enrolling members of the public, employees, executives in companies, public opinion formers and other audiences to take part in a qualitative research project. The term 'recruiter' (or 'interviewer' in some parts of the world) refers to a person who is specially trained in this process.

A working party on qualitative recruitment was set up in 1995 with the view to producing guidelines for improvement. After research and extensive discussions with people involved in the processes of recruitment, the following draft guidelines are in the final stages of approval as industry standards.

Sample definition
The precise sample definition should be discussed and agreed by client and agency before the recruitment process begins. This definition should include:

- the maximum and minimum numbers to attend each field-work session

- any previous attendance restrictions

- any subject-related restrictions

- any restrictions in relation to the recruiter's relationship with respondents

- the timing and duration of the fieldwork session

- any special requirements

- usage criteria and social demographic quotas.

The details of each factor may vary according to the needs of the research, each combination will relate to the specific project in question and costs will vary according to the degree of difficulty involved with any combination.

Recruitment procedure

The recruitment procedure should be discussed and agreed by client and agency before the recruitment process begins.

Possible recruitment procedures would include:

- personal contact through door-knocking, contact on the street or a specific site (e.g. store or school)

- telephone contact through client-supplied lists (databases), own networks, own lists, pooled contacts

- written contact

or any combination of all three. Again the details will vary according to the needs of each project and the process identified as being appropriate. Each of these will have ramifications for the cost.

Recruiter information

Once agreed, job-specific guidelines (or, where necessary, instructions) should be passed on to each recruiter, outlining the precise sample definition and acceptable recruitment procedures, together with an explanation of the reasons for the specification.

These guidelines should be accompanied by: a detailed briefing; a detailed communication path in case of queries; and appropriate documentation.

Communication

A two-way communication channel should be kept open during the course of recruitment by maintaining regular contact, encouraging regular progress reports, listening to difficulties reported by the recruiter and acting appropriately.

Verification

The accuracy of all elements involved in recruitment should be verified. This would include the precise sample and recruitment procedure where this has been restricted by specification, check-backs of an agreed percentage of respondents (made available to the client on request), and copies of the recruitment documentation (or a summary) signed by respondents, to confirm that all the details are accurate and truthful.

Verification can be undertaken at any stage of the recruitment process and up to four weeks after the fieldwork date.

Training

Training and re-training should be available to recruiters and should include:

- the rudiments of qualitative research

- the expectations of the role played and possible anxieties felt by respondents

- all aspects of the recruiter's role

- sample definitions

- all acceptable recruitment procedure methods

- the communication channels and how they should be used

- workload and time-management skills

- hostessing and etiquette requirements

- the verification process

- the role of the moderator

- reasons behind the guidelines used

- the problems that resettle from (and the action taken) in cases of miscommunication, mis-recruitment and fraud.

Recruiter status

The industry should accept the difficulties intrinsic to qualitative recruitment and value good recruiters in a way that elevates their status from 'bottom of the heap' to being a valued member of the team. This would involve:

- recognising good practice and the skills required to achieve it

- involving recruiters at early stages of planning and seeking their advice in cases where recruitment could be difficult

- encouraging openness and honesty

- providing accurate information

- paying appropriately.

These guidelines have been developed for the recruitment culture and preferred methods of practice in the UK. They may be suitable in whole or in part for other parts of the world and can be used as a template to check whether current country guidelines are satisfactory. Again, it may be worth contacting your local market research professional or trade organisation.

Validity and reliability in qualitative research

In plain English, the term validity means 'having some foundation based on truth' and the term reliability means 'able to be trusted, predictable or dependable' (*Collins English Dictionary*). Thus the phrase validity and reliability in qualitative research refers to the notions of accuracy, general ability and robustness.

Researchers and academics continue to argue not only about how to produce reliable and valid data and interpretations, but about what these terms actually mean. Positivism says that validity is reliability and reduces qualitative research to a survey-like science. The influence of post-modernism on all theory and practice has made the possibility of discovering the reliable truth a fallacy. The best that can be hoped for is to (re)present a valid truth.

We have also been made aware that all data are selected, interpreted and reported in terms of some explicit or, more likely, implicit theory. Hence all evaluations (including reliability and validity checks) are meaningful only by reference to a theory and the cognitive idiosyncrasies of the researcher and the reader alike (1).

The pragmatic practitioner and user of qualitative research will realise that a valuable, strong research study can be created by starting with an approach of objectivity, a corresponding rigour in method with systematic working practice, and a transparency and clarity of theory and presentation.

In this way validity can be pursued both in the research methodology and the strategies and techniques used. The final report can then be evaluated for its worth, correspondence and robustness. And it is here in the representation of the research, where claims making is carried out, that validity must be demonstrated and is ultimately assessed.

More recently it has been suggested that the concept of validity and reliability mean different things at each stage of a research project:

- when the project is generated, developed, clarified and evaluated, validity becomes the value or worth to the end user

- when the project is being done, validity becomes correspondence (agreement)

- when the research is replicated, verified and extended, validity becomes robustness and generalisability.

In the final analysis, a qualitative research study either has or does not have credibility in the context of previous research combined with the experience of those who are involved in the market, the category, the brand, the customers, the problem.

It is because of the very essence of qualitative research and the complexity of human nature it purports to study that perfect validity is, paradoxically, impossible to achieve.

REFERENCE

1. N. K. Denzin and Y. S. Lincoln, *Handbook of Qualitative Research*, Sage Publications, 1994.

Stimulus material

Many types of stimuli are used in qualitative research, as follows.

Adcepts – these are designed to explore advertising positionings, rather than the brand strategy proposition. Adcepts are best produced by the advertising agency since a dramatisation or metaphor for the proposition is required.

The form of the stimulus can be extremely rough: line drawings and handwritten headlines that reinforce the fact that adcepts are not ads help to avoid too much executional criticism on the part of the consumer. As execution *always influences response* it is a good idea to produce two or three different adcepts for each positioning that is to be explored.

Admatics – these are a development of animatics (see below). Storyboards are assembled into something more closely approaching the level of the finished commercial by using computer-generated and manipulated images. Admatics are quite successful in conveying both form and structure. They help to demonstrate movement and special effects, thus providing a third dimension to the material.

Analogy boards – these are helpful in overcoming problems of articulation and description. Used in both qualitative and quantitative research, an analogy board may comprise pictures of objects as diverse as a toothbrush, china cup, Concorde and sunflower. People are asked to select an image or images from the board that, in some way, has something in common with the brand (product, service etc.) in question. The question 'why is that?' is essential.

Animatics – key frames for a commercial are drawn (either black and white or full colour) and then filmed on video with an accompanying soundtrack. The effect of this is a somewhat jerky, animated TV film, using drawn characters to represent live action. Animatics are very useful for conveying structure, particularly sequence and timing, but less effective in conveying production effects.

Concept boards – these are designed to expose a new idea to consumers and come in many forms. There is no 'right' way. There are no rules! Our experience suggests that it is helpful to make the new idea (brand, product, environment) seem as genuine as possible – as if it exists already. Thus, showing a pack with a brand name together with drawn or scrap art illustrations to give clues as to its image context, can be helpful.

Flip-over storyboards – these are similar to storyboards (see below) but are mounted on a ringbinder frame and exposed to respondents in sequence in time to a taped soundtrack. They are useful for scripts that rely on a surprise ending that would be spoiled by revealing the last few frames at the same time as the beginning of the commercial, or for scripts where it is important for the voice-over/soundtrack to be timed to coincide with particular visuals/actions.

Jigsaw – this is a way of deconstructing the elements of a new product/service or existing brand. Consumers are exposed to a pre-selected range of elements – propositions, brand names, graphic styles, product descriptors, user images and/or photographic/verbal descriptions of concepts and asked to construct the 'whole' which best meets the needs of a core target market.

This technique is best used in extended creativity group discussions where respondents can work interactively. The final solution is not used as the final execution, but is used diagnostically to inform the design or creative briefs.

Mock-up editorial – the new product or relaunched (old) product is written about in an editorial style and presented to consumers as a cutting from 'Consumer News' in a magazine/newspaper.

This provides a more realistic context in which the new product/ relaunched brand can be evaluated, particularly if its core benefit is genuinely newsworthy.

Mock-up packs – sometimes it is worth exposing the new product concept in the form of a finished-looking 3D pack. If it is shown in a competitive context, it soon becomes clear whether or not it is seen to be a 'me-too' or unique brand/product and whether or not it is interesting and relevant to potential consumers.

Mood boards – these are usually collage boards of images designed to convey a mood – relaxation, energy, well-being, rebellion, etc. They often use colour to help convey the appropriate mood.

Music – short extracts of music can also be used to explore mood in relation to a brand, strategy or advertising execution.

Narrative tapes – these are audio-tapes. A voice artist narrates the dialogue and explains the action of the commercial. The characters are often described, the scene set and creative devices explained. They can be simple or complex, short or long, one voice or several, no sound effects or many. Some require key visual frames to illustrate a part of the commercial, others need no other support. They need to be short (under a minute), otherwise the audience loses concentration. They are often very successful in conveying structure, but less so in conveying form. They often lead to over-positive responses as respondents are free to imagine an idealised advertisement.

Packaging shapes and mechanics – these are often used for new product development and enable researchers to understand the rational and emotional elements of the product imagery that are communicated by packaging, shape/format and mechanical design. They are useful at the early stages of new product development when the emphasis is on understanding the rules of the product category and the brand parameters of the new product.

Photomatics – a form of animatic using photographs instead of drawn key frames, thus showing the characters and scenes realistically rather than as drawn representations.

Although photomatics can sometimes help to portray production elements (i.e. form) more realistically, they are still more appropriate for communicating the structure of the commercial.

Scrap art or *words and pictures* – respondents are given a pile of random words and pictures cut from magazines and asked to select any which they associate with a particular brand, product or service. This can bypass rationally held views and leads to a vivid picture of consumers' emotional beliefs and perceptions. It can also draw out subtle differences between brands that people may find very hard to express. What is important is not what words and pictures they select, but their reasons for the selection.

Storyboards – key frames for a commercial are drawn consecutively, like a comic strip, with the words sometimes written underneath and/or played on a tape recorder with special effects (for example a jingle, the sound of water, running footsteps).

Storyboards help to convey structure very well but, because they are drawn, are less helpful in demonstrating more finished executional and production details and emotional contexts.

Talkie tapes – these are mock interviews (unscripted to aid realism) with people such as the 'New Product Director', 'Advertising Manager', 'Head Teacher', 'Doctor', or anyone relevant who might be perceived to offer an informed point of view. In relation to the subject being discussed, the 'expert' divulges key points of view or facts that respondents will then discuss depending on their relevance to their own experiences and prejudices. Again, talkie tapes are useful in a quantitative interview to give product explanations more realistically than a written concept board.

Thought tapes – a mock consumer depth interview or group discussion which highlights known or conceptual needs, attitudes or motivations about a particular product category or brand. The dialogue is not scripted so that the tape sounds natural and realistic. Thought tapes are extremely helpful at the strategic development stage of advertising and marketing. They are also useful in quantitative interviews to provide realistic 'things that other people have said'.

Video collages – sometimes referred to as 'stealomatics', these are a useful way of showing consumers the proposed form of the advertisement – its filmic style (quick cuts, cinematic devices), its mood, tone of voice, type of music, appearance of characters, visual juxtapositions and so on.

They can also be used for strategy development by helping to illustrate which tone of voice is appropriate for the brand. Wacky? Authoritative? Sophisticated? Luxurious? etc. More recently, video collages have been created to convey 'brand essence'.

Visual collages – these are collage boards made of scrap art cut out of magazines or newspapers. They can be used to explore abstract concept areas such as freshness, balance, wisdom and so on, or can be used more simply to explore executional values (user imagery, casting or lifestyles). The benefit of visual collages is that they look nothing like advertising and are therefore not responded to judgmentally but instead help respondents to articulate their feelings about concept areas.

Vocabulary boards – these are lists of words to help respondents to articulate feelings about a subject for which they may only have a limited range of vocabulary. The vocabulary list consists of adjectives, verbs or phrases and is developed using language and terminology appropriate to the subject area.

Glossary

Definitions, where given, are not absolute. There is no one definition of a term or concept acceptable to everyone in every part of the world. The language we use is evolving constantly in parallel to our increasing understanding of the issues and in response to the growing complexity of our areas of enquiry.

The intention is to offer one definition or one explanation of a term or concept which can then be used as a starting point for discussion, elaboration or re-definition.

Ad-hoc Research. Research that concentrates on a specific marketing problem and collects data from a specified sample of respondents at a given point in time. Such surveys include pre-testing of a planned advertising campaign, customer satisfaction, or product testing surveys and Usage and Attitude studies.

Advertising Awareness. This is often used as a surrogate measure of the effectiveness of the advertising. Proof that advertising awareness is in any systematic way related to the sales effectiveness of the campaign is elusive. This is one of the thorniest areas of marketing, much has been written and sides are taken, so take care not to be naïve whenever dealing with this subject.

Advertising Recall. A measure of the content of an advertisement that is remembered. This is different from advertising awareness – a measure of remembering seeing the advertisement for a brand. Recall says something about the particular communication or dominant images left by an advertisement, but as an indicator of effectiveness it too is questionable. Note the same warning that applies to advertising awareness.

Attitudes. An ill-defined term generally used to mean consumers' set of knowledge, opinions and feelings about a brand, service or company; in the belief that attitudes are related to a disposition to purchase. Usually measured in research by a battery of statements to which respondents are asked to indicate how much they agree or disagree. However, what this measures is acceptance (or not) of formal beliefs at a verbal level, rather than attitudes. What is more, attitude studies usually omit to measure the relative importance, in terms of affecting disposition to purchase, of each attitude. So the interpretation of attitude research is largely subjective (see **Brand Image, Brand Personality**).

Awareness. A measure (quantitative) or an indication (qualitative) of the proportion of people who claim to remember or to be aware of some element of communication – advertising, packaging, promotions, editorial, a new service and so on. Awareness can be spontaneous or prompted.

Brand. A product or service to which human beings attach a bundle of tangible (functional product and service characteristics) and intangible (emotional and/or symbolic) meanings that add value. A brand has one strategic purpose and that is to differentiate itself from competitors.

Branding. Two meanings: (1) The process, which may take decades, by which a brand comes to have added values and involves long-term support by communications either above or below the line. (2) The associative strength between an advertisement (usually) and a brand expressed as a positive or negative relationship, i.e. 'well branded' or 'poorly branded'.

Brand Awareness. A measure or indication (see **Awareness**) of the readiness with which a brand springs to mind. There is evidence that brand awareness bears some relationship to the purchasing of the brand. Note same warning as with advertising awareness.

Brand Equity. A term developed in the 1980s to describe the financial worth of the brand to bottom-line profits. This term is often used in a different context to mean 'added values' as in 'understanding the brand equity(ies)'.

Brand Essence. The core values that define a brand. These remain constant over time even though the executional characteristics of packaging, advertising (and other marketing expressions) may change. By defining the brand essence with clarity, a brand owner creates a template against which all marketing and NPD activity can be developed and integrated.

Brand Image. The total impression created in the mind by a brand and all its functional and emotional associations. There are image facets which make up the totality – product, user, occasion, service and personality.

Brand Loyalty. A misleading term (consumers owe no 'loyalty' to a brand) loosely used to describe the extent to which buyers of a brand use it rather than other brands. In fact, people usually buy several brands, some more often than others. Brand 'promiscuity', as this normal behaviour is sometimes called, is an equally misleading term (see **Repertoire**).

Brand Map (see **Market Map**)

Brand Personality. A metaphor for the fundamental core values and characteristics of the brand, described and experienced as human personality traits, e.g. friendly, intelligent, innovative. An expression of the relationship between consumer and brand. One of the most important concepts in modern marketing and communications.

Brand Positioning. The compass points or parameters by which a brand defines its territory compared to competitors. These compass points can be described in down-to-earth terms such as the target market (for whom?), the key competitor(s) (against whom?), the specific consumer benefit differentiating the brand (why? when? for what?) Or they can be described in terms of emotional territory (e.g. Persil = caring, Nike = competitive performance).

Brand Proposition. A simple sentence or phrase that encapsulates the brand benefit, e.g. a brand with technical superiority, a brand that guarantees next-day delivery, a brand that deodorises as well as cleans. Often a brand benefit is translated into an endline that becomes part of the brand communication on advertising, packaging or promotions, e.g. 'the appliance of science', 'the world's most popular airline', 'never knowingly undersold'.

Buying Intention. A form of attitude measurement purporting to measure future purchasing intention after exposure to a test advertisement or other stimulus. There is some correlation with favourable attitudes to the stimulus. As a measure of actual future purchase, however, buying intention scores are questionable. Studies have found that they are correlated better with past buying behaviour than with future.

Cannibalisation. The degree to which increased sales of one brand replace sales of another brand or brands of the same manufacturer.

CAPI (computer aided personal interviewing). Computers are used to assist in face-to-face interviewing, whereby the interviewer keys respondents' answers directly into a computer (laptops are particularly handy), so avoiding errors in translation later and producing higher quality and faster results.

CATI (computer aided telephone interviewing). This is a type of telephone interviewing, using a computer during interviewing. The questionnaire appears on the computer screen, and the responses to questions are keyed directly into the computer. This speeds up the process, ensuring quicker and more efficient results.

Conjoint Analysis. Sometimes called 'trade off', this research technique reveals how people make complex decisions. It assumes that, in a real situation, such decisions (including those about purchase) are based upon a range of factors 'considered jointly' (hence the term 'conjoint'). It therefore emulates this situation by creating an interview format that forces respondents to make trade-off decisions very similar to those in real life.

Continuous Research. This involves regular interviewing using the same questionnaire so results can be tracked and forecasted. It can include the use of panels, retail audits and television viewer panels.

Creative Development Research. Typically (and preferably) small-scale qualitative research conducted on advertising and design material in the early stages of development. It helps to clarify consumers' responses and aids creative people in developing executions. Requires particularly well-developed 'creative' skills from the researcher. Sometimes called creative guidance research (see **Pre-testing**).

Customer Profiling/Analysis. The analysis of customer records to identify target markets, both overall and for specific products, brands, services and promotions. Typically, this will incorporate geodemographic codes taken from postcodes.

Customer Satisfaction Surveys. This expanding area of research attempts to assess the quality of service offered by a particular organisation and thus to define consumer perceptions of that company's brands or services. Theoretically this measure is a good indicator of customers' propensity to re-buy and remain loyal to the product or service. But research shows that even those claiming to be satisfied will switch if a more competitive or motivating alternative presents itself.

Demographics. Statistical characteristics of a population or user group: age, sex, socio-economic class, household size, family composition, education, etc. (see **Psychographics**).

Desk Research. The examination, analysis and collation of published research. Typical sources will include trade associations and government statistics such as the census, trade and consumption patterns of specific products or services and import/export data. The Internet has expanded the nature of this research so that it is faster, more extensive and likely to 'turn up' some unexpected facts or points of view.

Econometrics. Statistical analysis of large quantities of supply and demand data and their inter-relationships, using computers. Originally developed in the field of economics, econometric techniques are applied to the analysis of consumer markets (see **Modelling**).

Emotional. The 'affective' and intuitive feelings and beliefs surrounding a product or brand – 'how it makes me feel', e.g. First Direct makes me feel innovative, British Airways makes me feel safe. Different groups of people will feel differently depending on their relationship with the brand, product or service.

ESP (Emotional Selling Proposition). A term developed in the 1980s to describe the single-minded emotional proposition that is based on a motivating consumer proposition (the **USP**).

Executive Interviewing. Respondents are interviewed in their business capacity on a range of subjects, directly related to their commercial and industrial activity. The interviewing techniques used can include both telephone and face-to-face and may take the form of in-depth interviews or structured questionnaires. Interviewers conducting this type of research need to have the knowledge, experience and confidence to converse easily with senior management.

Fieldwork. General term for the interaction of researchers with consumers, customers or other stakeholders (e.g. employees, opinion formers, share holders). This includes both quantitative and qualitative sessions – hall tests, focus groups, depth and telephone interviews.

Frequency. The number of times within a specified period that an individual has the opportunity to see or hear a given advertisement or campaign in one or more media. For numbers of individuals (a target audience) frequency may be expressed as a single figure (average OTS – opportunity to see) or, better, as a frequency distribution (percentage having 0 or 1 or 2 or 3 OTS, etc.).

Functional. Sometimes synonymous with rational (as opposed to emotional) to describe the factual characteristics of a product or a brand, e.g. First Direct offers speed and efficiency of service through technology, British Airways has a worldwide network of routes.

Geodemographics. The analysis of people according to where they live. Based on information derived from the census, a classification of types of people has been developed according to residential characteristics. This classification has then been matched with postcodes to allow accurate customer analysis and target marketing. Literally, it is the fusion of geographical data with information on sex, age, socio-economic group and location.

Identification. A chord or empathy that can be built up between a consumer and a brand through understanding the nature of the relationship.

Incentives. When lengthy questionnaires or group discussions (focus groups) are used, respondents will often be given an 'incentive'. This is an inappropriate term, because the chocolate bar, money or product that they are given is to thank them for their time rather than to persuade them to participate (which could, of course, distort responses).

Life Cycle or **Life Stage.** A series of stages in the life of the typical customer, e.g. young single; young couple without children; couple with young children; couple with teenage children; empty nesters, pre-retirement families/couples; retired couples; retired and living alone. Usually a more meaningful discriminator than simple demographics or chronological age.

Lifestyle. This originally referred to a specific form of structured quantitative research that classified people by their attitudes, interests and opinions (AIO) to add to the discriminatory power of conventional demographics. Now commonly, but loosely, used to refer to differences in behaviour that relate to social values and attitudes as measured by any form of research (see **Psychographics, Life Cycle**).

Market Map. A graphical representation of different brands' (company) positionings, relative to each other, according to their respective ratings on the main dimensions of consumers' perceptions of the market. Better at illustrating existing knowledge than at revealing hitherto unsuspected relationships (see **Brand Image, Segmentation**).

Market Modelling. Conjoint analysis (see above) produces output that makes it possible to build a market model which can predict a product's attractiveness when placed alongside a range of products already available. 'What if ...?' modelling can be used to identify optimum product profiles for any given market segment. Other forms of market modelling are also available.

Modelling. Econometric method of trying to establish correlations between observed variations in marketing data, for use as explanation of cause and effect, and for the prediction of future effects (given that the causes can themselves be predicted or controlled). A simplified version of reality which needs careful interpretation and should not be regarded as proof (see **Econometrics**).

Mystery Shopping. This has become a popular form of research among large organisations such as supermarkets, DIY stores and banks to find out how their staff treat their customers. A 'mystery' shopper who is a trained observer experiences the normal buying process, and then prepares a report on the level of service received, measured against pre-agreed criteria.

Need States. The complex web of rational, emotional, environmental and personal triggers that lead to brand or product choice. A helpful model of thinking to explain repertoire behaviour.

Observational Research. This includes mystery shopping, audits and customer behaviour studies, and is defined as research where interviewers are required to report on activity they observe, rather than asking questions. There are two kinds: participant observation where the observer asks questions to clarify the meaning of the observed behaviour; and classic observation where there is no possibility of asking questions.

Occasion Image. The impression created, either explicitly or implicitly, about the kinds of occasion for which the brand is believed to be most appropriate.

Omnibus Surveys. This is a form of ad-hoc quantitative research where clients can buy space on questionnaires (either telephone, or face to face). The interview will cover other topics, as well as their own. Clients benefit from sharing the cost of the survey and gain information that can be analysed on a regional, class or age basis.

Open-ended Questions. An open-ended research question requires the interviewer to record the answers verbatim. Alternatively, questions may force respondents to choose one of a given set of answers (closed questions), or may pre-code the answers (where these are predictable). Open-ended questions are less likely to suffer from the bias of pre-judging what the answers will be but are more time consuming to analyse.

Penetration. Usually refers to the proportion of homes/individuals in a given universe who buy (or use) a brand or product field during a specified period of time. Cumulative penetration refers to the proportion who buy at all, over longer periods of time. Most frequent purchasers will be captured within a short time, but infrequent purchasers may not make a purchase – and thus will not be counted within penetration – for many months, even for fast moving consumer goods.

There is thus an intricate relationship between penetration and frequency of purchase. An increased frequency of purchase will show up as higher four-weekly rates of penetration, even though cumulative penetration over, say, a year remains unaltered.

Less often used to refer to the proportion of a population who are reached by a medium (e.g. radio penetration, cinema penetration).

Planning. The process of translating data (both consumer, customer and market) into an effective strategy. It is concerned with understanding people, their relationship with brands and products, how creative ideas work and how to develop and enhance successful brands. Originally developed in advertising agencies, planning is becoming an important function in all sectors of the communication industry.

Pre-testing. Qualitative or quantitative techniques for evaluating communication material (advertising, packaging, corporate identity, internal communication, promotions etc.). Because pre-tests are carried out in 'laboratory' conditions, care must be taken over the interpretation of the results. Pre-tests are not predictions of market share or share of voice.

Product Image. The impression created about the characteristics of the product or service. These may be perceived or real attributes and are generally conveyed through communications, packaging or real experience.

Proposal. The response from the agency to a briefing document. Companies commissioning research do not usually obtain proposals from more than three agencies as, done properly, they can take much time, effort and expense.

Proposition. Currently adopted by corporate or service organisations (financial institutions, airlines, utility companies, hotels etc.) to encapsulate the essence of the identity. This requires holistic and integrated expression through communications, environments, products/services and, importantly, staff/management behaviour (see **Brand Proposition**).

Psychographics. A refinement on demographics whereby personality and social values are measured and used to classify people (see **Lifestyle**).

Questionnaire. Writing questionnaires that will elicit the right information accurately is a deceptively difficult art. The precise wording, the question order, the choice of open-ended or pre-coded questions, all affect the nature and degree of response. Time spent on questionnaire design (including pilot testing) will usually save time in analysing the results.

Recognition. Another way of trying to assess the extent to which consumers have seen a particular element of communications. In contrast to unprompted recall, respondents are shown all or part of the advertisement (or pack, promotion etc.) and asked if they have seen it before. While this leads to some overclaiming, it is generally more reliable than unaided recall (see **Awareness**).

Recruitment. The process of selecting and finding participants to take part in a market research programme. Criteria for inclusion will be carefully calculated and may be specified in terms of demographic features, such as age, socio-economic group or region, behavioural patterns, such as product usage, and psychological profiles.

Relevance. Usually used to describe whether or not the advertising or brand proposition has any affinity with a particular segment of consumers or customers.

Repertoire. In many different sectors, people buy a repertoire of different brands, some more often than others.

Research Brief. Research will only be as good as the brief. This should include the brand's current positioning in the market, its full history and competitor activity, the current and potential target audience, the overall aim of the research, as well as the timescales involved and the allocated budget for the study.

Salience. (1) The importance a brand holds for different groups of people. It is a measure or indication of emotional closeness to, or distance from, a brand; it is different from awareness. (2) The extent to which a brand comes readily to mind (e.g. measured by first mentions in answer to a brand awareness question) or the most frequently mentioned brand in connection with a set of associations.

Segmentation. The division of a market into discrete segments, classified by user characteristics and requirements/needs or by product benefits. Though segmentation is often a convenient tool for the marketer, care needs to be taken that it does not create artificial divisions, i.e. it should conform to consumer perceptions of the market or to their purchasing/ownership behaviour (see **Positioning, Market Map**).

Semiotics. The theory of signs in language. In research it is used to identify and evaluate the true meaning behind consumers' linguistic responses and to decode their cultural frames of reference. It employs specialist techniques to override the problems of conditioned or expected responses by providing a deeper understanding of consumers' motivations.

Sensory Test. The examination of some or all aspects of products that are perceived by the five senses. Key users of this type of research are companies involved in the food and drink, tobacco, household goods, fragrance and cosmetics industries. It is of particular use to R&D departments in helping them to optimise their recipes or formulas in the light of consumer preferences.

Service Image. The impression created about the nature of the brand's service capabilities. Similar to product image for service brands.

Socio-economic Classification. Otherwise called social class. Stratification of society, for purposes of market research definition, into classes; based principally on occupation of the head of household, the classification bears some relationship to social status, education level, culture and to preference between certain media vehicles (e.g. newspapers) and certain categories of goods. Various classifications exist, of which the most widely used in the UK is that developed for the National Readership Survey as follows.

Social Grade	% Adult Pop.	Head of Household Occupation
A	3	Higher managerial, administrative or professional
B	14	Middle managerial, administrative or professional
C1	22	Supervisory or clerical, junior managerial
C2	31	Skilled manual workers
D	19	Semi and unskilled manual workers
E	11	State pensioners, casual or lowest-grade workers, unemployed

Tracking Study. Research to monitor the effects of marketing activities on the performance of brands and markets. Carried out at intervals, or continuously, a typical tracking study will measure brand awareness, purchasing and attitudes, and advertising awareness and recall. It seeks to provide a better explanation of the precise effect of a given marketing stimulus and why (see **Attitudes, Awareness, Brand Image**).

User Image. The impression created, either explicitly or implicitly, about the sort of person who is likely to be a user of the brand defined demographically, by life stage, lifestyle or attitude.

USP (Unique Selling Proposition). Rosser Reeves invented this phrase to describe a single-minded approach to advertising strategy, based on a proposition to the target consumer, which will sell because it satisfies a real want, which is unique to the brand (or uniquely presented).

Viewing Facility. A venue for holding group discussions or individual interviews that has a two-way mirror. This allows clients and/or their agencies (advertising, design) to watch and listen unobtrusively.